This book is dedicated to anyone who has never had a book dedicated to them before. Now you have.

Six Inches for the Holy Spirit

(Part three)

Piss and Bleach

Chapter one

Out of all of my mates I was the only virgin left now. Those jammy bastards. The treacherous, disloyal, jammy little bastards. This was annoying but at least I had the beginnings of my gang. Yes, it was true that they were awful and pretty much useless, but I had to start somewhere and they were all I had. So far, anyway. I bet Al Capone and the Cosa Nostra and the Triads and the Crips and the Krays and all the rest of those other tasty cunts didn't start off their criminal empires with fully formed, cut throat, blood thirsty motherfuckers either. I bet they also started off with their insipid, lazy, cowardly, weedy, bottom of the barrel, mummy's boys, stoner, nerd, mates and sort of built up from there like I was going to have to.

Beggars can't be choosers though so I just had to make the best of it. I had our Wayne, Diamond, Just Clint, (formally known as Black Clint) Squint, Billy, Sandy and Kev. From this day forth collectively known as, The Bin

Boys. Sandy would just have to wear the name because I wasn't about to call us something like, "The Bin people; affiliated with the trans community" or some new age, inclusive, hippy shit like that just because he liked putting on girl's clothes and having a big wank in his bedroom mirror. Yes, I'd been radicalised by Sally and was now a confirmed and committed feminist, at least until I'd given her one anyway, but it was still early days and very confusing for a cultural shit cunt such as myself.

   A gang name couldn't be too complicated or convoluted. It would be bad business to kick the fuck out of someone and leave a calling card next to them saying something like, "Congratulations you've been visited by Johnny and the Bin boys plus Sandy, who feels like he's a girl who has been cruelly trapped inside the body of a boy, but she's quite happy with her big, thick cock, although apparently she'd like a massive pair of tits once she's saved up enough money." It's too long to read plus all those words could be expensive if you had to pay the printer per character. Nope, it was the Bin Boys and anybody who disagreed could suck my dick. Especially if it was Sandy but he or she .. they? would have to be dressed up as

Madonna and be wearing those little silky panties he or she or they had on the other day when I had to wank him or her or them off in those public toilets.

   Our Wayne had proved himself in battle at least and Sandy, who for a bird, or nearly a bird or whatever the fuck she or he they are was very quick to kick the living fuck out of anyone stupid enough to give he or she or them any lip, so that was at least something. The rest of them had never thrown a punch in their lives though, but on a more positive note, they'd certainly received a good few. That was something not to be taken for granted. Unless you've had a proper hiding you don't really get it until you do. I've seen a lot of kids who have done years of Kung Fu or Karate or some other film inspired martial arts bollocks who thought they were the dog's bollocks until they got a punch to the head and all that training dribbled down there legs.

   Personally I could take a right good kicking. I'd been beaten all to fuck so many times I didn't even feel pain any more. Physical or emotional. I saw that as a strength. Physical and emotional abuse at an early age, although perhaps not for everyone, seemed to be working pretty well for me. If the last few weeks were any kind of gauge I was clearly a mental case and I was happy with that because it suited me.

This was not the time for introspection and self-indulgence however. I needed to lose my virginity pronto. If I didn't pop my cherry before I was sixteen I'd never live it down. Round our way the average age was around twelve or thirteen - much younger if you were a Catholic or your uncle was staying in the spare room- so people were probably already looking at me as if I was weird. I'd had a few near misses but so far I'd never actually put my penis into a vagina and emptied my load into it and time was ticking. Tick tock, tick tock, tick tock.

I was livid though and still could not believe that my so-called mates had used my notoriety to lose their sexual innocence. The perfidious cunts. The least they could have done was to have let me have first dibs. 'Hey Diamond I hear you know Johnny McQueen would you like to bend me over and give me a good seeing to before spraying my tits with your love sauce?' 'Sure baby doll but it's only fair that Johnny gives you one first as he's the sole fucking reason that you're even talking to me because before

Johnny pretty much single-handedly wiped out all the bad guys so that we no longer live in fear, to smash one up you on the strength of that would be just plain immoral.' But no they used my name to get their sordid little ends away. I hated them for that but I also had to admire them too. The bloody fucking cunts.

I pulled out a cigarette, lit it and inhaled deeply. I'd certainly come a long way in a relatively short time. Yes I was still a virgin that much was true, but I was still pretty pleased with my progress when it came to becoming a criminal mastermind. I'd left the way clear for myself to accomplish all the dreams I had about being the number one gangster around these here parts but this wasn't the time to pat myself on the back and start wanking off about it. I could have definitely done with a wank though. I could always do with a wank. Every time I achieved anything of any significance I rewarded myself with a wank, so I figured I was due one.

It seemed like years ago when that cunt Butch put that dog clip on my ear and set in motion a chain of events that resulted in an awful lot of people getting royally fucked up but in reality it had only been a couple of weeks. I looked across the playground and watched all the kids going about their day without a care in the fucking world. This was all down to me. Nobody was getting beaten up and bullied and any kid who was lucky enough to have any pocket money was now able to keep it. For the short term anyway. I'd created a paradise but it wouldn't last long. Sooner or later there was going to be some other tricky little upstart who had the same dreams as me and want to exploit this new found utopia. I could not let that happen. I scanned the playground for potential adversaries and found one. I put my arm around Diamond and whispered in his ear,

'Diamond.' I breathed, 'I want you to go over to Steve Callaghan and punch him in the face.'

'What? What? Eh?' Replied Diamond.

Diamond looked surprised and confused so I asked him again.

'I want you to walk on over to Steve Callaghan and punch the cunt right in the face, please.'

'I don't want to do that Johnny.' He replied.

'Why not Diamond?' I enquired.

'Well for one he's hard as fuck and furthermore I don't really have a reason.' Diamond quite rightly told me.

'Did Sarah Harding suck your cock this morning Diamond?' I asked him.

'Well yes as it happens she did Johnny.' Diamond replied with a broad grin.

'And why do you think one of the hottest girls in our year did that to someone like you Diamond?' I asked him.

'Because I'm cute?' He replied unconvincingly.

'Have another guess Diamond.' I replied coldly.

'Because I know you Johnny?' Replied Diamond, finally understanding the situation.'

'And what do you think would happen if I cast you out of the Bin Boys?' I asked him.

'Who the fuck are the Bin Boys Johnny?' Diamond replied.

'Oh yeah sorry mate, The Bin Boys is the name of my gang. I forgot to mention that.' I replied.

'And we are the Bin Boys because we always hang around the bins Johnny!' He replied excitedly.

'Spot on Diamond! Spot on!' I replied to him with equal excitement. 'Now I like you Diamond, you're a good friend of mine and we've been together through thick and thin but as the leader of the Bin Boys sometimes I have to make difficult decisions, and I've just had to make one. Thick and thin Diamond, thick and thin. Now for you the thick was you getting to cum down the throat of Sarah Harding this morning. Or was that the thin? Which one of those two means the good one?'

'I don't really know Johnny I've never really thought about it.' Diamond replied.

'Me neither Diamond, me neither' I replied. 'So for now we are just going to have to assume that the thick part of it is the good bit and the thin part is the shit parts otherwise we are going to be here all day and I'm desperately in need of a wank. Unlike you it would seem. You jammy cunt. No offence.'

'None taken Johnny.' Okay Johnny. Thick good. Thin shit. Got it.' Diamond replied.

'Brilliant. Right then so the good part of you knowing me is that you've had your dick sucked. Correct?' I told him.

Diamond hesitated.

'Fuck me Diamond let's put this another way.' I continued. 'Up until very recently have you ever been anywhere near getting your cock sucked? Have a good think about that. In fact have you ever had anything at all to do with the fairer sex apart from wanking off about them from the relative safety of your bedroom or the east block bogs… before I blew the fuckers up? I enquired of him.

Diamond looked up to the sky and scratched his chin.

'Well there was this one time…'

I had to cut him off.

'Spying on your Nan having a bath does not count Diamond.' I told him. 'We've all discussed this and we came to the conclusion that you are just a sick little deviant and even though, yes, you were admittedly the first of us to ever see real tits in the flesh, however gross those tits turned out to be, it was just too gross to really count.'

'Okay well in that case no Johnny.' Replied Diamond solemnly.

'See? Well there you go then! If it wasn't for me you'd still be trying to suck your own cock. So to sum up, if you don't go over to that big cunt and punch him in the face I'm throwing you out of the Bin Boys and you can spend the rest of your life wanking off over your nan's old tits. Capisci?' I told him.

'Eh? Bin Boys?' He replied.

Fuck me it was torture and I was tempted to punch the cunt in his own face but he was a mate and apart from being thick as dog shit sometimes and a coward most of the time, and a sexual deviant all of the time, he was still a mate. I took a deep breath and said,

'The fucking Bin Boys is the fucking name of my fucking gang Diamond for fuck's, fucking sake mate.'

'Oh yeah! The Bin Boys! Replied Diamond. 'I remember! Sorry I was a bit preoccupied with you wanting me to punch Steve Callaghan in the face and the consequences of such an action on my own face so I can't really think straight at the moment.'

'Totally understandable Diamond and I totally get it. If I was in your position I'd also be full of trepidation. I'd be shitting myself actually because he will definitely kick the fucking shit out of you. That's pretty much guaranteed mate.' I replied.

'Well why are you making me do it then?' Diamond asked.

It was a good question.

'Listen Diamond,' I told him, 'I'm not making you do it. It's both hurtful and a tad unfair for you to suggest that. All I'm saying is that if you don't do it, and you have every right to refuse, and I won't think any less of you than I do already, the chances are that Sarah Harding will drop you like a fucking bad habit when she finds out that you are no longer a member of the fucking Bin Boys... The Bin Boys being the name of my gang of course. I know you're stressed. It's a stressful time for all of us. Well not all of us obviously, just you, but I do want you to know that I get it.'

Diamond had a difficult decision make. If he punched Steve Callaghan there was a very high probability that he'd get his head kicked in but if he chose not to that was almost certainly the end of his sex life, forever.

The poor cunt was visibly shaking and his bottom lip was starting to tremble. I did feel sorry for him but there wasn't much that I could do. With great power comes great responsibility and all that shit so my hands were pretty much tied. I could have chosen one of the others obviously but fate had turned over a card and Diamond's terrified face was on the fucker. Diamond was called Diamond because every time he got nervous his dick got hard, as hard as a diamond cutter, so my only real concern right now was if he got a hard-on during the process and made the whole thing a bit off- key and undermine what kind of statement I was trying to make.

'But why Johnny?' Diamond whined,'It would be a lot easier for me to go over to him and lay one on him if I knew why?'

'It's not really a need to know kind of thing Diamond.' I relied. 'I'm the leader and I give the orders and you are a foot soldier so you only need to follow orders. It's best for everyone otherwise chaos will ensue. Fucking hurry up mate I really need a wank and, unlike you lot, it would seem, I'm going to have to do it myself.'

Finally Diamond looked at me with resignation in his eyes, gave out an audible sigh, puffed himself up as best he could and strode purposely forwards in the direction of the unwitting Steve Callaghan.

   Steve wasn't even a bad lad really he was kind of nondescript and kept himself to himself and his little gang of mates. He was the leader of his gang though and he was a big cunt. Unfortunately for poor Steve though he was a potential obstacle in my attempt to scramble up to the top of the criminal tree and I had to set out my stall by making an example of the poor cunt.

I called Diamond back.

'Hang on Diamond.' I shouted, 'before you knock the cunt out I want you to walk past him then give the impression that he's said something to you then walk up to him and point at him in a threatening manner. Then chin him. Oh yeah and do all this in a very theatrical way because I want everyone to see. Got that? Oh and here's the important bit. Once he's laid you out I'll stroll over and kick the fucking shit out of him and then do a speech about me being the new daddy around here and all that. Scum style. Then we can all fuck off and you can get your dick wet inside Sarah Harding or if you don't feel up to it, she can at least take you to A and E.'

Diamond was not in a good way.

'I'm not going to knock the cunt out Johnny!' He cried, 'I've never thrown a punch in my life! I'm going to die!'

'Don't be so fucking silly Diamond, you soppy cunt. Just chin the fucker and see what happens. Maybe you'll get lucky and he'll hit the deck and you'll be a hero and hot chicks will form a long line, a long sexy line Diamond my old pal, my old buddy… A long sexy line to your genitals.' I told him trying to jolly him up a bit.

'I don't want to Johnny. Ask one of the others!' He pleaded.

'Listen mate, everyone is going to have to prove themselves at some point. It's not all about eating pussy and smoking weed. It's about discipline and commitment to the cause. It's about transforming our lives and clawing our way to the top and fucking well staying there. Now if you don't go over to Steven Callaghan and punch the cunt I'm going to throw you out of the Bin Boys and you'll be eaten up by these fucking wolves in no time at all.' I told him as I waved my hand theatrically across the playground. 'It's your choice though. I'm not going to force you. Squint, Kev, Sandy, Black Clint, I mean Just Clint, they're all going to have to prove themselves at some stage. Maybe not today, maybe not tomorrow but soon and ... um ...for the rest of their lives.' I told him as the others gathered around also clearly shitting themselves at this news.

Just Clint spat on the ground, put his fingers in his belt loops and said, 'Johnny, what the fuck did that bit mean, pilgrim?'

I had to admire Just Clint's dedication to his cowboy act even under extreme stress.

'Which bit just Clint? I sure did say a lot of mighty fine words back there darn tootin' but I can't rightly remember it all due to the amount of drugs I've recently taken... Gawd blimey love a duck and no mistake.' I replied, getting into the spirit of it and adding a bit of cockney just for added fun. Just Clint wasn't really a cowboy but he loved to play the part and who the fuck was I to stop him? No one. Not yet anyway.

'The last bit pardner,' Just Clint replied, ' why you kinda tailed off at the end a bit there Johnny and it didn't rightly make a whole lot of sense see?' He Drawled in his God awful fake cowboy accent.

'That was a quote from Casablanca Black Clint, sorry I mean just Clint now, but I had to bend it a bit.' I told him, 'I was going to save all the Westerns quotes for when it was your turn. Now I don't want to keep speaking with heap big, fork, fucking, tongue, all the good long day, so I'd be much obliged if we could all shut the fuck up and get on with it. Comprende?'

I was starting to get impatient and all my drugs were beginning to wear off and I just wanted to go home and give myself a good seeing to. Damned that Sandy in his little silky panties turning a boy's head. You'd have to be a right fucking bender not to be turned on by his big, thick cock and balls bulging out of those little things.

I'm not trying to be a cunt Diamond and I don't want to see you get hurt. I'm just trying to shove my finger into the dyke of anarchy and revolution before it bursts its banks.' I told him.

'Dyke.' Squint sniggered.

Then we all sniggered. Everyone except Diamond who was still a bit distracted.

'Listen Diamond my drugs are wearing off and as it doesn't look like I'm going to have sexual intercourse any time soon so I'd very much like to get home and bash one out before they leave my system. So would you kindly either shit or get off the fucking pot. Please.' I asked him for the final time.

'Okay! Okay! Okay fuck it. I'll do it.' Diamond suddenly said, almost to himself.

He then started taking huge, deep breaths trying to psych himself up.

'I can do this! I can do this! It's just mind over matter ain't it? Piece of piss! I've just got to visualise smacking the fucker. Yes that's it! I've just got to picture myself punching him on the chin and knocking him out! Yeah then picture myself standing over him while everyone is cheering! Yeah cheering and clapping me and patting me on the head and saying, "good boy Diamond! Who's a good boy!?" It's me! Diamond is a good boy! Johnny I'm a good boy!'

'Yeah' I laughed, 'That's right Diamond is a good boy!' And I patted him on the head and scratched him behind the ears.

Diamond had clearly lost his fucking marbles. I've seen this happen a few times. The poor cunt had got himself into such a state he'd lost his sense of self and evidently now thought he was some kind of dog, possibly a Labrador or more likely one of those nervous little fuckers who piss themselves at the first sign of any kind of trouble. I decided that the only thing to do was play along so I patted my legs enthusiastically and said, 'There's a good boy!'

He bounded towards me and I ruffled his hair and told him again that he was indeed a good boy and also a clever boy.

'Right then be good boy and run over to Steve and punch the cunt and I'll give you a treat! How's about that then!? Go on! Go on boy! That's it!' I shouted at him eagerly, egging him on. This was all getting a bit fucking mental by now but it was all a means to an end. After one last ruffle and a pat on his stupid fucking head he set off in the direction of the unwitting Steve Callaghan who was about twenty yards away chatting to his mates and oblivious to what was about to unfold. I was full of pride and admiration for Diamond and also extremely intrigued to see how all this would all pan out.

Within no time Diamond had reached Steve and his gang. He barged through the assortment of boys and then stood in front of his victim. Steve caught his eye. They stared at each other for what seemed like an eternity and then inexplicably Diamond started barking. He was barking at Steve. Right in his face. He was barking loudly in his face like a real, actual dog. It was odd to see. Very odd. A crowd was starting to gather. Steve just looked confused. Then the barking stopped and Diamond cocked his head to one side in a kind of quizzical manner. This is it! I thought to myself. This is the money shot. Diamond is going to throw that punch and it's all going to kick off. Boom! But Diamond didn't throw a punch. Nope. Instead of throwing a punch Diamond started to lick Steve's face. Nobody knew what the fuck was happening. Diamond least of all I suspected. Steve, quite rightly in my opinion, pushed him away and told him to fuck off. But Diamond wasn't finished with him. Not by a long chalk. Diamond then proceeded to walk around him while growling and whimpering. Once again I thought that he could still pull it all back if this was the moment he unleashed the mother of all punches and laid Steven Callaghan on the proverbial canvas. No such luck though. No, the whole thing just got more and more bizarre.

'Listen mate, I don't know what the fuck is going on here and I don't want any trouble but if you don't fuck off I'm going to knock you the fuck out.' Steve, quite reasonably in my opinion, said to Diamond. At this point I wanted to knock the cunt out too because he was making a right royal spectacle of himself and by extension he was making me look like a right cunt too.

Diamond didn't seem to be taking any notice and by this stage I think he was somewhere else. Possibly on another planet. A planet on which he was getting his dick sucked with a big joint in his mouth and not this planet in which he was parading about like some kind of hybrid, half human, half canine, cunt.

Steve then turned his attention over to me. He looked pleadingly at me and I just shrugged. He knew what was occurring and was clearly looking for a way out that didn't involve me making an example of him. I admired Steve for his intelligence and had to make a quick decision.

'Come here boy! Diamond come here boy! Who's a good boy?! Diamond heal!' I shouted over to the soppy cunt.

Diamond seemed to come out of his dog trance for a brief moment and he looked up quizzically.

'Get here now Diamond!' I shouted again. This was certainly not going to plan and I was in danger of looking like a right mug and I wasn't about to let that happen.

I marched over to where this pantomime was being played out.

'Hahaha! Good one Diamond! You've won the bet!' I shouted at him as I pulled out a fiver and tried to hand it to him. That should have been that but Diamond was sunk deep into his character again and just stared at me. Then he started growling.

'Diamond mate that's enough now. You've won the bet so let's get out of here. We've all got things to do.' I laughed. There was a large crowd now and I was struggling to find a way out with my integrity intact.

'Come on buddy. Look Sarah's over there and she's got treats!' I said getting increasingly desperate.

Diamond looked over to where I pointed and when he couldn't see her; because it was obviously a lie, he started snarling. I had to admit that it was quite a convincing performance and in any other circumstance I would have applauded him but I couldn't be seen to be rewarding bad behaviour. I decided to try a different approach.

'Fucking stop it now Diamond, enough is enough. We've all had a good laugh but stop it now because you're acting decidedly odd.' I told him.

Diamond looked at me with big, sad, puppy eyes. He then looked at Steve and then back to me. He then pulled out his cock and pissed all over Steve's legs. Steve's immediate response was to call him a dirty cunt and punch him in the head which resulted in Diamond being laid out unconscious on the playground tarmac.

I walked over to Steve.

'Do you and your boys want to work for me?' I asked him.

'Yeah alright.' Steve replied.

And that was that. Not what I'd planed but not a bad result really. Not for Diamond obviously but that was his own fault. Fear will do some pretty crazy things to a person. I sauntered back over to the rest of the boys. Then I looked coldly at just Clint and said, 'Right then Black Clint it's now your turn'

Black Clint looked like he'd just shit himself.

'Only joking you stupid cunt.' I laughed.

'Your fucking face!' I continued. 'Fucking priceless mate! Right then I'm off for a wank. See you later you fucking virgins.' I said and started to walk off.

You're the only virgin around here Johnny. You fucking virgin.' Quipped Squint.

'Yeah that's why I'm going to pop round your mum's and giver one up the Gary Glitter and put an end to this once and for all.' I replied.

'Sounds good. I might come with you and get my brown wings.' He replied.

"Let's all go!' Black Clint chimed in, obviously feeling a bit more chipper.

'Someone throw water over Diamond or whatever you have to do to wake him up and I'll see you lot later because I've got an appointment to keep with Sam Fox and one of our Wayne's t shirts!' I told them.

Then I fucked off.

Chapter two

I hopped on my bike and headed home. It was a home now too. I'd cleaned it all up and if I did actually ever get to take a bird there, hopefully they wouldn't just start vomiting or self-harming as soon as they stepped in. All the shit and piss and blood and spunk stains had been scrubbed clean and the place smelled of bleach and that stuff you spray to make the place smell nice when you can't really be arsed to do it properly. 'Woodland meadow' it was called; although to be honest it smelled more like what I imagined a chemical castration would smell like. Nevertheless it was a vast improvement on what it was doing its utmost to cover up which I can only describe as being a heady concoction of childhood trauma, clinical depression, various sexually transmitted diseases and a tenacious yeast infection.

  I actually looked forward to going home these days. Before we kicked the shit out of our parents and threw them out I'd always tried to avoid going home at all. It wasn't exactly what you'd call cosy and welcoming. The heating was never on and there was never any food and there was always the chance of getting a good hiding. There was always fags and alcohol though; and loads of stuff that had been nicked and waiting to get fenced. All that shit was behind us now. I was even paying the rent. Our rent man was too scared to come round ours because he was always getting threatened by my mum and dad. We didn't pay our rent for months at a time. Or our electricity. My parents had always paid just enough to keep us from being evicted. But recently I'd changed all that. I wanted us to be legitimate council house occupiers and that was because I didn't want any cunt from the council coming around snooping about from now on.

  The bailiffs had been round to ours on a regular basis ever since I could remember but all that had to change and I now had the money to put everything right. I wanted to be an upstanding citizen and be able to walk the streets with my head held high. I didn't want to be a scum bag any more. Some people love to be seen as scoundrels and vagabonds and play the system to their own advantage, but not me. I'd already had my fill of that life. Yes I wanted to be a criminal mastermind but I didn't want to wear it on my sleeve. As far as all these legal fuckers would know the McQueens were now the epitome of model citizens in every way and would no longer be drawing attention to themselves by being horrible fucking scumbags.

  A few days previously I had spotted our rent collector; he always scooted past our house as fast as he could because he knew it was a waste of time trying to get any money from us. I knew his name was Eric. We all knew him round here as, 'Eric the rent.' He was old as fuck and always wore a suit and tie and carried a big leather bag on his shoulder. Eric was a very nervous man. This was presumably due to the amount of times he'd been beaten up and robbed for the contents of that leather bag over the years. Fuck knows why he didn't just quit but regardless of all the harassments and muggings he always tuned up round our way on a Tuesday morning come rain or shine and to be honest I'd admired the daft cunt's tenacity.

   As I watched him run past our house from our living room I knocked hard on the window to get his attention. The knock was loud as fuck and he'd clearly heard it because I saw his whole body stiffen but he kept on running. I didn't blame him. He was well trained in knowing when to keep his old, bald head down. A tap on the window was seldom good news in his world but I was just about to make the cunt's day. I ran from the living room, into the hall, and out of our front door in a thrice and shouted over to his rapidly fleeing body.

'Eric!' I bellowed, trying to sound both authoritative and jolly.

 No response or acknowledgment was issued forth.

I shouted again.

'Eric you soppy cunt! Come back! I want a word mate!'

Still no response.

'Fuck me Eric its good news!' I hollered at the top of my lungs.'I'm not going to harm you! I want to pay our rent!'

This last sentence got his attention and he immediately stopped in his tracks and looked back towards me. He starred at me hard for a good couple of moments trying to gauge whether it was some kind of trap.

I waved a pile of notes in his direction and grinned. This act did the trick and he tentatively started to walk back towards our house. He was still wary because over the years he'd seen every trick in the book that was played out to get to his precious leather bag full of rent money.

'I'm not going to mug you Eric! If I wanted that bag I would have had the fucker off you by now and you'd be laying on the ground in a pool of your own blood, begging for your life!' I laughed.

Eric didn't get the joke though. In fact he looked like he was just about to leg it again.

'Fuck me Eric I'm joking you silly sausage!' I shouted over to him, watering down my language in order to try and put the cunt at ease.

He looked at me again and eventually said,

'Didn't you bum that kid to death in the park a few weeks ago son?'

What the fuck? Why did every one in the whole world know about that?

'No! No I did not bum a kid to death in the park a few weeks ago you cheeky cunt! How very dare you! That was our Wayne! ... and I'll have you know that it was consensual. Probably. Did Kenny die then? That's no loss. He was a right little cunt. Did they all die? I hope that Mickey is dead too and Debbie... Benny? Davie? and Matty? All Dead I hope. The fucking pricks.' I replied, fucking incandescent with indignation.

'Well I heard it was one of the McQueen brothers and just assumed it was you.' Eric replied innocently.

'Of course it wasn't me you daft old cunt! ...No offence. No wonder you're always getting your head kicked in spreading rumours like that all across town! Bloody cheek! What if I started telling everyone that you tried to touch me on the bottom!? What then?! You'd be strung up mate that's what! We don't tolerate kiddy fiddlers around here I'll tell you that!' I replied, angry as a mother fucker.

'No offence son but I don't think anybody would believe that I tried to touch your bottom. If I was going to risk getting strung up for child molestation I'd pick someone an awful lot sexier than you. No offence like. Your next door neighbour for example. Now there's a right little sort! I'd do time for giving her one I'll tell you that! And the mum too at a push! My standards have dropped a lot as I've got older. This is what happens son. One minute you only fancy the top dolly birds and then as time goes by you'd fuck anything! Well not the likes of you obviously but pretty much anything else! Why only last week this old lady couldn't make her rent so I gave her a couple of days grace after she agreed to eat my arse while wanking me off! The rusty trombone think it's called. I'm a big old softy really. ..'

'Fucking hell Eric stop talking!' I shouted at the dirty bastard.

'Oh grow up you scrawny little cunt why the fuck do you think I do this job? Out of loyalty to the Council!? No son, it's for all the blow jobs and rim jobs and the Mexican wheel barrows and the cream pies. The best news I get in a day is when some sexy little thing can't pay her rent. You should see some of the single mothers I've shagged over the years! I reckon half the kids around here are mine! Not you though son. I always drew the line at your mum. Even I have standards.' He continued earnestly.

We both laughed at the last bit.

Well fuck me what a turn-up. The wily old fox! And there was I, up until now anyway, feeling sorry for the old cunt. At least he didn't fuck my mum. Well not recently anyway. I was convinced of that. Nobody would have stooped that low. I was glad that I probably wasn't his son, the ugly cunt. Fair play to him though.

'Hey! Hang on a minute please don't talk about Sally like that! She's a very intelligent young lady and not a piece of meat for you to objectify!' I told the cheeky bastard.

'Fuck off son! Don't give me any of that old pony! I bet you've had a good few knuckle shuffles over her since your knackers dropped! I bet you've had a few over the mum too you dirty dog!' Eric laughed, and he gave me a conspirational wink which made me want to literally murder him.

'How dare you suggest such a thing! Sally is a good friend of mine and I'd never do anything that base!' I replied very unconvincingly while feeling myself go bright red.

Suddenly I heard a familiar voice shout from somewhere above.

'Pants on fire! What do you mean you've never had a wank about me Johnny you little liar! I'm hot as fuck!'

It was Sally. Fuck me here we go again.

I was confused. Did she want me to have a wank about her now or not? Did she want me to objectify her and treat her like a piece of meat? I wasn't sure of anything any more but one thing that was for sure and that was the scientific fact that after that little speech I would be having a wank about her as soon as I was able and that meant getting rid of Eric the rent as soon as possible.

'And as for you! You mucky old cunt Eric!' Sally continued,'how dare you fantasise about shagging me and my mum at the same time!' Why I could have you sacked you filthy bastard!'

'Now look love I was just having a joke with this young man here. I meant no harm. Of course I wouldn't like to ... um... make love to you and your dear mother at the same time.' Eric stammered, clearly wrong footed by the sudden situation he'd found himself in.

'Saying that... Your family is well behind on the rent though and all I'm tentatively saying... that is if you or your mum or both of you did feel like writing me a furry cheque or even giving me ...um... let's see now ... topless relief perhaps or a quick one off the wrist into a pair of your PE knickers or some such then I'm sure we could come to some kind of mutually beneficial financial arrangement...' He continued.

Fucking brass neck on that cunt, I thought to myself. All these years I'd been pitying him and he'd been filling his boots abusing his position in order to shag all the fit birds round here. Of course part of me admired him but most of me was a bit appalled.

I looked up to where Sally was but she was no longer there. Probably gone to see her mum about Eric's deal. My head was all over the place now and I didn't really know what was happening. This situation was about to get sorted pretty quickly though.

   The next thing I knew was Sally bursting through her front door and using her ten hole Doctor Martens to kick the living shit out of Eric the rent. The first kick was right to his nuts and he went down like a sack of potatoes. He groaned and tried to plead for mercy but we all knew it was too late for that. Sally was all red in the face and spittle was coming out of the side of her mouth with the effort she was making beating him up. At one stage as she bent down to punch him in the face I could clearly see her tits pop out of her shirt. I was a gentleman though and didn't immediately get my dick out and start wanking off. I did get a hard-on though but this was only after I watched her bend over right in front of me in order to get a better angle to clout old Eric and I got a magnificent view of the crack of her arse coupled with a fleeting glimpse of her black satin knickers. This beautiful and highly erotic sight brought back an image of me stood over our kitchen sink wanking off over the very same pair when they were hanging on her mum's washing line a few days previously. Fuck me I had enough wanking material for ages now!

Then Sally's rather course language brought me back to the moment at hand.

'You horrible, shitty little man! I'm going to fucking kill you! You dirty, disgusting, fucking, shit cunt!' She screamed as she kicked and punched and scratched old Eric who was just crumpled up into a ball desperately trying to protect his head and genitals as best he could given the circumstances.

I wondered if I should have joined in but to be honest she was doing such a cracking job and I didn't feel it was necessary. Plus I didn't want to miss any of the action because it was sexy as hell. Between kicks and punches I could see that Eric had a look of stoic resignation about him and I quickly came to the conclusion that he'd been in this situation many times before during his illustrious career. All he had to do was not die and sooner or later it would be over and he'd be on his merry way.

After a disappointingly short time Sally had worn herself out. She stood up straight, put her tits back in her bra, pulled up her jeans and tied back her hair. She then looked down at Eric who was now covered in scratches and bruises and a very hilarious looking Doctor Marten footprint on top of his bald head. 'Cunt' she said contemptuously and spat in his face. She then turned on her heels and went back inside. The show was over.

'Fuck me Eric you just got fucking owned mate.' I laughed. Eric looked up at me and winked. 'You win some, you lose some son. Now help an old man up please.' He looked rather a pathetic site so I took pity on him but as I did so I couldn't help but noticed that his cock was as hard as mine.

I dropped him back to the floor. 'Oh you sick fuck Eric!' I shouted at him disgustedly while trying to hide my own erection.

'Listen you little prick, if the next time I'm getting a good hiding off a teenage girl and her tits fall out and I don't get a hard-on you have permission to shoot me in the back of the fucking head. At one point I got a right good sniff of her little cunt too! Now fucking help me up, I've got work to do!' He shouted at me.

I helped him to his feet and dusted him down. Then I head-butted him which knocked him out cold. How dare he get a sniff of Sally's fanny before me!? And he'd seen her tits! I felt both betrayed and violated. I should really have killed him at that point but I needed him. I then propped him up against our garden wall and waited until he came round. All my neighbours seeing him in this state wouldn't do me any harm with them because he was obviously a proper cunt to all of them. Eventually he came round and once his head had cleared and he knew where he was I slapped him across the face a few times like I'd seen in films and threw a bucket of cold water over him.

'Hey what are you doing!? You're supposed to do that while I'm unconscious not after!' He groaned.

'Well you were bleeding all over the place and plus you're a cunt so I'll do what I want. You're only alive because I need you alive you filthy old bastard.' I replied. 'Anyway shut your fucking mouth. From now on you only speak when I tell you that it's okay to speak. You cunt.' I replied, still livid that he'd had the presence of mind to inhale the heady scent of my future wife's vulva while he was getting his head kicked in.

'You wouldn't kill me! You wouldn't dare! I'll have you know that I'm a very good friend of a certain Paul Simonon … also known as …'

'You're a fucking mate of that fucking ginger nonce Simmer? Well fuck me it's a small world. So am I!' I replied delightedly.

This must have been why he was so fucking sure of himself. He was under Simmer's protection and thought he was untouchable.

'I'll tell you what son, I wouldn't go around calling Mr Simonon a nonce as that might be very bad for your health.' He replied, looking up at me in a kind of triumphant way that really did make me want to murder him right then and there.

I was livid that he thought that I was scared of that scrawny little strawberry blonde sex case so I kicked him in the head and his lights went out again.

In hindsight I wish I'd dragged the fucker into our house before I'd done that because he was very difficult to move in that state but fuelled by only anger and two lines of amphetamine I somehow managed to drag the cunt into my hallway where I tied him up and let him stew for a bit. A few weeks ago I could have given him to our Wayne to use as a sex toy but since he'd met old Dorothy he'd calmed right down. He was pretty much normal now.

Who would have thought that all our Wayne needed to become an upstanding member of society was the love of a good woman? Or in our Wayne's case the love of a raddled old semi- retired prostitute. To think I was willing to give up my precious cherry to that hag makes me retch now. I can't remember why she got the arse and rejected my offer to free me from this virgin curse but she did and in retrospect it's probably for the best anyway. They say that beggars can't be choosers but I wanted my first time to be beautiful and loving and romantic. Well maybe not beautiful and loving and romantic exactly but I'd have liked it to be with someone who wasn't some decrepit old corpse with a fanny that resembled an empty head-lock. Call me a snob but that's got to be the minimum standard. I don't want to look back on my life and remember my first time with horror or shame. Somewhere deep down I knew that it was probably a long shot but in an ideal world I'd always hoped to lose my virginity while shagging Sally and Pali at the same time while they both lezzed off. Obviously I'd be willing to take it down a notch or two with the right lady. I wouldn't mind if it was with a page three girl or the dark haired one off Bananarama or even that Toyah as long as I didn't have to listen to their shit music. I bet Bonnie Tyler would give a good account of herself in the sack but I wouldn't take her out. Annie Lennox could fuck right off even if she begged me to give her one. I think after Sally and Pali and Cait O'Riordan from The Pogues, Sinead O'Connor would be my number four. Especially if she kept those Doctor Martens on. Maybe I should write to them all and ask them if they'd be interested in taking my virginity? I didn't know where they lived though and I didn't even own a pen let alone an envelope or stamps so I decided to leave it up to fate. Or Jesus. Or a mixture of both.

In a fit of desperation I'd decided a few days earlier that if I lost my virginity before my sixteenth birthday I would see it as a miracle from God and I'd become religious again and if not then He could officially fuck off. I thought that this was fair. I'd even got down on my knees by the side of my bed and prayed. I started off like it was no big deal and prayed for the poor and the weak and that then snuck in about losing my virginity at the end. 'Dear God, hope this prayer finds you well, please help the needy, and them starving Ethiopians and if you could do one of your miracles and help me to lose my virginity to some half decent bird then I swear I'll believe in you again. Thanks in advance, all the best, yours, Johnny. Amen.' It was worth a try. Actually this act brought back a memory I had from years ago when I was around six or seven when I asked God to intervene when my dad was beating up my mum and to His credit about twenty minutes in my mum clubbed my dad around the head with a pint glass which just seemed to have come out of nowhere and he was knocked out which gave my mum time to kick him repeatedly in the nuts and fuck off round to Auntie Joan's, so you could say he'd already done me a favour. Although if I could go back in time I would probably have have kept quite on that occasion and let them fight to the death.

I saw this documentary on gigolos once where these good looking French cunts would stand outside posh hotels in Paris and wait for rich old ladies to come out and hope that they'd get paid to give them one. They'd be wined and dined and then all they had to do was shag these old birds and get paid loads of money. Some of them were given expensive presents too like watches and designer clothes and even cars. Since then I've always fancied myself as a gigolo. Maybe I should stand outside of the Dolphin and see if any of the old birds in there would pay me to slip them a length? There's a lot of ropey birds come out of there of an evening though; many of them nearly as fucked up looking as old Dorothy. What if they asked me to lick them out and I puked into their old growlers and then they refused to pay me? No I was just going to try and be patient and let nature take it's course.

I was well busy anyway what with expanding my criminal empire. Maybe I should just concentrate on that first then when I was truly minted I'd just go to Thailand or one of those other third world countries and just buy a woman. One of my dad's mates did this once. Apparently he go pissed one night in Bangkok or wherever and ended up sleeping with this Thai bird and when he tried to bin her off the next morning she wouldn't leave and got all upset because apparently he'd bought her the night before and now it was his responsibility to take care of her. I think in the end he gave her fifty quid in their money and told her to fuck off. My dad's mates talked a lot of bollocks though so this might not be true. I'd definitely pay fifty quid for one of the fitter ones though but I'd get rid of her before she got too old because that lot don't age well. Plus you've got all that screeching. Plus you've got all those lady-boys over there too of course. I'm not going to lie, some of the ones I've seen in those channel four documentaries could easily pass for real birds and if I was over there and one night and I was in a nightclub and got off with one without even knowing and ended up hanging out the back of it while off my nut on whatever drugs those cunts take over there I'm not sure I'd be too bothered if come the next morning when we both woke up with raging hard-ons and he shyly asked me if I'd be a gentleman and take his swollen member into my mouth and give it a suck until he emptied his load down my eager throat. I mean I wouldn't be shouting about it the next day but I'm certainly no racist and if that was the custom then who the fuck am I to not participate like some jumped up colonialist? No way mate in fact I'd probably go back to the same night club the next night just to immerse myself into their culture just so they didn't think I was one of those Brits who just want to go to these places and eat fish and chips and get a cheap tattoo. I'm not sure if bumming a lady boy or getting bummed off one would actually count as officially losing my virginity though, so for now at least, I'm going to stay local and see what other options where available.

Eventually Eric the rent woke up and we had a little chat and put a few things straight.

'Eric ... Eric ... Eric mate... ' I whispered in his ear. I suspected that he was trying to kid me so I took out my lighter and gently set fire to the thin bit of skin on his wrist. That did the trick and he jumped up suddenly wide awake.

'What's going on! Where am I? Who are you?' He whimpered while trying to look all frail and elderly.

'Fuck off Eric I don't have time for all that shit. Stop acting like a clever cunt or I will actually set you on fire.' I replied. I wasn't having any of his bullshit now that I had the measure of the cunt. He worked for Simmer and he used that power to shag all the poor hot mums in our neighbourhood and even though a tiny part of me did in fact admire the cunt's audacity even by my standards it was morally repugnant. Especially given his advanced years. I gave him a slap, which to be honest was probably out of pure jealousy and said,

'Right then Eric me old mate, the way I see it is you've got two options.'

Eric looked up me in bewilderment.

'Eric if you play me for a cunt for one second longer I'm going to put you in a coma mate.' I told him. This did the trick.

'Okay son. Okay. There's no flies on you are there? You're too clever for me that's for sure.' He replied, trying a different tact.

'Eric I will cut one off one your hands and shove it down your fucking throat if you don't stop fucking me about. I'm a busy boy and you are doing my fucking nut in so just don't say anything until I tell you that it's okay to talk again. Okay?' I replied.

Eric now looked genuinely terrified this time.

'I said Okay Eric?'

This was met with silence.

'Eric you absolute cunt' I screamed, 'We don't have much time mate! Our Wayne will be here in a minute and if he sees you all trussed up and vulnerable looking, muscle memory is going to kick in and he's almost certainly going to rape you. In your old, saggy white arse! Why are you playing for time? Nobody is coming to rescue you mate. You're the baddie in this scenario and I'm the hero! Simmer isn't coming through my front door, guns blazing to come and free you mate. You're fucked. And if you don't stop taking me for a cunt when our Wayne gets here you are literally going to get fucked! ...in the arse... and the mouth. Yeah it's going to be arse to mouth. Both yours!'

Still silence from Eric's end.

'Right that's it. I'm going to fuck you myself and then I'm going to kill you. To death. You cunt.' I told the cunt.

Finally, as I was unbuttoning my jeans he said,' Is this still part of the test?'

'Part of what fucking test Eric?' I replied.

'Well you said that if |i spoke without your permission then you'd set fire to me or something.' He replied absolutely petrified by now.

'Oh yeah I did say that didn't I! Although what I actually said was that I'd cut off one of your hands and shove it down your fucking gob, or words to that effect, but to be fair to you I'll hold my hands up and admit that I didn't actually make myself clear. So if our Wayne does happen to come in and try and rape you I'll try to pull him off you. Although as you know he's a big cunt but given the circumstances I will do what I can... You may reply to that with no consequences.' I told him.

'Was that a question then son? I must have missed it. Can you repeat it please?' He replied. To be honest I think I'd fried the poor cunt's brain and my own too a bit so I decided to get it all done an dusted as quickly as possible so he could be on his merry way and I could have a nice long wank about Sally's tits and knickers and arse crack.

'The way I see it Eric, you've got two options.' I repeated. 'Either you fuck Simmer off and come and work for me, or I kill you.' I told him.

'In that case I'll fuck Simmer off and come and work for you son.' He replied.

'Good choice Eric!' I replied delightedly, ' you're clearly a pragmatist! A pragmatist and an utter scoundrel. I like that about you. Right then here's the deal you rancid old cuntstickle... Your job is basically the same but without the bit where you fuck all the women who can't pay their rent, because that's immoral and also disgusting at your age. If I find out that you even suggested anything remotely like that with anyone around here I will kill you. Also Sally and her mum will no longer being paying rent. I will be paying their rent from now on and also I will be paying me and our Wayne's rent. Finally when the time comes you will be offering an assortment of drugs to every one who pays rent. So basically you knock on their door and take there rent like normal, and don't forget no blow jobs or fingering or anything at all sexual if they can't pay for a while because...?'

'Because you'll kill me.' Eric replied matter of factly.

'Correct.' I replied,' but obviously if they're clearly taking the piss then you tell me and then it will be my problem to sort out. But if they're just normal upstanding council house fuckers, then you say, 'would you like any drugs today?' And then if they do, which they will because their lives are so shitty, you say, 'okay cool', or whatever old people say, and then you tell them what drugs you have and how much these drugs are and then you bring me all the drug money and take the rent money to wherever the fuck that goes and you stay alive. Oh yeah and If you try and take one single penny of my drug money I will kill you. If you behave I will increase your wages but for now you will just be getting paid by the council because you are a despicable cunt. How does that sound? And before you answer please don't forget that if you disagree with anything I've just said, I will kill you... You may now speak.'

'Okay son.' He replied meekly.

I'd broken him and now I owned him, a bit like my dad's mate who owned the Thai prostitute except I wasn't letting Eric free any time soon. He belonged to me now.

It was different with the electric metre reading collection cunt that came around because the council kept changing them. This was presumably so that the same guy wouldn't keep getting robbed and beaten up when he came round our way. I caught up with one a few days after dealing with old Eric. He also shit himself but I managed to persuade him that I wasn't going to harm him and then I gave him two hundred quid in electric arrears, signed something and he fucked off. He said someone would be round every two weeks to empty our electric meter and I said to tell his bosses that it would now be safe to come round our estate without any trouble. Then I told him to sell my drugs for me and he readily agreed.

It was infuriating that everyone obviously thought that it was me that bummed Kenny on that bench but I was quite pleased that everyone also thought that I was mental. In fact I loved it that everyone thought I was mental. There were a lot of hard cunts around our way but only a few were proper head cases in fact as far as I could tell it was just me and Simmer and Stan the Man. I think it was the moment that something snapped in my brain on the day Butch put that Dog clip on my ear that that I became free. It was at that moment that I realised that I was at the bottom and I had absolutely fuck all to lose. That was the moment of emancipation. If I died tomorrow I'd die happier than I'd ever been and I'd go out with a smile. I'd achieved a lot in a relatively short time. With the help of my darling brother I'd beaten up Mickey and his gang, both my parents, my uncle Sean, I did feel a bit guilty about that one but one has to be one hundred percent ruthless in this game.

Every villain knows that the moment you become soft that's the beginning of the end. That's page one shit in my book. I'd literally set fire to Butch and his bum chum mate and they were both now dead, I'd kicked the shit out of that posh nonce in the bogs,and then killed two of Simmers Hench- men. If I did get old I guess these acts of violence could well come back to haunt me but right now, while I reflected, it all just gave me a massive boner.

Chapter three

As I cycled up the road to our house I could see Sally from next door was leaving to go to college. I didn't even plan it. Due to everything that had occurred over the last few weeks I simply didn't have the time to stalk her any more. This was just plain luck, or possibly divine intervention. Like every other time my heart started pounding and I could feel myself sweating and shaking. I had to do something cool to impress her so as I pulled up I tried to do a broadside by sharply turning my handlebar to the left while pulling hard on my back break. This was accompanied by me doing what I thought was a pretty good impression of screeching tyres as the gravel flew up. It was fucking mint. As I came to a triumphant halt I looked up and tried to give the impression that I'd only just seen her and this type of cool shit was just me being me. Cool as fuck.

'Oh hi Sally. I didn't see you there. Hows it hanging?' I asked her, nonchalant as a mother fucker.

'How's fucking what hanging you absolute walking abortion? My cock? Is that what you mean? Cunt.' Sally replied coldly.

She never ceased to amaze me with her command of the English language.

'What? No I mean, how are you?' I replied.

'Fuck off Johnny.' She replied. And then just like that she fucked off.

   As I watched her pert little ass cheeks swaying to and fro while they fought for breath in her spray-on jeans as she stomped off down the street, for the first time ever my cock didn't get hard. I didn't know what had just happened then but one thing was for sure and that was that I wasn't about to run inside and have a wank about her. I was actually mad as fuck with her unwarranted vitriol towards me and to teach her a lesson I had a wank about Pali... And a bit of a one about her mum too, just out of plain spite. It was her own fault and she'd brought it upon her self. I didn't even feel that guilty about it until I'd shot my load into our bathroom sink and all over the new mirror thirty seconds later. Then I felt I'd somehow betrayed her so after about twenty minutes I had a wank about her too and felt much better.

   Two hand shandies on the bounce must have tired me out because the next thing I knew I was laying on my bed and our Wayne was shaking me awake. As I started to come round I just prayed that my cock wasn't still out.

'Our Johnny! Our Johnny! Wake up! You've fallen asleep with your cock out again!' Our Wayne was shouting gleefully.

I slowly opened one eye hoping that I was still dreaming and having some kind of anxiety driven nightmare but the sight of both our Wayne and his ragged old missus staring down at me soon put me right.

'Men always need a nap after they've shot their bolt.' said Dorothy matter of factly as if it was the most natural thing in the world to be chatting away while a teenage boy was laid out on his bed with his jeans and pants around his ankles and his cock still in his hand. And judging by the cold, sticky sensation I was now feeling, it would seem that I also had spunk all over my belly. My only saving grace, in the scheme of things, was that because it was the second load I hadn't come all over my new duvet cover.

I decided to play it cool.

'Oops sorry guys I just had some bird round and we were doing so much sex I must have passed out when I orgasmed! Where is um ... Linda? Did you pass a really fit dark-haired lady on the stairs? Perky tits? Probably just wearing a thong and a contended smile?'wearing a thong?' I enquired with a cheeky wink.

'Linda? Wow not 'the' Linda! Not flipping Linda flipping Lusardi Johnny! Wow our Johnny was that page three stunner Linda Lusardi who we passed on the stairs just then?' Cried our Wayne with mock excitement.

'Dorothy! Bloody hell did you hear that? Our Johnny just had page three stunner Linda Lusardi up here! That's why his penis is out and his stomach is covered in sperm! For a minute I thought he'd just fallen asleep after having a wank like all the other times! Gosh that's a relief isn't it Dorothy! That's much less embarrassing!' He continued sarcastically.

'Hang on a minute! Why that explains it!' Replied Dorothy getting hold of it too. Then she turned towards the bedroom door, looked passed it and said, 'Well fuck me gently you old rogue Johnny, I thought it was her but couldn't believe me own peepers! It is! It's page three stunner Samantha Fox taking a shit in the bathroom with the ruddy door open too! Ooh Johnny she looks battered son! You must have really whacked her twat all to ruddy buggery!'

Then it was our Wayne's turn again. He's a fat cunt but he turned on his heel like a London Taxi cab turning on the preverbal sixpence and as he theatrically flung open my wardrobe doors he shouted, 'Look Dorothy, unless my very own eyes are playing tricks upon me, he's got young Sally from next door hidden in here! And who is this concealed behind my dear brother's gold medallions and silk shirts and designer suits? Why if it isn't Mr Patel's quite delightful daughter Pali! ... and they are wearing bikinis and kissing each other! Almost certainly because of our Johnny getting them so hot and horny! Where you making love to these two as well Johnny? No wonder you fell asleep dear brother!'

Our Wayne was even speaking like an old person these days due to hanging out the back of Gandhi's nan. Fuck me, If I'd had a gun at that moment I would have shot them both and then myself. Well I'd have definitely shot

Dorothy. I've pretty much always wanted to shoot her though but love is love and our Wayne was happy so as long as that was the case I'd have to grin and bear it.

A few weeks ago our Wayne could hardly string a sentence together but since he's been getting his dick sucked by Mother Theresa here he's transformed into a cross between Shakespeare and Frank fucking Carson. It was fucking check mate and I had nowhere to go from here. All I could do was pull up my jeans, tuck my cock back into my underpants and join them.

'Okay Okay you got me! Come out from under the bed you two the game is up!' I shouted.

'Wow Johnny! Even more hot dolly-birds stashed away you little devil? Who've you got under there then?' Enquired Dorothy with fake wonderment. 'Marilyn Monroe and Audrey Hepburn?'

'Wow at least keep it relevant Vera Lynn!' I replied, 'No, for your information it's Mum and auntie Joan!' Then me and our Wayne pissed ourselves laughing and by the smell coming off her, I think Dorothy had just pissed herself.

'I really must put a lock on that door at some point. That could have been embarrassing.' I said, trying to sound ironic.

'Why? What for Johnny? To keep out all the pussy?' replied Dorothy cuttingly.

'No babe to keep out the living dead! Fuck me sideways, you're not going to let me forget this in a hurry are you Dorothy.' I sheepishly replied.'Although luckily for me you'll be dead of old age soon anyway ah you'll not see another winter I'll wager.' I laughed.

Nobody else laughed though. I could easily have snapped the old crow's neck there and then but as I said, I didn't want to upset our Wayne.

'Sorry Dorothy that was out of order. You've probably got weeks to live.' I continued. I could have gone on like that for ages but I could see our Wayne wasn't happy so I relented.

'I'm just joking for fuck's sake! I'm embarrassed! Nobody wants to get caught with his trousers down. Especially when they're covered in their own jizz.' I said, as I frantically started trying to wipe dried spunk off my stomach.

'And skid marks Johnny! You've got skid marks in your under crackers too!' Laughed our Wayne. I briefly thought about murdering the pair of them but then, luckily for all of us Dorothy threw me my t shirt and said, 'Oh don't worry about it Johnny love! I've seen much worse than that son. Why that's nothing compared to what I've witnessed over the years! Fuck me I could tell you some right stories! There was this one time I was paid to throw my own shit at a police commissioner! That was a long time ago mind you. It's been a long time since I've passed a solid enough stool to hurl at a high ranking member of the law establishment. They're more like cow pats these days. Isn't that right our Wayne?'

Our Wayne grinned and nodded.

'The one I threw at him was beautiful though.' She continued. 'I remember it like it was yesterday. It flew through the air like one of them fat Cuban cigars. Hit him right in the fucking face! The saucy cunt. And the dirty bugger ate it right up! Fifty pounds I got for that! And that was back then!'

Fucking hell. Well that little story put everything into perspective.

'I'll tell you what, I'll give you both fifty quid to fuck off out of my room. How does that sound?' I told them.

'Sounds great our Johnny!' Replied our Wayne. So I did and they did and when the coast was clear I couldn't help but peer inside my wardrobe door just to see my miracle had occurred yet. The same old sight of cheap clothes, the pile of porn mags and screwed up tissues strewn all over the floor told me that it hadn't. Not so far anyway.

'What do you two love birds want anyway?' I asked them after I'd had a shower, changed and come downstairs to where they were sat in the living room waiting for me. Dorothy was sat on our Wayne's lap like it was the most natural thing in the world for a twenty year old boy to have an octogenarian prostitute as his missus. Council estate stuff personified.

'Fuck me Dorothy you look absolutely radiant! Don't tell me you're pregnant!' I quipped.

A dust ball drifted across the floor. Well that's double standards to say the least I thought to myself. It was a different scenario ten minutes ago upstairs when they were taking the piss out of me. Laughing their fucking heads off they were. Suddenly a thought came into my head. And it was, ' Fuck me if I ever do have sex I just want it to be normal, every day, straight- forward, run of the mill, love making. I don't want to be eating anyone's poo or anything off-key like that. Not to start off with anyway. To begin with I'm only going to do finger banging, licking out, getting sucked off and vaginal intercourse.

  Sure if Sally or Pali wanted to piss down my back or on my balls while we were coked off our nuts then I'd probably just have to go along with it in case they thought that I was some kind of prude, but I'd have to draw the line at big toilet. I bet Sally and Pali's shits would be perfectly formed though. Pali's probably even more so than Sally's. I had no real explanation as to why I thought this I just did. In my mind both of them would produce a perfect shit but Pali's would just take the gold, or in this case, the brown. I just think that because her family have a few quid that she'd eat a better diet than Sally. More roughage. Sally is poor as fuck and probably lives on a diet of own brand tomato soup and cups of tea like me and our Wayne did up until very recently. Although she's less poor since I've been paying their rent.

That's it! That's why she thinks I'm a cunt again! Because I'm paying her rent she thinks I'm going to ask her to write ME a furry cheque! Actually that's not a bad idea. No, I'm not that kind of sick pervert. Or am I? No! No Johnny! Bad Johnny! Stop it! I was actually quite proud of myself for not thinking of that until this moment so well done me. No harm in asking her mum for a nosh though I guess. No, I can't do that. She's okay now but what if I marry Sally and she becomes my mother in law? I'd be at the alter knowing that my bride's mum had swallowed by jizz. Or what if I slipped her a length and got her pregnant?! She'll give birth to Sally's half brother or sister! And then what if me and Sally had children they'd be their own nan's cousins or something! That's proper council estate stuff and as I didn't want that kind of life any more I decided to leave any ideas of giving Sally's mum one to the odd tug during one of my more lack-lustre and mundane wanks when I couldn't think of anything better.

Our Wayne stopped nuzzling old Dorothy's scrawny neck and looked up at me. 'No, my darling girlfriend is not pregnant but if she was I'd be delighted.'

'Ooh been there done that our Wayne! You're a sweet heart for saying that though!' squealed Dorothy delightedly, and then she stuck her tongue down our Wayne's mouth and I felt bile rise up into my own.

'Fuck me gently, you two love birds must stop with the public displays of affection! You're putting me off thinking about my dinner.' I told them while trying not to gag.

'Ooh what are you having Johnny? Me and Dorothy are blooming starving because we've been making love all morning and didn't have time to eat!' Our Wayne giggled as he put his fingers through what was left of his bird's hair.

'I was thinking about having a line of speed to be honest brother.' I replied.

This was true. I was starting to feel awful and thought that a nice little livener would be just the job. I wasn't going to do it until these two had fucked off though because I was getting horny again and wanted to draw one off. I don't know whether it was my new found infamy or just the fact that I had a bit of time to myself these days but I was wanking off even more than usual recently. I was smoking more and drinking more and taking more drugs too. It was ace. I was in control of my own destiny for the first time ever and I was loving it. I was going to keep driving forward no matter what or die trying. This was the life for me and fuck the consequences.

   As I was reflecting I suddenly remembered head-butting that poncey cunt in Del's clothes shop. Well it wasn't his shop, he was just doing security there. That was a good day. I'd headbutted the new romantic shop assistant, nicked loads of clothes and then fingered Del's wife. She wanked me off too, and stuck a finger up my arse. 'These are what memories are made of' I thought to myself. I could have given her one but Del came home unexpectedly early -ironically due to me knocking out Simon Le Bon- or whatever her name was, which was a blessing in disguise really because her fanny smelled putrid to say the least and it had lingered on my own fingers for days afterwards.

   I prayed that Sally's fanny smelled a lot better than June's. And Pali's obviously. I loved them both but if I ever got the chance I'd have to do I quick litmus test and dip my finger into them before even contemplating licking them out or sticking my cock into them. What if they wanted me to shag them and when it came down to it their minges stunk like fuck? What would I do? How do you tell a lady that her growler is fucking rank without hurting her feelings and ruining the mood? Would the rotten stench of their respective growlers change the way I felt about them?

My own cock stank for years up until very recently. All our cocks stank. Me, Squints, Diamond's, and Billy's too. Not black Clint's though. His mum still washed his cock by all accounts. Gets right under his five-skin and everything. 'Cleanliness next to Godliness' is his mum's favourite saying. We all thought it was just an excuse to get her hands on his big thick, love pipe. Yeah he was adopted and he didn't know who the fuck his real mum and dad were but, as they say, 'when God closes a door the cunt opens a window,' because black Clint had been blessed oin the trouser department.

I'd read somewhere that there's a lot of pressure on black men because everyone assumes they've got hug cocks but apparently this isn't always the case. Some black men are walking around with small dicks just waiting to get laughed at I guess but not our Clint, he was limping around with a big smile on his chops due to his huge cock. He was happy to get the fucker out too. More than happy, and if I had his dick I'd be showing mine off at every opportunity as well.

   Clint's cock was indeed a big one but compared to our Wayne's it was average. Our Wayne's was gigantic. It would take your fucking breath away if you saw it. And many people around our way had seen it. Before he met Dorothy and calmed the fuck down with the mental stuff he was always getting his out too. The only difference between them was that Clint would politely wait until he was asked. If Wayne saw even a half decent bird he'd immediately unzip and flop it out and wave it about to attract her attention, which it always did. I never knew what he expected to happen as he exposed himself. Did he think that the birds would swoon and giggle and fall upon it with wanton unabashed sexual intent? I hope not because this never happened. Not even once. In fact the opposite always happened, which was for our Wayne getting a kick to the cock, and due to its size these women seldom missed. Anyway that was all under the bridge now and these days our Wayne was to all intents and purposes a stand up citizen and it had been ages since the coppers had been round telling him to keep it in his trousers or face the full force of the law.

Our Wayne had never really given one flying fuck about that though. Not until recently anyway. Now, because I guess, like me, he had something to lose, i.e. his freedom and therefore access to Dorothy's vagina and God only knows what else, he now keeps that mighty anaconda all wrapped up.

I often wondered if I'd change my character if or when I ever lost my virginity. Would I suddenly become all mature and aloof? What if the opposite happened and I suddenly became the frightened little weakling I was before my head popped? That wouldn't do at all. Maybe it would be better for my career if I stayed a virgin forever. I can see the headlines in the local Argus.

"100 year old virgin billionaire dies! The notorious Johnny McQueen died today reaching his one hundredth year with his virginity still intact. Best known for being the most brutal but handsome, cool and sophisticated of all the criminals, Johnny was found dead early yesterday morning by his sister in law Dorothy with his trousers and pants around his ankles and spunk all over his belly. Two old but still fit grieving lesbian mourners wailing outside one of his many mansions named Sally and Pali sobbed, 'We begged him to give us one and then come all over our faces and tits and that but it was always job first with our Johnny. That's why we became lesbians because it was Johnny or no cunt... Although he did bum that kid who was nailed to a park bench that time...''

I really needed to make it clear to this whole town that it wasn't actually me who bummed Kenny in the park, but our Wayne. I wasn't usually a grass but fuck that shit. Fuck it, there's no way I want to be remembered as a criminal overlord virgin. Nope I want to go down in criminal overlord history as the most ruthless mother fucking criminal overlord to have ever lived. And the one who shagged the most birds and the one who was least fucking likely to bum some horrible, little, bully, cunt who had been nailed to a park bench.

'Listen guys, I love you both dearly obviously but what do you actually want? It's halfway through the day shouldn't you two be making sweet love to each other?' I asked them again.

'Our Wayne has already sloshed a couple up me so far Johnny so we thought to give him a bit of a rest we'd come and see you for a bit. That way his gigantic balls can fill up again and later he can empty the bastards all over me. Spunk is very good for the skin Johnny and your brother produces ruddy fucking gallons of the stuff. My skin has never looked better! Or smelled better. Come over and have a look and a sniff! Come on don't be scared our Wayne isn't the jealous type. Are you our Wayne?' Giggled Dorothy.

That was a lot of information to take in. It was lucky for me that the only appetite I had was for drugs and not food because all I could do was picture our Wayne spraying his considerable load all over her naked body as she writhed and lurched in sexual abandonment. Wave after wave of my own dear brother's hot, salty man milk cascading over the mummified corpse of his missus. Volley after volley of our Wayne's dirty concrete embedding itself into the folds and crevices of Dorothy's ancient, worn out, leathery skin as she lay there like a two hundred yeah old tortoise who'd lost its shell. Our Wayne's bollock juice firing out silvery arcs of his love load bruising the connective tissue of his beloved as they landed. Thankfully these gross images were cut short by the disgruntled tones of my beloved sibling.

'Please don't touch or smell my missus our Johnny. Nobody touches my Dorothy. They can do what they like with Candice but only if they pay.' Replied our Wayne gruffly.

'Fine by me mate. Fine by me.' I replied, relieved to have been let off the hook.

Candice was Dorothy's prossie name. I admired the way that our Wayne could separate the two. They were both equally fucking gross in my eyes though. I think the only difference was a cheap, ill fitting acrylic wig and makeup that had been thrown at her by a left handed toddler. In her full regalia she looked like an Elizabethan street walker who'd died of the plague but nobody had the heart to let her know.

'Well that's a lovely thought but next time ring because I am very busy.' I explained to them, hoping that they'd get the hint and fuck off.

'But we don't have a phone here Johnny.' Our Wayne replied.

'Exactly. Now if you don't mind I have a very urgent appointment with a gram of speed and it really can't wait.' I told him.

'Oh yeah, Mum and dad and Mickey and Kenny and Matty and Benny and Debbie are all alive but they are all in intensive care. And Uncle Sean is in a bit of a state but he's back at home. His home. Not here obviously. Apparently they're all very angry and hell bent on revenge. Oh and Simmer is going to shoot you in the legs and then get a horse to rape you for nicking Eric the rent off him.' Our Wayne suddenly informed me in such a matter of fact tone that for a minute it didn't really sink in.

'I say we kill them all.' He continued while at the same time planting the most gentle of kisses around Dorothy's haggard face and rubbing his hand between her legs so vigorously I had to get up and open a window.

'We could go to the hospital first and smother them all with pillows, I saw that in a film once, then we could go to the Dolphin and stab Simmer to death and then kill uncle Sean on the way back home. I can't remember why we hate uncle Sean though Johnny. I hear he's not too happy that you beat the shit out of him and put that watch up his bum. Although I'm not surprised. Nobody is going to like that are they Johnny? Having a watch shoved up them. I bet that hurt on the way up and on the way down! I heard that you shoved it so far up his bottom that he couldn't find it himself and he had to go to A and E and a surgeon had to fetch it out with a big pair of those forceps that you use to pull out babies when their heads are too big or they come out bum first or something.' He rambled, clearly more preoccupied with feeding Dorothy's rancid old pony than telling me what the fuck was going on with these, so far, undead fuckers.

'You were a breach birth our Wayne!' Dorothy suddenly chimed in.

'We hate uncle Sean because he's my dad's brother and he came around that time to try and tell me off for beating the shit out of our parents... And he more than likely bummed you when you were little and that's probably why you were a right mental and were always getting your cock out.' I replied. The last bit was poetic licence but I wanted our Wayne to have a valid reason to kill the cunt.

Dorothy butted in again and said, 'Ooh no I don't think you're uncle Sean would have bummed you our Wayne. I knew your uncle Sean very well. Especially when his lovely wife was pregnant. You get to learn a lot about a man when he's hanging out the back of you. No you weren't his cup of tea at all. If he was going to have bummed anyone it would have been you son. You see he was smitten by your mother boys, absolutely smitten, and you, Johnny, were the spit of her when you were little. So if he couldn't have fucked her then you would have naturally been the next best thing in his eyes I'd imagine. Although he did fuck her of course. He fucked her a lot. Especially when his lovely wife was pregnant. And she was pregnant an awful lot. He fucked a lot of women did your uncle Sean. And not only when his lovely wife was pregnant either! Your uncle Sean loved the ladies you see? And we all loved him. He was a real gentleman between the sheets and he knew his way around a lady's vulva too! That's a posh word for cunt! He was the definition of, what we used to call back then, a cunt -hound. Fuck anything he would! If it had a cunt he would do his utmost best to fuck it. It was his tongue game for me though boys! There's not a lot of men will lick out a prostitute. Especially at the end of a hot, busy day. Your uncle Sean would though. He couldn't get enough of it. I'd say, come on now our Sean I've had a lot of cock up me today son but he wouldn't care! He'd be pulling down me knickers and munching away like a mad thing while me previous trick was still climbing down the ruddy stairs with his baby gravy still warm inside me! He'd be slurping and belching and making an awful racket between my legs but fuck me gently did that paddy mother fucker make me cum! I'd be dripping in fanny batter before you could say Jack ruddy Robinson! And he wouldn't waste a drop! If I knew he was coming over I'd make sure he was my last client because I knew that I wouldn't even need a bath that night because my snatch would be licked clean as a ruddy whistle! And me dirt box!'

'Fucking hell Dorothy that's a lot of new information to take in! What the fuck! Please stop fucking talking babe!' I pleaded. But Dorothy had a distant and wistful look in her eyes and nothing was going to get in the way of her depraved stagger down memory lane. Wayne also seemed to be engrossed in her sordid tales.

'Oh grow up Johnny you ruddy little prude! It's only natural!' Dorothy replied indignantly.

'Yes Johnny let my Dorothy speak please! It's always good to learn new things about our family!' Said our Wayne.

'Okay our Wayne if you're happy then I'm happy but if you get nightmares you won't be climbing into my bed tonight I'll tell you that for fuck all!' I replied.

'Thank you our Wayne.' Dorothy told him and then she stuck her tongue down our Wayne's throat and frantically pulled at his fast expanding cock. Mercifully this only lasted for a few minutes before she pulled away and said, 'No! Mummy finish baby off later!'

'Oh Come on mummy! Not fair! Our Johnny won't mind if you finish off baby now will you Johnny?' Cried our Wayne using some kind of fucked up sexy baby talk right in front of me like I wasn't even in the room.

Having to listen to that made me cringe so deeply that I literally didn't know how to respond. This was definitely the most fucked up thing I had ever witnessed and that included the time our auntie Joan sat on my face and made me puke and the time Del's bird June was noshing me off and her wig came off in my hand as I got the jester's shoes which somehow resulted in her false teeth flying out of her mouth and hurtling into their bathroom sink and spin around the fucker like a grinning roulette ball. Although the time I watched Butch go up in flames was also quite the occasion. Especially when his ear fell off his head. It looked like a pork scratching and I nearly picked it up and ate it just for the laugh it would have no doubt got. Oh and also, now I'd come to think about it, that time our Wayne threw that dart straight down Jimmy the Greek's fucking stupid, fat, throat in the Dolphin and he shouted, 'one hundred and eighty!' And everybody laughed as he choked to death. I'd seen quite a few fucked up things recently but I had to concede that this little scene was taking the fucking biscuit.

'No our Wayne!' I shouted, 'Bad baby! Mummy will not finish off baby now! Baby will just have to fucking well wait until mummy is back in her own fucking gaff so Johnny doesn't have to see baby's cock explode all of baby's fucking jizz all over Johnny's clean fucking carpet! Now baby and mummy best fuck off because Johnny has many things to think about and I can tell you both right now that one of them won't be the thought of you two doing this mother and son shameful role play fuckery!'

'Hang on I never got round to finishing me ruddy story!' Cried Dorothy.

'Yes our Johnny! Dorothy never got round to finishing her ruddy story!' Said Wayne and before I could argue she was off again.

'Right then where was I?'

'Our uncle Sean used to love to lick you out after you'd been spunked up in by loads of men I think. ' Replied our Wayne.

'Ah yes. As I said, your uncle Sean certainly knew his way to a lady's heart and that was most definitely through her cunt. A woman will put up with a load of shit if her fella knows how to fuck her right! That's a fact boys. Same goes for the fellas too! As long as two people are compatible between the sheets then everything else is secondary. Look at your parents for example! It was no secret that most of the time they ruddy hated each other all to buggery but as soon as they got into bed they fucked like demons! Insatiable they were! Couldn't keep there ruddy hands off each other in the early days. The dirty beggars would be at it at every opportunity. Then the drink and the drugs took there toll. Everything in moderation that's the key boys! If you take it gently you can get off your tits your whole life! Look at me! I still like a little line of Charlie on a

Saturday night! Don't I our Wayne!? It really gets me fired up! Especially when we're rimming and Got full bladders! Doesn't it our Wayne!?'

Wayne nodded enthusiastically and the lump in his trousers jumped enthusiastically too.

Jesus Christ. I wanted her to stop talking so badly but she was having such a good time holding court there was nothing anyone could have done to stop the old crow. Plus our Wayne was looking at her with such pride it would have been cruel to have thrown her out of our living room window, which is what I so sorely wanted to do at the moment.

  The old bag of bones was right though. Fucking and fighting was all our parents did and we were there to witness it all. Every grunt and groan. Every scream every moan. And the explicit language that they used was fucking appalling. It was no surprise that I've always sworn like a cunt after being brought up in a house- hold like this one was. It was also not a surprise that I was a fucking psychopath and I definitely blamed those two for that. I also blamed them for our Wayne's poor taste in women.

'I little dab on the tip of our Wayne's todger keeps him going for hours on end too! Don't it our Wayne? Fucks me bandy he does! He's given me a renewed love of the cock!' Dorothy giggled.

 Old people should not be allowed to attempt giggling or trying to be sexy or anything that was not age appropriate in my opinion. Especially not while they've got my brother's cock in their arthritic old hand in plain sight of every bastard. I'd never even been able to eat in front of her without gagging and now I've got all these new images in my head. If I ever had therapy I hoped they didn't charge by the hour because I'd be skint just listing off the filth and the fury I'd seen so far.

'Up the shitter!' Dorothy suddenly shrieked.

'Excuse me Dorothy?' I replied.

   Had the old bag's head finally popped? I hoped so. That way we could cart her off to the loony bin and we could find our Wayne some bird nearer his own age or at the very least one who was still alive.

'Up the shitter!' She repeated. 'Our Sean! He loved to shove it up me Gary! Don't get me wrong boys in my, considerable experience, all men like a bit of up hill gardening from time to time, it's not unusual, but our Shane he was a gentleman! He wouldn't just try and stick it in dry like most of those other dirty buggers. No, he always spent some time to get to know it! He'd nurture it you see lads! He'd lick it and toy with it and play with it and tease it until you were begging him to put a large dent into tomorrow's stool! I can safely say, hand on heart, that your uncle Sean was the only man to have ever given me a browngasm!' She squealed.

Old people shouldn't be allowed to fucking squeal either or make up words like browngasm.

'... Apart from our Wayne of course. He also knows how to get the best out of my rusty sheriff's badge. It must be in the genes. There's been many a time when our Wayne has been giving me one and I've thought of your uncle Sean!' She continued, while trying her best to look coquettish, although from where I was sitting she looked like she was either having a stroke or a shit. Possible both.

Fuck knows why are Wayne's cock was so stiff because mine had crawled down deep inside my ball bag and it was going to take a lot of psychotherapy to get it back out. At least it seemed likely that if I ever got the opportunity I'd be good at sex, especially bum games. According to Dorothy this was evidently an innate McQueen talent. I wasn't sure if that was my cup of tea though; especially if all bird's bum holes smelled anything like old June's or auntie Joan's did. As for actually eating a lady's balloon knot, I wasn't sure I was ready for that step just yet.

After listening to Dorothy's startling and twisted revelations I think that now all I wanted to do was meet a nice girl ask her on a date and then afterwards shyly ask for a peck on the cheek and let our romance blossom organically. Poetry and flowers and long walks with my beloved were the order of the day for me after hearing all that mad shit.

Licking someone's tea towel holder and then putting my penis into it seemed like something a long way off. I wasn't sure that even if I did want to do that how would one go about broaching the subject? We'd definitely have to have a shower first. Especially me. There was no point worry about this advanced stuff at the moment anyway. That kind of thing would just have to wait until I'd got to grips with the more run of the mill, every day kind of sex. For the time being my priority right now was trying not to vomit as I tried not to think about our Wayne's tongue deep inside Dorothy's mummified anus.

   I tuned back in.

 'Some nights it was only a lower colon full of warm man milk that kept out the cold!' Dorothy cried,' It could be the difference between life or death back then! Especially in the early days when I was walking the ruddy, fucking streets! Sometimes I'd give a gentleman a half price gobble just to get something warm down me throat! Times were hard for a working girl until she got herself established.'

A picture came into my head of a young Dorothy walking the streets in of Victorian England touting for trade amongst the cart horses and plague victims. She was still ropey looking. 'Half a crown for up the bum deary? 'Nah you're alright love I'd rather stick it in this geezer with leprosy cheers.' I decided that I'd have to cut her off because she was already putting me off the whole idea of sex all together.

'Girth!' she suddenly cried out. 'Girth! Your uncle Sean had girth and length! Double bubble like our Wayne here!' That's what us girls like! A big fat one! A lot of folks say that it's not the size of it but what you do with it, but that's bollocks boys! That's a myth spread by men with tiny cocks! Us ladies need to be given a right good seeing to by someone with a big bugger who knows what to do with it!' Our Wayne here took to it like a duck to ruddy water! Didn't you our Wayne?'

Wayne nodded sagely like he was some kind of fucking Lothario rather than someone who had learnt the ropes from this Iron aged cave slut.

'Enough is enough now Dorothy you're making me feel ill.' I told her. 'Please shut the fuck up now! It was lovely to see you both and thanks for the information. I'll be in touch when I've formulated a plan. Now if you'd kindly fuck off that would be great.'

'Oh that's charming! We come over to see you and tell you all we know about the welfare of your parents and those other shit cunts and now we're getting hoicked out without even a thank you!' Dorothy replied indignantly.

'Okay, thank you now fuck off please.' I replied.

 I thought I'd been extremely patient with them. Especially given the circumstances. Dorothy had pretty much put me off ever even contemplating having sex now and the images of her and our Wayne would be sure to haunt me forever.

'Wayne mate, why don't you take Dorothy to the Bingo or some other old person thing?' I asked him.

'Oh gosh yes! We are going to the Bingo! Come on Dorothy or we will be late! Dorothy bought me my own dabber Johnny! Look at this beauty?' Exclaimed our Wayne as he whipped out an oversized pen type thing and waved it in my face!

'Oh and I know where that'll end up if I know you our Wayne! You saucy little bugger!' Shrieked Dorothy.

'Yes! Right up your cunt!' Replied our Wayne.

'Fuck me mate why did you have to be so explicit?' I asked him. 'I think it was implied that it was going up her vagina so there was no real need to say it out loud now was there? Can't you just keep a few things to yourself? Just to keep the magic alive like? Now I've got that image etched into my brain for eternity along with all the others.'

'Oh come on now Johnny don't be such a ruddy prude! You're just jealous that my Wayne here is getting his dick wet and you still haven't broken your duck!' Dorothy contemptuously replied.

Fuck me I'd warned Dorothy a good few times about talking to me as if I was some kind of cunt rather than the next criminal over lord and I was now livid as a mother fucker.

'I'll tell you something for nothing Dorothy.' I told her, ' If you weren't our Wayne's missus I'd have put you threw a meat grinder and fed you to pigs by now.'

'Actually I don't think you'd even have to bother putting her through a meat grinder before feeding her to pigs because I think pigs could eat a whole human Johnny. Especially a small one like Dorothy.' Wayne replied.

'I think that depends on the breed of pig actually our Wayne.' Replied Dorothy clearly not taking my threat seriously.

Then our Wayne said, 'Actually come to think of it I don't think pigs can digest human hair or teeth so you'd be leaving behind evidence Johnny.'

'Well that wouldn't be a problem in my case lads because I can't even remember when I had me own hair and teeth!' Laughed Dorothy. Then we all laughed.

'Here! Take this little assortment of drugs and pass them out to your bingo buddies!' I said to our Wayne as I tossed him the bag.'Tell them that the speed will help them pay attention to the cunt who shouts out the numbers and the vallies will get them off to sleep once they get back home. Give them out free and then when they're all addicted we'll start charging.'

Wayne caught them and stuffed them into his pocket, nodded his head and said, 'Will do Johnny. See you later brother.'

'Yeah see you later brother.' I replied.

'See you later Johnny.' Dorothy said, and she flicked out her tongue like some kind of dying lizard. I didn't know if she was trying to be sexy or it was just some kind of sex worker tick but either way it made me feel extremely queasy.

'Yeah see you later Dorothy. I replied. 'Don't pull a muscle picking up your dabber!'

Dorothy replied by sticking up her middle finger and then she said, 'Two, four, six, eight, Johnny's going to masturbate!' And then she cackled and made a wanking motion with her hand and then mimed throwing the imaginary spunk in my direction. I then mimed catching it in my mouth and swallowing it and then rubbed my belly and said 'yum yum.'

Then we all laughed and mercifully they fucked off.

Chapter four

After they left and I had a nice fat spliff and a nice long wank my mind was clear enough for me to be able to sit down and think about my next move. I thought about it for a good ten minutes before deciding that our Wayne was right. Everybody needed to die. It would be a lot easier if everyone who had in any way wronged me or got on my tits would just be taken out of the picture. I didn't really want to be looking over my shoulder for the rest of my life waiting for some cunt to avenge themselves and the only way that this was not going to happen was if they were all dead. All I needed to do was formulate a plan. I decided that was enough thinking for the time being and a good solid start so I thought I'd let the idea ferment for a while and see what came up.

In the mean time I decided that I would go and see my friend and mentor Stan the man. Stan was once the criminal overlord around here but he'd retired now. This was very unusual because criminal overlords usually got killed long before the age of retirement and it was this fact that everyone admired about him. Plus he was also mental so even if you didn't actually admire him you had to pretend you did because he still had a lot of clout.

Not dying at some point along the way seemed to be very difficult in this game. Stan had been shot and stabbed and had the shit kicked out of him many times but he just refused to die. I loved that about him. Fuck knows why but he liked me. Maybe he saw me in him. Or was it him in me? Anyway he'd always had a lot of time for me when I used to run errands in the pubs for him and anyone else who'd give me a few quid to put a bet on for them or take something somewhere no questions asked. He still lived in the same council house that he'd been brought up in even though he'd obviously made a fortune out of being a gangster. He always wore nice suits and hand made leather shoes but apart from that and his Rolls Royce you'd have never guessed that he used to run this town.

I walked up to his door and rang the door bell.

'Hello Johnny son!' I heard coming from his fancy intercom. I looked up to where he had his closed circuit camera, grinned and then leaned into the intercom and said, 'Hello Stan. Can I come in please?'

'Of course you can my boy!' came the tinny response. Then the door started buzzing so I pushed it open.

'I'm in the front room Johnny. Come on in!' He shouted.

I instinctively took off my shoes and walked into his front room marvelling at the décor. Stan's front room made Liberace's gaff look like a protestant had designed it. To get in you had to push through a beaded curtain made up of a thousand tiny jewels and there were mirrors and crystals everywhere you looked. The ceiling and walls were made up of hundreds of mirrored tiles and a crystal chandelier hung regally in the centre. Hanging over the fireplace was a picture of a crying boy and there were naked statues of muscular Greek men in various athletic poses dotted all over. All the furniture was gold-plated and the mirror tiled floor had a Persian rug laying on it majestically. It always reminded me of a cross between Aladdin's cave and an amusement arcade and was seedy as fuck.

'Come in! Come in Johnny! Such a delight to see you! Come closer and let me have a look at you my dear boy!' Said Stan from the back of the room.

I looked over to find him sat on his Golden throne. He was naked apart from a pair of gold lame' underpants and a pair of socks and brogues. He also had a budgie perched on the end of his finger.

'As you can see Johnny I wasn't expecting visitors. Do you remember Percy here?' He said, as he gestured towards the budgie with a wave of his free hand.

'Yeah sorry for disturbing you Stan it was a spur of the moment thing. Yes of course I remember Percy! Percy want a cracker!? Percy want cracker!?' I replied, talking to Stan first and then to his budgie.

'Fuck off you soppy little cunt!' Replied Percy.

We both pissed ourselves laughing at this.

'He recognises you Johnny!' Said Stan gleefully. 'He's getting on a bit now but he still knows a soppy little cunt when he sees one!'

We both laughed at this. Stan had lived with his mum until she'd died. He'd never had a wife or any kids that anyone knew about but he loved his budgies. Ever since I'd known him he'd always had one on the go. Percy was getting on a bit now and he was losing all his feathers but he could still talk and up until very recently was a lot more articulate than our Wayne.

I leaned in towards Percy and said, 'Who's a fucking nonce cunt then Percy?'

'You are you mate! You are mate!' Replied Percy right on cue.

Neither of us ever got tired of this and we doubled up with laughter again.

'Put it in your mouth son or I'll cut off your fucking ears!' Percy suddenly blurted out.

This was followed by silence. Stan looked a bit sheepish so I pressed on with what I'd originally came for.

'Uh yeah anyway Stan I'm here for a bit of advice actually.' I told him.

Percy was now kissing Stan on the mouth.

'Percy love daddy? Daddy love Percy.' Stan was saying to Percy. People loved to get kissed by their pets. Before Satan fucked off our dog was always licking his bollocks then licking our Wayne's mouth. Sometimes I'd burst into our bedroom and our Wayne would be laying on his bed stark, bollock naked and Satan would be laying next to him and both of their cock's would be hard. Once when I caught them Satan was wearing a pair of my mum's knickers. I never asked any questions because I didn't want to know the answers. I knew the answers anyway. The dirty bastards. At the time I didn't really give a fuck because I thought that at least if he was fucking our dog he wasn't sexually assaulting some random passer by.

There was one time when I shamefully rubbed dog food all over my cock and balls and arse hole and tried to get Satan to lick it all off just to see what all the fuss was about but he started to growl and snarl and wasn't at all interested. A part of me quite admired his loyalty to our Wayne to be honest although it might have been more to do with the own brand dog food I'd bought for the occasion. It tasted okay to me though and loads better than anything my mum had ever given us.

'You know me Johnny. I'd do anything to help out a young boy in distress. ' Stan told me between Percy's kisses. It was true that over the years Stan had helped out many a vulnerable young boy who needed a place to stay. Any lad who had run away from a care home or borstal or his own family because the new step dad was a bit too hands on in the bedroom for example, Stan the man would always find room for them in his gaff. They could stay rent free until they got back on their feet or at least until they'd reached puberty.

'What can I do for you Johnny? Do you need to lie low for a bit? You can hold up here if you like? It wouldn't be a problem. He continued. I couldn't help but notice a bit of movement coming from his golden under crackers.

'No that's very kind of you Stan but that's not why I'm here.' I replied.

'Are you sure Johnny? It wouldn't be a problem. I've got plenty of drugs and booze and satellite television! I can get films from all over the world on that! Plenty of mucky films if you know what I mean Johnny!' He replied becoming a tad more insistent.

'Fucking nonce cunt! Fucking nonce cunt!' Screeched Percy.

Fuck me Stan must have been called that an awful lot for his fucking budgie to have picked up that particular phrase I thought to myself. I decided that I'd better get to the point before Stan started to get himself at it. I took a deep breath.

'As you are no doubt there have been many changes in me and our Wayne's circumstances. I decided to smite the fuck out of all my enemies and that's what I did...'

Stan immediately interrupted.

'So I hear Johnny. So I hear and very impressive it was too by all accounts. Now would you do me a favour and go into detail about exactly what occurred please? Just in order for me to know the facts. And don't miss anything out please. Don't worry about any of the gory details because I've seen and done it all over the years.' Stan replied, as he put Percy back into his cage and reached for his oxygen mask. He'd always had a tank full of some kind of substance by his side but nobody had ever found out what it was. He put the mask over his mouth and inhaled deeply.

'Right then son let's have it.' He gasped. 'And don't forget to go into detail.' The next thing I knew his little gold under crackers were around his ankles and he was pulling manically at his worn out old todger. Whatever he was inhaling certainly had an effect on it because within a few strokes it was as stiff as a brush.

'Start with your parents Johnny!' He gasped.

'Well Stan, as you know our dad is a real cunt...' I began.

'Don't fucking look at me Johnny!' Stan shouted at me which immediately put me off my stride.

'Fuck me Stan yeah sorry.' I told him. I was sorry too. I didn't want to embarrass him.

I looked at Percy who was pecking away at his own reflection in the little mirror in his cage oblivious to the mad scene that was taking place outside of it.

'Don't look at Percy either! He's mine! All mine!' Shouted Stan. Whatever he'd taken had also turned him into some kind of psychotic loon because he was now frothing at the mouth and cavorting and gyrating all over his throne.

'Nonce cunt! Nonce cunt!' Percy suddenly screeched and he started to hysterically flap his wings about. It was fucking mayhem now and I didn't know whether to continue or not. 'Get on with it boy! This stuff only lasts for a few minutes!' Stan shouted. I decided to just look at the creepy fucking crying kid hanging over the fireplace and crack on as best I could.

'As you know Stan my dad is a cunt...' I began again.

'Just give me the abridge version Johnny! I can only do this once a day!' Stan gasped.

'Right then Stan, Me and our Wayne got tired of our dad being a cunt so we both nearly kicked the cunt to death. We punched and kicked him unconscious and stamped on the cunt's fucking head until he'd pissed and shit himself and then we left him for dead. Then mum tried to manipulate our Wayne so he head-butted her and then we laid into her and kicked and punched her until we couldn't even recognise the slag, apart from the smell obviously. Oh yeah and before that we beat the fucking shit out of that Mickey cunt and his gang, I head-butted his bird and then kicked her in the cunt and Benny got fucking ruined and then I nailed that little cunt Kenny to a park bench and our Wayne scuttled him while I went to get chips. He was always asking little kids to get their dicks out you see Stan?' At this bit I accidentality looked over at Stan but luckily his eyes were screwed tightly shut and he was wanking off like a teenage monkey on crystal meth so I pressed on as fast as I could.

'What happened then?' I said, ' Oh yeah then I went into school and this cunt butch and his little bum chum mate, no offence Stan.'

'None taken Son' replied Stan without missing a beat.

'Yeah so he was the one that started the ball rolling by putting a bulldog clip on my ear Stan.'

'Bulldog clip? What's a bulldog clip?' Stan asked.

'Well Stan it's a kind of clip that you used to ...'

'Oh fuck it we don't have time! Get to the bit where you set them on fire Johnny!' Stan bellowed.

'Oh yeah so butch and his cunt mate thought they were going to have all my money and gear off me but I was too wily for them and ended up poisoning the fuckers with antifreeze in a bottle of vodka and then I threw a Molotov cocktail down one of the east block bogs and blew everything all to fuck including those two. You should have seen that Butch running out all on fire you would have creamed your pants Stan!'

At this point I took a chance and glanced over to him just at the exact moment that he shot his load while moaning, 'Percy want a cracker! Percy want a cracker!' As Two big arcs of knuckle juice hit the polished floor one after the other in quick succession.

Stan then let out a contented sigh and said, 'That's enough now Johnny. Good lad. You sure showed them son.' Then he opened his eyes, looked at all the spunk and said, 'Fuck me son that's not a bad load for an old timer now is it?'

'Nonce cunt! Nonce cunt!' Shrieked Percy again.

'Yeah that's quite a respectable amount Stan. Fair play to you mate.' I replied.

'Do me a favour and get a cloth out of the kitchen and mop that little lot up will you Johnny? I'm not as young as I was and I don't want to go slipping in it and taking a tumble. And pass me a wet wipe while you're at it' He asked me.

'Yeah no problem Stan' I told him and that's exactly what I did.

After he'd given himself a little dab around his cock and balls he slipped his underpants back on and said, 'Right then our Johnny down to business. What can I do for you?'

'Hang on Stan do you want me to swill this cloth out or throw it in the bin?' I replied. It looked like a brand new cloth to me and if he didn't want it I'd have it for my own wank rag.

'Just run it under the tap for a bit, give it a squeeze and leave it on the side please Johnny.'

'Bollocks', I thought to myself, I could have done with that because I was running out of our Wayne's t shirts now that he spent most of his time over at Dorothy's gaff.

As I came back into the living room Percy was back on Stan's finger peaceful as a mother fucker as if the last ten minutes had not actually occurred and all was calm again. I told Stan about my parents and Mickey and his mates unfortunately not being dead and that now for some unknown reason they were bent on revenge. Then I mentioned that Simmer wasn't going to let me take over some of his operations even though I was polite and offered the cunt a fair cut of the profits and the fact that he literally told me to fuck off and then threatening to have me killed just because I'd nicked Eric the rent off him.

Stan sat on his throne like Rodin's, The Thinker; The only difference being that rather than naked, Stan was wearing his shoes and his little golden underpants which were now splattered with spunk.

I looked across at him in total awe. No wonder we all looked up to him. He was a living legend. Eventually he spoke.

'Here's what you're going to do Johnny. First off we're going to smoke a joint then I'm going to give you some money and some drugs and some weapons. And then we're going to have ourselves a nice little turf war.'

'That sounds like a great plan Stan.' I replied.

' I don't want anything to do with it though Johnny.' He continued. ' I'm retired now so keep me out of it... I'll be on the sidelines but if you get desperate I'll be more than happy to give you a little leg up, but this is your caper son. I'll supply you with everything you need to begin your quest to become a crime lord but the rest will be up to you. I'm here if you need me though. All I want are the gory details. If you win then all power to you but if you fail then you'll pay the consequences like everyone else who's had a go and came up short. Although if you do die, and the chances are that you most definitely will, I will avenge you. Actually I'll tell you what son, on my ma's fucking grave if some cheeky no mark cunt even lays their hands on your beautiful veal like skin or you get a scratch on that handsome boat race of yours I'll shoot every cunt in the fucking head! The cheeky cunts! Who the fuck do they think they are son? Hey? Hey? Those fucking chancers! Fucking CHANCERS they are Johnny!'

'Fucking chancers Stan. That's what they are! The cunts! Chancer cunts Stan!' I shouted back.

'Chancer cunts! Stan shouted back. 'Same deal if any cunt hurts your brother too!' He continued. 'And that old brass he's shagging! Granted she's no oil painting but back in the day when I was sloshing one up her she was a right sort! Very accommodating to me she was Johnny. Let me round the back as long as I spat on it first! She had a gift that one. She could take one look at you and know exactly what you wanted. She some how knew I was a poofter even before I did. She had a lot of skills did Candice. A lot of skills if you know what I mean Johnny.'

He was getting all red in the face again now and starting to get himself at it so I causally mentioned the joint.

'Yes! Let's fire one up son!' he beamed.

Danger averted. Stan was a volatile and unpredictable fucker but get him on the ganja and he'd mellow out in no time. He rolled a joint with one hand in under thirty seconds and it was tight as a duck's ass hole and a beautiful piece of art. Then he lit it, took two big tokes and passed it to me and said, 'Listen Johnny, I've been lucky. I'm aware of that. I should have been dead a long time ago but here I am. Now I'm going to tell you exactly what I said to Simmer all those years ago. I'll give you a hand but you do all the donkey work. And the thinking. But if you do need me to do any thinking for you, you know here I am. But you need to have your own system you see Johnny?'

'Yeah Stan I've got a few ideas.' I replied.

'Back in the day, for example' he continued, 'you could burst into a bank holding a shooter and everyone would shit their pants and do what you fucking told them to do. "Put the money in the fucking bags you slags or I'll blow your fucking heads off!" That's what I used to shout. I was known for it. "Put the money in the fucking bags you slags or I'll blow your fucking heads off!" It was like my catchphrase you see Johnny? I fancied myself as a bit of a Butch Cassady, Jessie James kind of villain you see? Handsome with a bit of a swagger you know.'

'Yes I can see that Stan. You've got a bit of Al Capone mixed with Larry Grayson about you too I've always thought.' I said.

Why that's very kind of you to say son. Thank you.' He replied.

'No need to thank me Stan that's just the fucking truth mate. We all think the same. You're all our criminal heroes rolled into one with a bit of glitter thrown in the mix. Ask any cunt.' I told him. And I meant it too.

'That's lovely to hear Johnny.' Stan replied, 'that's actually made me quite emotional. Now where the fuck was I?'

'Robbing banks Stan.' I told him.

'Oh yeah that's right.' He continued, 'so yeah anyway it ain't like the old days now Johnny. You can't just walk into a bank with firearms these days. Too many fucking cameras for one. And clever cunts. You're always going to get your "Have A Go Hero" these days. I blame Hollywood. Some silly cunt who thinks he's going to save the day and get in the fucking newspapers. "Have A Go Hero defies armed robbers!" Splashed all over the front page of the Sun."Have A Go Soppy Cunt" more like. It don't usually pan out like though see Johnny?'

'Doesn't it Stan? I replied.

 Fuck me that joint was strong and I was finding it difficult to keep up now but it was still fascinating to hear even though I was immediately forgetting what he was saying. We passed it between us as he spoke.

'Yes son. In my experience life ain't like the movies. The last time I tried to blag a bank some little no mark in a shiny suit tried to wrestle me sawn off from me own bloody hands! He'd obviously been watching too many action films and thought he'd try and impress his boss, the soppy cunt. He started doing all this fucking kung foo shit so I ended up having to blow one of his arms off.'

'I bet he didn't like that Stan.' I giggled.

'No he did not!' Stan laughed. 'You should have seen the daft cunt after that! 'Sit down you cunt!' I shouted at him, but I might as well of saved me breath because reality hit him right there and then and he went into shock. Especially after he saw his fucking arm lying on the floor!'

'I bet that was a sight Stan.' I said.

'It fucking was Johnny.' Stan replied, 'He weren't no hero that day I can tell you that for fuck all. In fact he shit himself!'

'He actually shit himself Stan?' I asked.

'Yes mate. He shit himself.' Stan replied.

'Because you shot his arm off he shit himself?' I replied.

'Well yes.' Said Stan, 'unless it was a coincidence but my first thought at the time was it was because I'd blown his fucking arm off and he wasn't too happy about it.'

'So he shit himself!' I laughed.

'Yes Johnny. He had nowhere else to go see son?' Satn continued. ' You can't fight with only one arm! I think that he knew that as soon as he saw one of his lucky charms lying on the bank floor next to him that he was fucked. He'd be all off balance see? Ask any boxer how many arms is ideal for fighting and the majority of them will tell you two! At least two. Two would be the minimum. A left and a right. Even your amateur boxer will tell you that son.'

'Yeah that makes sense to me too Stan. So without two arms the only thing left in the cunt's defence was to fucking to shit himself?' I asked.

'Well I don't think he did it on purpose to be fair to him.' Stan replied. 'No I don't actually think it was a defensive strategy per-se. But you never know son. Maybe that's why we shit ourselves in these sort of circumstances? At the end of the day we are all animals after all.'

'Are we Stan?' I replied.

'Animals? Or do I mean mammals?' Stan continued. 'Fuck knows but most things shit themselves when they get scared. I reckon it comes from right back in fucking cave man times actually Johnny.'

'Do you Stan?' I replied. I was off my fucking nut now and so was Stan by the sounds of it.

'Yeah because let's say you're just about to get eaten by a dinosaur or something. Yeah let's just say that some cave man cunt and his missus is out hunting and gathering and what have you and this fucking, fuck off tyrannosaurus Rex cunt comes running out of the jungle and starts chasing you. What's the first thing you're most likely going to do Johnny?'

'Give my cave bitch two dead legs and make a fucking run for it Stan?' I replied.

Stan looked at me for a good long while then mercifully he started pissing himself laughing.

Just then an image came in to my head of Sally in a sabre tooth tiger skin bikini staggering about with two dead legs and looking at me like she could kill me and I suddenly felt guilty and there and then I decided that if this sort of situation did ever actually occur I would stay and fight and I'd tell Sally to make a run for it even though she'd say that she was staying too because what would be the point of living if I was eaten by a dinosaur.

'I wouldn't really do that Stan. I think what I'd actually do is shit myself.' I told him.

'Exactly Johnny. You'd shit yourself! That way the old dinosaur is gonna be all like, "I'll be fucked if I'm going to eat that dirty cunt! Fuck that shit I'm off to eat something less fucking disgusting like one of them big triffids or a bit of veg." I reckon that's why a lot of these big fucking things ended up vegetarian to be fair.' He continued.

'Do you Stan? Because of all the cave man shit?' I asked. I thought I was going to keel over although I did like the idea of sexy cave birds running about gathering nuts and berries and that while wearing little bikinis made out of woolly mammoth fur. It gave me a bit of a twitch to be fair.

'Yeah. The way I see it that's got to be evolution you see son? After a while your dinosaur is going to associate cave men with shit so eventually they think, fuck that I'd rather eat a tree or a bit of hedge.' Stan continued.

'Vegetarian Dinosaurs. Makes sense to me Stan.' I replied.

Stan passed me what was left of the joint and said, Hang on, what were we fucking talking about before vegetarian dinosaurs Johnny?'

'I can't remember Stan.' I replied. I could hardly see straight by now and I also couldn't feel my face.

'Can't remember what Johnny?' Stan replied looking puzzled.

"About the dinosaurs Stan.' I replied.

'Dinosaurs? What fucking dinosaurs?' He asked me.

'The vegetarian dinosaurs Stan!' I told him.

'Oh yes! The vegetarian dinosaurs! What about them?' He said.

I put my head down in shame and said. 'I don't know Stan.'

'No me neither son. I wonder why we were talking about vegetarian dinosaurs? Fuck me that's good puff ain't it Johnny.' Said Stan.

Then we both started giggling. We were fucking curled up for what seemed like forever then out of the blue Stan got out of his chair and looked my straight in the eyes and blurted, 'Shit! We were talking about shit! The geezer in the bank!'

'Shit Stan? Bank? What geezer? You've lost me mate. What do you mean, the geezer in the bank Stan?' I asked him.

 I didn't have a fucking clue what he was on about because my short term memory had gone and it didn't look like it was coming back any time soon.

'I blew this cunt's arm off while doing a bank!' He shouted at me triumphantly.

'Why did you do that Stan?' I asked him. Was he fucking mental? Yes I'd done some damage to a lot of people but they'd all deserved it. I hoped that this poor cunt in the bank wasn't just some poor cunt who got in the way of a bank robbery.

'Fuck me Johnny it's all coming back to me! We were talking about the cunt who tried to grab my shooter so I had to blow one of his fucking arms off to calm the silly cunt down!' Stan cried.

'"The Have A Go Hero" cunt!' He he shit himself! Stan! Yes I remember!' I shouted as it all came flooding back. Yes he did deserve it! The cheeky cunt.

Stan was off and running again. 'Yeah that's right!' He shouted. 'The next day the headline should have been, "Stupid Kung Foo Cunt Shits Self During Robbery!" And I'll tell you what Johnny, fuck knows what he had for lunch that day because it fucking stank too! Putrid it was son. Really turned my stomach. I remember it like yesterday. One bird fainted and I'm still not sure to this day if it was because I'd shot that cunt's arm off or if it was due the fucking stench coming from his trousers. The biggest ball ache wasn't the stink though son, it was the fucking claret all over the money!'

'Awe no not claret all over the money Stan!' I cried.

'Yeah mate, we had to throw away nearly a grand because of that cunt bleeding all over it!' Stan told me. 'He was spurting blood out all over the fucking gaff! If he'd just kept his head down everything would have been cushty but no he had to play Billy big bollocks! It still makes me angry even after all these years. It put us behind too Johnny! The saucy cunt! We only just got out before the fucking old bill turned up. The whole thing was a fucking nightmare as soon as he grabbed my arm. The cunt.'

'Oh that saucy cunt!' I replied.

'Well that was it for me son' Stan continued. 'That was the last time I ever robbed a bank. That jumped little cunt absolutely ruined it for me. There was no fun in it after that. In the good old days you'd run in, take the fucking loot and fuck off within a blink of an eye. Everyone knew what to do back then. Us robbers would rob the place and the punters would keep their fucking heads down and nobody would get hurt. We'd have the loot and they'd have a good story to tell their mates the next day. Simple rules of the game. Win win. Promise me one thing Johnny, if you ever find yourself in a bank that's getting robbed by men with shooters just keep your fucking head down and do as you're told. It's as simple as that.'

Stan then looked from side to side like he was making sure nobody else was listening even though it was only us two and Percy sitting in his living room and he leaned over towards me and in a sort of loud whisper he said.

'I'll tell you something now that I've never told anyone else Johnny. I'm old now and I don't care. About six months after that incident I tracked that man down and found out where he lived. I walked up to his door, knocked on it and when he came out to see who it was I shot him in his other arm and that fucker came off too.'

'Fuck me Stan.' I replied.

'Yeah I did and I'm still happy that I did because he ruined a lot of things for me that day.' Stan replied. ' I could have got nicked because of that clever cunt. Anyway as he was flaying about on the ground like a fucking upturned beetle I explained to the cunt that if he went to the law I'd shoot him in the bollocks and blow his wife's tits off. I could see his wife you see Johnny. She was standing in their front room with a right look of horror on her boat. Terrified she was.'

'Did she have big tits then Stan?' I asked him.

'Eh? What do you mean? What difference does it make?' he replied.

'Well were they big enough to have been shot off? Like if she stood side-ways?' I replied. 'Could you have shot her tits off? Bang! Bang! First leftie then rightie. You know like when some cunt throws knives at a bird on a spinning wheel like on magic shows or the circus. Not that I've ever been to the circus. You know, the geezer stabs the balloons from between the bird's legs and just misses her head and that. She holds a balloon in her gob and her fella throws the knife and bang! A big round of applause because she ain't dead! It's always Russian cunts with bald heads throwing knives at hot birds in a sparkly Lyotard. Not the birds, the geezers. The birds are always fit. You ever shagged a Russian bird Stan? Oh no probably not.'

'Oh I see well yeah, as it happens I do recall that they weren't a bad size.' Stan replied. 'More than a handful. I reckon if I'd had a couple of knives I could have stabbed her tits off. No I've never shagged a Russian bird son. I shagged a good few Russian lads though. Very athletic they are. Cold but taught... very pale too... I used to be good at throwing knives. Took a man's ear off once. On purpose like. So yeah I do recall that they were of a reasonable size and also firm. I don't know why I've remembered that because as you know I'm not really a breast man but even I could see that if I hadn't have been born a raving egg I would have probably found them very attractive. I did get a hard-on though but it wasn't because of tits it was because she was absolutely scared shitless. That's what gave me a boner. It was the power I had over them you see Johnny?'

'You sure it wasn't the geezer Stan?' I asked him.

'No son it wasn't that cunt.' Stan replied. 'He wasn't my type at all. It was definitely not the geezer. It was the fact that I knew and they knew that I had the power of their life

'or death in my hands.

'Yeah that would have given me a boner too. Especially if her tits were as big and firm as you reckon they were.' I told him.

Stan then said, 'Power is sexy Johnny. You'll find that out. But anyway listen to this bit. You'll never guess what.'

'What Stan? What happened then?' I asked him.

'He'd only gone and shit himself again!' Stan laughed. 'And not only that, it was exactly the same fucking smell as the last time. I mean I would have been well within my rights to have shot his missus because it was obvious to me that it was her cooking that caused his shit to smell that fucking foul.'

'How to you know it was her fault Stan? I asked him taking a long drag on his joint. 'Maybe he did the cooking? You can't assume that just because she's a bird that she did all the cooking. Even back then I bet there was loads of men who did the cooking. That's not fair to assume that just because she was the one with the tits and the fanny it was her fault that his shit smelled that bad. What if you shot her thinking it was her that made his arse smell that fucking putrid and it turned out to be him who did the cooking?'

'Well she was wearing a fucking apron Johnny! Stan replied.

'Oh well then that's fair enough then Stan.' I told him. 'It was probably her that did the cooking then. A lot of top chefs are men though Stan so you can't just go around assuming that birds all do the cooking and men go out and do proper work. Have I ever told you about the fit bird next door to me Stan? She's fucking hot as fuck but you can't say she's hot as fuck because I think she's one of them feminists. I don't think she's an actual lezzer though. I hope not anyway because I want to marry her one day. I'll invite you to the wedding Stan. You can be guest of honour. Actually I think her dad is dead or something. He might just have fucked off I'm not sure but if she doesn't have anyone to walk her down the aisle maybe you could do it! Like I said though, she's a women's libber so she might ask one of her lesbian mates to do it. Or a bender. Come to think about it as you're one you might be alright.'

We were both very stoned now.

'This Sally seems like a lovely young lady and if she turns out not to be a lezzer and you end up marrying her I'd be more than honoured to walk her down the aisle son.' Stan told me. 'I knew a lezzer once. She was a big piece. Used to do the door at the Dolphin. If it was a disco or we had some strippers in like. Hard as fucking nails she was. Nice girl unless you tried to get in for free obviously. I saw her pick up a bloke once and throw him at a bus. Well to be fair to her I think she just threw the cunt into the road just as a bus was coming past. Crushed every bone in his body it did. He was flat as a veritable fucking pancake. Served the cunt right though, it was only three quid to get in. He lived to regret it though.'

'Fuck me did he live then Stan?' I asked.

'Who?' He replied.

'The fucking geezer that that got thrown under the bus by the lesbian?' I replied.

'No of course not! The fucking bus flattened the cunt! He was dead as a fucking door nail Johnny! We all had to tell the coppers that he was depressed and he'd chucked himself under the fucker otherwise she would have got done for murder.' Stan replied while looking at me like I was mental.

'But you said he'd lived to regret not paying the three quid to get into see the strippers! Or was it a disco?' I replied.

'Did I?' Stan replied. 'I thought that was just something you said? Well anyway he did live to regret it. For a about five seconds as he flew through the air before hitting that fucking bus and going under it!'

This made us both laugh like fuck.

'Don't get me wrong son I know that shit stinks.' Said Stan seemingly out of nowhere. 'Of course it does because it's shit. But this was beyond the normal realms of what shit should smell like.'

'Eh?' I replied not knowing what the fuck he was talking about again.

'The armless bank cunt Johnny!' Stan replied.

'Oh yeah the guy who shit himself! The kung foo bank guy cunt with the wife with big tits and the apron!' I shouted.

'I can still smell it to this day Johnny' Stan continued, 'sometimes it feels like it's haunting me. Following me around you know? Sometimes I'll be out and about doing me little chores and that when suddenly out of nowhere I'll get the same whiff of that cunt's shit. And nobody else can smell it Johnny! Only the other day I was in The Dolphin just having a pint with some of the old firm and I smelled it again. "Can you smell that Reg?" I said to Reg. And Reg went, "What? I can't smell nothing Stan." and I said, "Reg you must be able to smell that! It's fucking foul!" And Reg said, "Nah I can't smell anything Stan." But

Johnny I could smell it Johnny. I could smell it like it was coming out of my own arse hole!'

'Did the cunt ever grass on you Stan?' I asked him.

'Did who grass on me?' Stan asked. 'Reg? No! Reg ain't no grass Johnny! Why would Reg grass on his old pal? I'd have blown his fucking head off! The cheeky cunt! Why do you say that then Johnny? Reg a grass is he? That what you've heard? Now I come to think about it I wouldn't trust that cunt as far as I could throw him. The cunt.'

'No Stan, not Reg! The cunt with no arms!' I replied.

'Cunt with no arms Johnny?' Stan replied.

Fuck me this conversation wasn't going anywhere now because we were both truly fucked.

 I got up and walked into Stan's kitchen and stuck my head under his cold tap. I let the water run all over my head until I felt relatively normal again. Then I dried my hair with a tea towel and went back into the living room.

Stan was still sat on his thrown staring into space. When he saw me he clicked back into life.

' I used to like that Simmer. He began.'He was an odd little ginger kid but he was sexy enough in his own little, odd way. He wasn't exactly your go-to kiddie for someone like me and my dark urges but you'd still smash. He was what I'd call niche but once in a while... it's like when you eat steak every day for so long that you get sick of it so you have something that you wouldn't normally go for. Like a tin of tomato soup or a tin of sardines, you know... anyway I took him under my wing and I helped him on his way to the top... What I liked most about the cunt was that he was a lonely boy and clearly mentally ill. A lonely nut job will always do well in this game Johnny. You need to be a bit mentally unstable and ideally a psychopath to get to the top at this caper. He was like... You know, a cat killer type... Your psychopath doesn't give a fuck about consequences you see son? I remember when I was about your age watching my father throw a bag of kittens into a river and rather than getting all upset like some little nancy boy, it gave me a raging hard-on. Hearing their pitiful last meows gave me enormous pleasure. That's when I knew that I wasn't all there in the nut Johnny boy. A few days later I put a pencil up my dog's Derek and the same thing happened.'

'So killing stuff and putting stuff up dog's arse holes gave you the horn? And that's how you knew you was a nut-nut Stan?' I asked him.

'Well yes but not just that Johnny. Any type of violence... and young tearaways too obviously.' He replied.

Fuck me, I thought to myself, you had to weld a lot of power to say things like that out loud.

As he rambled on I drifted off into a stoned haze and started getting inside my own head. What if I'm the same kind of nut job as Stan? I hoped that these two things weren't essential to being a loony tunes because neither of them were my cup of tea. I thought that it was cruel as fuck to put kittens in a bag and throw the poor cunts into a river to drown. And as for putting pencils up a dog's arse hole, well that was completely fucked up in all sorts of ways. If I had put a pencil up Satan's ring piece he would have bitten my face off plus I'd never be able to look him in the eye ever again.

Dogs know when they're having the piss taken out of them but I think they play along because they know the hierarchy. They're pack animals and instinctively they know the pecking order so I reckon if you start putting things up their arse holes they'll lose all respect for you. Plus it's just fucking wrong. I'd love to see Stan put a pencil up a cat's Derek. It would go mental and scratch him all to fuck or even worse give him such a disdainful look of disgust he'd end up topping himself. That nearly happened to me once. Although knowing Stan he'd probably find it erotic or something equally mental. I was relieved to know that I was just a psycho when it came to extreme violence involving humans who had wronged me and not a psycho who tortured or stuck blunt objects up the ring pieces of animals.

 My mind then went back to the time I was really stoned one night and I deciding to go to the playground and have a wank on the slide. There wasn't any kids around obviously. I'm not a nonce. Unlike Stan. I just liked the idea of shooting my load and seeing how far I could get it down the chute. I even kept records. So anyway I went to the playground, climbed up the slide and started bashing away, just loving the feeling of the wind in my hair and around my bollocks while listening to The Pogues on my portable cassette tape player. I was just getting into my stride as, 'The Body of an American', had just started playing and I wanted to cum just as it properly kicked in and a few seconds later, as I gave it a few swift ones off the wrist, right on cue I emptied my load, and at that very same time I had the audacious idea to stand up in order to try and break my previous record.

I knew this was a bit of a cheat but it was my game so I could change the rules to suit me. So with my eyes still closed, in order to hopefully give myself a nice surprise when I reopened them, I frantically started pumping away until I got the vinegar stroke and after two almost inaudible grunts and I was done. Just after this potentiallly record breaking and momentous event I heard the distinct sound of meowing. An upset sounding meowing too. An upset, disgruntled and annoyed sort of meowing to be precise. This was immediately followed by the sound of hissing so I looked down and it turned out that I'd just emptied my balls over a fucking cat! It must have been sleeping at the bottom of the slide or something. Or maybe it was looking for mice or maybe it was on the pull, fuck knows. Anyway it was none too pleased that I'd ejaculated all over it and by the light of the street lamp I could quite clearly see two separate blobs of spunk reflecting off black fur. I remember thinking that it looked quite beautiful in its own way. It looked to me like two moon beams glistening on a calm, black sea but I was stoned so maybe it just looked like a cat covered in spunk. The next thing I knew I'd caught this fucking cat's eye and it looked at me with such anger and resentment I immediately felt myself blush. I always feel guilty and sinful after cumming anyway but that time I was completely engulfed with self-loathing and shame and it was a good couple of weeks until I had an outdoor wank after that just in case I bumped into the fucking thing again.

I know Satan and our Wayne got up to some weird fucking shenanigans together but I couldn't even tug one off in front of the dopey cunt. Satan I mean obviously. I'd been wanking in front of our Wayne since I learned from uncle Sean how to do it. Well not literally in front of him but in the same room. Wanking in front of one's brother is one thing but call me a prude if you like, wanking in front of animals is morally wrong. And fucking them too in my opinion. And I know that's a thing because Squint had a

VHS which his dad got from work and one day we all sat round his and watched it. It was called, Nature's Teat vol.6 and in this video really fit American birds with huge fake tits and shaved fannies were sucking off dogs and horses and also getting fucked by the dogs. Mercifully they only wanked of the horses into each other's faces. It was both disgusting and hilarious. I mean Diamond got a boner of course but the rest of us were just fucking pissing ourselves laughing. It was the look on the dog's faces that was so funny. They all looked a bit bemused by it all. I don't know how much these women were getting paid but it wasn't enough. I hoped the dogs got a few quid too. How do you even advertise for that service? "Oi mate we're making a film, can we borrow your dog for a bit? Does it bite? How does it react to getting its little cock sucked?" I don't know if the dogs' were credited at the end of the film because I don't really pay that bit too much attention to that part.

Dog coming over Tracey's tits..................... Bruno.

Dog getting sucked off by Candy................. Rex

Dogs involved in interracial orgy .... Bandit, Spot, Buddy, and Mr Fur Ball.

Maybe some animals are specifically bred to be in the porn industry? Maybe that was the only life they knew? Maybe in that industry there were animals that became stars in their own right? I suddenly had a picture of Satan pulling up outside our house in a limo. The mirrored window would come down and he'd pop his head out. "Woof woof!" He'd bark and this would mean, "Hi guys I'm big in porn now so you two can fuck right off!" Wayne might be a bit jealous but I'd be happy for him.

As I sat in Stan's living room, stoned off my nut I suddenly wondered if I could kiss a girl that's sucked off a dog. Not a French kiss anyway. If Sally came up to me one day and demanded that I give her one but then said that she'd just sucked off a dog I think I'd be in two minds whether to give her one or not. That is how disgusting a dog's cock looks to me when it's hard. I know that Sally would call me a sexist pig for this but after I'd watched that tape the only thing I could think about was what if these women had children, or would one day, and then their kids came across the tape and saw their mums blowing dogs and getting scuttled by them and how this would affect them mentally.

I bet our mum had sucked off dogs for money. And our dad too probably. The dirty bastards. They probably didn't even get paid. I bet they just did it for the craic. I bet they were out in the park off their nuts and a dog came along and dad would be all like, "hey Julie! Suck off that dog for the craic!" And mum would be all like, "yeah okay!" And then she'd call the dog over and the next thing you know she'd be glugging back dog spunk like it's going out of style. And my dad would be licking its little hairy bollocks. The dirty buggers. Fuck me I hope it's not genetic. I don't want to wake up one day and suddenly get an urge to suck off dogs. If I had to fuck an animal though it would be a big cuddly brown bear with its claws removed or a swan. But that's it. Or maybe a panda.

'Johnny! Johnny! Are you listening to me son? This is all part of your education lad!'

Oh yeah. I was in Stan's gaff. Fuck me I was miles away then.

'Johnny!' Stan was shouting at me.

'As I was saying Johnny, there was a lovely looking girl who lived across the road from us when I was a nipper.

Beautiful she was. All the boys fancied her but not me. Ivy her name was and to all intents and purposes she had it all. Tight little arse and big tits and lovely hair too. She looked a lot like the Duchess to be honest. Me mum. Lovely blonde hair and blue eyes she had. You know the score. But she did fuck all for me. Sexually speaking. Many a time I tried pulling my pudding over her but it wouldn't budge. Not a fucking murmur Johnny. She had a brother called Frank. He had poliomyelitis. More commonly known to you and me as your polio. It was very common back then you see son? Anyway this polio gave Frank a pronounced limp you see son and for some reason, known only to the good Lord himself, seeing him limping about always gave me an enormous erection. I used to look out of me mum's window, cock in hand, just waiting for him to leave his gaff and when he did I'd be tugging away at me old man nineteen to the dozen until I'd shot my bolt all over the nets. I think it was the vulnerability. I got to know his habits you see Johnny and I'd follow him sometimes. We are all creatures of habit you see Johnny. As a species we like routine. This gives us comfort. Make a mental note of that. Anyway Frank would typically leave his house at seven forty five in the morning, go to where he was doing an apprenticeship as a joiner, have his break at one and leave at five thirty in the afternoon and then come straight home. Weekends he didn't do a lot. Probably on account of his gamy leg. So one day I was following him about here and there with one hand in me pocket giving the old man a little squeeze just to keep it angry when all of a sudden as he crossed the road he was hit by a car. There weren't that many cars around back then so it was proper bad luck to be honest. So Frank gets hit by this car and the impact threw the poor cunt right up into the air and over the top of the fucker thing and he comes to a sprawling halt behind it. Well the driver was a decent fella and he gets out to take a look and then he starts being sick by the side of the road. Proper convulsing he was so poor Frank was obviously in a bad way... Anyway I suddenly felt this peculiar feeling come over me and at first I wondered if I was crying. I'd never cried before you see Johnny so I didn't know what it felt like. Anyway so then I realise that the feeling is coming from me nether regions so I look down at my trousers and I see a wet patch forming and at first I thought I must have pissed myself with fright but then I suddenly realise that it was Harry Monk and I'd actually cum in me ruddy kecks! See Johnny now that isn't a normal response to have in a situation like that. I knew it was wrong but I couldn't do anything about it could I Johnny? For some reason the good Lord, in his infinite wisdom, had decided that I was made up differently to everyone else.'

'It does seem that way.' I agreed.

'It can get lonely Johnny.' Stan continued. 'That's why I think I took a shine to Simmer all those years ago. I could sense something in him that I had. A deep sense of Isolation. Isolation and alienation son.'

'Yeah it must be shit Stan.' I replied, not really knowing what the fuck to say.

'... But your ginger doesn't age well Johnny.' Stan continued. 'And it's difficult to get to sleep next to one. They look quite scary when they're asleep. It's the eye lids. Plus they give off a certain smell that's quite disturbing actually. Especially during the summer months... Anyway he's got too big for his boots recently and some of the things he does to those boys well... anyway never mind all that now. Yes I think it's time we have a little coup d'etat around here.'

Fuck me that was a lot to take in. I quickly thought about someone throwing a bag of cats into a river and a cripple getting run over by a car and then looked down at my crotch. Merciful nothing was moving. I felt an enormous sense of relief. I was obviously mental but not as mental as Stan. At least I fancied age appropriate birds. And at least I could actually feel stuff even if it was only lust and revenge. Ivy sounded a right little sort but I guessed she was old as fuck by now although maybe still worth a squirt. Maybe she still lived locally and I could pop round and ask her if she remembered Stan and would she like to take my virginity. If she had any old photos of her as a younger woman I could maybe stick them on her back and give her one from behind. I was getting desperate now. No harm in asking Stan though.

'What happened to Ivy then Stan?' I asked.

I knew that there were probably more pertinent questions to ask him but if she still lived in walking distance I could nip round, give her one and be back here before Percy could say, "nonce cunt! Nonce cunt!" And then my virginity would be done and dusted and I could get on with being a criminal overlord without any distractions.

'Who?' Replied Stan.

'Ivy, the crippled lad's sister.' I reminded him.

'Oh yes Ivy. Ivy got pregnant by a bus driver when she was fifteen so they carted her off to the nut house and nobody ever saw here again. The poor cow.' Stan replied.

The nut house! Our local loony bin wasn't too far away! Maybe I could break into the place and let all those rampant sluts have there way with me! Maybe Ivy is still there! Maybe I could break in and find Ivy and free her and she'd be so grateful that she'd agree to let me give her one!

'That's a shame Stan.' I replied. 'Especially if she was a looker. I bet she got a right old seeing to by those orderlies. I watched a programme about it once. Dirty bastards. What a waste. Oh well never mind. What about Frank? Did he die in the road on that fateful day when you creamed your jeans?' I wasn't a fan of loose ends.

'No Johnny he didn't die actually.' Stan replied. 'And you're going to laugh your tits off at this bit. The irony was that as he flew through the air and landed in the road he broke both his bloody legs, including the gamy one obviously and he ended up having two plaster casts! Hold up in bed for nearly three months he was but anyway when they took the casts off he was right as ruddy rain! He could walk as normal as you or me! It was a miracle really.'

'Did you still wank off about him after that Stan?' I asked.

'No son. Those days were gone after that' Stan replied. ' As soon as I saw him walk out of his front door with two normal legs my heart sank and my cock went limp.'

'What happened to him then Stan?' I asked.'Did he fall in love and get married and have kids and all that kind of shit that they all did back then or was he a bummer like you Stan? No offence?'

'None taken son.' Stan replied. ' No, he didn't have time for any of that because about two weeks after getting back on his feet he got hit by a lorry and was killed. Proper flattened the lad that lorry did. They had to scoop him off the road with shovels by all accounts. He obviously had no road sense at all, the stupid cunt. Fuck knows what I saw in the daft cunt really. He was obviously thick as fucking pig shit. I think his mum put her head in a gas oven soon after. She was found the next morning by her husband. Dead as a dodo. I think he went doolally soon after too and ended up in the same nut house as Ivy. They didn't have much luck that family.' He replied.

'Well at least the pair of them would have had someone to chat to I guess. In between her getting a good seeing to off the orderlies.' I replied, trying to put a bit of a shine on it.

'I loved hearing about the old days Stan.' I told him.

Fuck me then here we go. Stan is giving me the chance to be the boss of this town and I'm not going to let him down. Money, drugs and weapons were just what I needed. Especially the drugs.

'Stan do you mind if I skin up in here too mate? I'm gasping for another joint.' I asked him.

'No son, not at all. You crack on.' He replied, ' You're only young once Johnny. I'll tell you what why don't you do some more of my gear? This lot is special.' Stan replied and pulled out a big plastic bag from one of his many secret drawers. 'This is the dog's testicles. Straight off the boat from Jamaica, if you know what I mean. You can tell me what you think. Personally I can't take it so much any more. It's the old ticker you see Johnny too much rich living for too long. It'll get you in the end. I only do me gas these days. And me vallies of course. And a bit of speed. And the Charlie obviously. And the whiskey. I wouldn't be able to sleep without a drop of me whiskey. I'm on me lithium too but that's only to stop the voices in me head, they don't really do much apart from stopping me murdering cunts. Oh and these new- fangled ecstasy pills! A mate of mine got them from Amsterdam a few weeks ago. Fuck me Johnny I only took three and I was up all night dancing! Sinatra! Bing! Deano! Even a bit of Elvis and that new fella, Barry something, the shirt lifter one with the huge snozzle. All loved up I was Johnny. I kept thinking about me ma. I just wanted to give her a big hug and tell her that even though I did used to give her a dig on occasion I still loved her. I would have hugged anyone that night. Even a copper or Simmer. That's how strong they were! Come to think of it I think it was the first time in my entire life that I didn't want to torture something or someone, but about two days later I felt like I'd lost a large part of my brain. Bloody superb they was. I'll let you have some. They'll sell like hot cakes.'

I loved to chat about drugs. Whatever that gas was didn't really appeal to me but I liked the idea of the ecstasy pills. They sounded awesome. I rolled a joint and sat down on Stan's big fluffy pink couch being careful to use one of his big gold ashtrays that were dotted about. I knew that Stan had a little soft spot for me but I also knew that if I burnt a hole in his fruity sofa I'd find myself stuffed into a sack and thrown in the river and no amount of mood stabilisers would be enough to stop that from happening. I took a long drag and said,

'I'll tell you what Stan, why don't we do do one of those new Jack and Jills you got from the Dam? That way I'll know what I'm talking about when I'm selling them.'

'Well I shouldn't really Johnny.' Stan replied hesitantly. 'That last lot really took it out of me for days. But as it's a bit of a celebration what with you being my new protege and all that. Fuck it let's do one each!'

Stan then sauntered over to his gold writing desk and pulled out a draw.

'Here you go son get your laughing gear around one of these little bastards!' He said and threw a big bag of little white pills at me.

There must have been thousands of them.

'Why do they have the letter D stamped on them Stan?' I asked him.

'The D stands for Doves Johnny.' Stan replied. 'It's a brand name like Vim or Hoover or Cambridge University Press! If you get a pill and it's got a D on the fucker you know you're in for a good time see? It's all about marketing Johnny.'

'Oh Yeah. I like it. It makes a lot of sense. I should create my own brand Stan.' I replied.

'You should son. Look at me. What do you think when you look at me? What's my brand?' Asked Stan.

I looked him up and down and even though he was sat on a throne naked apart from his spunk stained gold undies and his socks and shoes I couldn't help but throw him a bone.

'I'm gonna say, "well dressed, homosexual psychopath" Stan.' I told him.

Stan chuckled with delight and said, 'I'll take that Johnny!'

I loved him and I looked up to him so I didn't say what I really thought which was, "dirty nonce cunt" although it was obvious we were both thinking it.

   I took a long drag of the joint and thought about myself and wondered what people think when the they saw me? A few months ago I was a scruffy little no mark wanker and if anyone thought about me at all it was with more than likely with either pity or contempt. These days I was certainly a lot cleaner that was for sure. I washed every day now and I was pretty certain that even up close a passer-by could no longer smell my penis. And surely I must be commanding a bit more respect? I'd already noticed that kids at school were treating me differently. As I walked across the playground it was all, "Hello Johnny!" "Hi Johnny!" "Alright Johnny?" I knew that they didn't suddenly like me and it was through fear that these cunts had started to acknowledge me but it was better than nothing.

Nobody really liked Simmer or Stan. They respected them and were scared of them but nobody particularly liked them. I didn't fear either of them. Up until recently my life was so utterly shit that if someone had put a gun up to my head I would have pulled the trigger for them. I had nothing to lose. I was just existing. I still didn't really have much to lose but at least these days at least had a three point plan.

1. I wanted to be a criminal overlord.
2. I wanted to shag loads of hot birds.
3. I wanted to be respected and or up to and including, feared.

I'd add more to this plan as time went on but for now these were my main objectives.

Personally I loved Stan. A lot. Yes he was mental and a nonce but he'd always been kind to me and although he had on more than one occasion tried to lure me into his clutches and bum me, he always took no for an answer. Over the years he was the only person who had ever paid any attention to me or showed me any kindness and for that I was grateful and for that I loved the old cunt.

'Johnny! Johnny! Are you even listening to me son? Let's neck a couple of these pills now because I don't want to be still off my nut when Coronation Street starts!" Stan shouted.

I came to again.

'Yeah Stan let's do it!' I replied.

I then tore open the bag and necked two.

'Fuck me Johnny go easy son! Those are strong as fuck!' Stan gasped in horror as he watched them go down my throat.

'Stan, I've been taking drugs since I was a toddler! I've got the tolerance of a bull! I'm sure I'll be just fine' I replied.

It was true. I was already a proper old hand at taking drugs. I had my first beer around three years old and my first whiskey at five years old and I'd been smoking fags and weed since I could talk. I was a late starter with speed though because I remember mum and dad laughing at me on my seventh birthday when they gave me some base just to watch my face contort although I got used to it pretty sharpish. My first line of coke was given to me by my dad on my tenth birthday and I'd been doing a combination of all of these drugs since then.

The only drug I never touched was the brown because I'd seen what it did to my parents and their friends and to me it didn't look like that much fun. Stan also put me off the gear years ago.

He said something like, "Johnny once you start on the gear that's all you'll ever want to do. It'll take your dreams and your soul and you'll do absolutely anything to get it. You mark my words son sooner or later you'll be sucking cocks for five pound wraps and you'll be happy to do it. You'll swallow the load of a down and out and say thank you afterwards. I've seen it happen with my own eyes." Or words to that affect.

He definitely mentioned it taking your soul and the sucking off tramps bit and that was enough for me. I decided after that little speech I'd only do heroin after a doctor told me I only had about three months to live.

I walked over to Stan and handed him a pill. Stan took the pill, crossed himself and said, "The body of Christ." And then he necked it and washed it down with a whiskey.

'Amen Stan. Amen.' I replied.

'How long does it take to kick in then Stan?' I asked him.

'I think it depends son. When was the last time you had anything to eat?' He replied.

'Fuck knows Stan. Two days ago? I can't remember.' I told him truthfully.

'Well in that case it won't be long at all son.' He laughed. 'Listen Johnny far be it for me to ever tell you what to do but if you're going to be the Don around here then you're going to have to start looking after yourself a bit better. Don't get me wrong son, you're still extremely shaggable but you can't live forever on a diet of fags and booze and amphetamines. That's a recipe for disaster. You need to have a clear head in this game. All the greats have become unstuck when they let the drink and the drugs get the better of them. I always took it easy on the drugs when I was active. I had me mood stabilisers obviously and me Charlie of course and the booze of course but I never done so much as to let it cloud me judgement or get all paranoid. You can't start thinking that every cunt you thought was your pal was really a snake or a grass or some cunt that wanted your title. Saying that, sooner or later, most cunts will stab you in the back though Johnny. At the end of the day you can only rely on one person. And that's yourself. Never trust no cunt. Not even your family. Especially not your family. And especially not YOUR fucking family son. When your mum and dad used to work for me I knew they were stealing off me from day one. They would take more drugs than they'd sell most of the time. They could have been rich as kings if they'd stayed clean and kept their fingers out of the till. Johnny, I know they're your family and this is going to sound harsh but if it wasn't for you and your Wayne I would have topped those two treacherous cunts years ago. Your Wayne has always been a real diamond. He ain't got a bad bone in his body that one. Say what you like about the retards son but most of them wouldn't hurt a fly. Although I did see one rip the legs off a dog once.'

'Did you Stan?' I said.

'The dog spooked the cunt see Johnny? A dog is very perceptive animal you see Johnny. Or is it a mammal?'

'I think it's both if it's got warm blood and can produce milk Stan.' I replied.' Non-mammalian vertebrates include fish, birds, and reptiles. And insects too I think. It's hot in here isn't it Stan? Are you getting hot? I'm sweating like nonce in a playground. No offence like.'

'None taken son. Yeah it is getting a bit warm in here Johnny. Anyway, whatever the fuck it is, a dog will instinctively know if someone isn't the full shilling and it spooks the buggers. They can sense it somehow. I remember it like it was yesterday. Me and this other cunt was going round collecting rent see? And we knocked on this one door and this old lady answered it. Terrified she was and with good reason too because she was fucking weeks and weeks behind and we'd been told that if she didn't cough up on this particular day we had to go in a take anything that had a value to it and then break her legs. It was horrible work really Johnny but I was just starting out and that's the kind of shit jobs you'd be given to sort of harden you up. You'd be roughing up old people and young mums and breaking arms and legs all for a couple of bob back then. This was way back in the day and I was a young man and I wanted to prove myself. Make a bit of a name for myself you see? I'm not going to lie to you Johnny, between you and me, I fucking loved it. I'm not proud of myself but secretly I used to hope that they couldn't come up with the readies so that I could give them a nice little slap. Anyway the old bird said she couldn't pay and started sobbing like they all did and giving us the hard luck story and all the time I was waiting for the right moment to bang her out when all of a sudden this big fucker comes to the door. He must have been about seven fucking feet tall and about twenty stone. He looked fucking demented. Proper scary looking cunt he was. He had no fucking hair and his skin was translucent, is that the right word? It was fucking see-through. White as a fucking sheet he was with these mad red eyes. Well we had this fucking Alsatian dog we used to take around with us in order to intimidate those poor cunts and when this fucking dog set eyes on this big, mad, hulky looking cunt in the doorway with his fucking size and white skin and those red fucking eyes he started going mental and snarling and growling and barking. It was fucking mayhem. Anyway then the nutter guy starts to get himself at too he starts shrieking and jumping up and down and then he starts slapping himself on the head. Well me and this other cunt didn't know what to do. My instinct was to pile onto the cunt and start giving him a few digs but before either of us could do anything this old bird starts giving him a slap herself and starts yelling at him to calm down. "Calm down you silly cunt! Jeffery!" "I'll lock you in the cupboard Jeffery!" "Do you want that Jeffery you big fat spastic cunt?" "Do you?" "Do you Jeffery?" Or words to that affect anyway. I know his name was Jeffery because she kept saying it and I know she called her own son a spastic cunt which even I thought was a bit strong... Well Jeffery clearly didn't want to go into no cupboard because the mere mention of it made the soppy cunt even worse and he started having this kind of seizure. His big red eyes rolled back into his head and he started heavy breathing and saying, "Jeffery no go cupboard mummy!" "Jeffery no go cupboard mummy!" Well the fucking dog sees all this going on and he starts getting himself at it even more and before any cunt could do anything to stop him he springs up at this fella barking and snarling and that, all ready to bite his throat and put the cunt out of the game.'

'Fuck me Stan.' I said.

'Yeah son the whole thing had turned into a veritable pantomime by now. Stan continued. 'So anyway the fucking dog jumps up ready to put it all to bed when

Jeffery suddenly comes to and he catches this fucking dog mid flight and quick as you like he snaps the dogs fucking neck. I can still hear that sound plain as day Johnny. "Crack!" and just like that, silence. The fucking dog is dead. Not one more sound comes from the cunt. So Jeffery is now standing in his mum's doorway holding this dead dog in his two hands, the dog was the size of a fucking pony by the way, but in the hands of Jeffery it looked like a fucking puppy. Anyway Jeffery looks down at the dog and then at us and then at his mum and for reasons known only to the good Lord Jesus himself and Jeffery, he suddenly grins and says, "sweets!" and then he takes the dog by its two front legs and pulls! He pulled the dog's fucking legs off Johnny!'

'Fuck me Stan.' I replied again.

'Fuck me indeed Johnny. Fuck me indeed.' Replied Stan.

'What happened then Stan?' I asked him.

'Well naturally we fucked off. Left the dog there and everything. The fucking dog was no good to us was it? Dead as a fucking door nail it was and thus about as useful as Anne Frank's drum kit.

'Who's Anne Frank?' I asked him. ' Is she a shit drummer then?'

'What?' Stan replied. 'No Johnny! Anne Frank was this little Jewish bird who was hiding from the Nazis during world war two!'

'She live around here then Stan?' I asked him trying to do a quick calculation in my head as to whether she'd still be shaggable.

'Anne Frank? No she's well dead! She lived in Amsterdam!' replied Stan.

'Aww that's a shame. What happened to her drum kit then?' I asked him.

'Johnny son I'm telling a story here!' Stan replied indignantly. ' And you keep putting me off! I'm losing my train of thought! If you've got any questions leave them until the end please!'

'Fuck me sorry Stan.' I replied trying to sound apologetic. It's just that I've always quite fancied myself as a drummer. Traditionally the drummer is the band member who takes the most drugs you see? Plus you get to sit down. So I was thinking that seeing as though this Anne

Frank bird didn't need it any more then maybe I could have it?'

Stan then looked at me and I know for a fact that he was deciding whether or not to kill me so I shut my mouth. Luckily for me he must have decided to let me off and then he continued the story.

'Anyway, the geezer with me, whose dog it was, started to get all emotional so I ended up giving him a slap to straighten him out which was something I guess. And then we carried on with the business of the day.'

'Well what happened to the old bird and Jeffery? Did you go back under cover of darkness and burn the house down or something?' I asked him.

Stan replied, 'No son. It's quite a funny story to be honest. After we finished work we went back and told the geezer who we was working for, Northern Tony I think the cunt's name was, anyway yeah we told him what had happened and he laughed his fucking head off. The next thing I know it's a few days later I'm walking into the Nag's head and I hear this voice say, "Sweets!" So I look up and it's only fucking Jeffery! Northern Tony has only gone and recruited the mad bastard and he's now doing the door at the Nag's!'

'Fuck me.' I replied.

'It's a funny old world sometimes.' Stan chuckled.

'Actually, I'll have you know that our Wayne isn't a retard any more Stan.' I told him. ' I think that by all accounts, it was some kind of act just so he could opt out of life until it improved. Once he kicked fuck out of mum and dad and all those other cunts you had a wank about back there, and then started sloshing one up old Dorothy, he's cheered right up. He can even be a sarcastic cunt on occasion.'

'Well I never! That crafty old bugger! Good for him Johnny! Stan replied. 'Well that's great news! Glad to hear it! Sarcasm eh? Not everyone can do sarcasm son. That shows true intelligence. Well I'll be fucking damned Johnny that's a real turn up because he'd convinced me he was a right fucking head case. No offence like.'

'Non taken.' I replied.

'So all those times he got his cock out and started waving it about and chasing birds down the street was all an act then?' Said Stan.

'I guess so Stan.' I replied.

'Like one of those method actors! What a genius! And the drooling and the monosyllabic utterances and reluctance to engage in any kind of conversation? All an act? 'Stan asked.

'Yep. It seems that way Stan.' I replied.'I think it was his way of escaping from the horror of our existence. Clever if you ask me. Personally, my own tactics were, in no particular order, drugs, cutting sarcasm, music and habitual masturbation. But each to his own. We are both free now. '

'You still like your drugs and your masturbation though son.' Said Stan.

'Yeah, you know me Stan. I replied. 'I love a good tug. Especially when I'm off me nut. Which is pretty much always. I'm still a sarcastic cunt and I still enjoy music too though. Come to think of it even if we had an ideal childhood I don't think I'd have turned out that much differently to be fair Stan. Have you got pins and needles in your head Stan?'

'Yes as it happens I do have pins and needles in my head Johnny. Me heart is racing nineteen to the dozen too. I think we're on our way son.' Stan replied.

'I do feel fucking odd Stan. Even for me. I'm sweating like a shitting nun. Is that right? Shitting nun? Or is it colder than a witch's tit? I'm cold now Stan. Are you cold?' I asked him.

'I am quite cold now as it happens Johnny. It's just take off don't worry you'll be fine. Just go with the flow and let it wash over you.' Stan told me.

'No I like coming up Stan. It's different to speed. It's more subtle.' I replied excitedly.

One of the many things about drug taking was the thrill of uncertainty. If you had a beer for example, you'd pretty much know what to expect. You start to get a bit pissed and on and on until you wake up the next morning in a shit filed bed but with drugs you can never really predict what the fuck is going to happen, until it's too late. This was the best part for me.

Knowing that I could be dead at any given moment really made me feel alive. I loved it. If I wasn't destined to be a criminal overlord I'd happily find gainful employment taking experimental drugs until that fateful day when one would metaphorically snap my neck and pull my fucking legs off but what a way to go.

Then Stan started up again.

'I've only really ever done drugs seriously since I retired see Johnny? Now I do them all the fucking time. I have to son. Just to block out the memories. I've done some terrible things in my time. Terrible, terrible things. Even for me Johnny. I'm a psychopath. A certified psychopath. Doctors have had a good look at me and they've all come to the same conclusion. I'm a nutter. But I can't block out some of the more vile and cruel things I've done. I had to do them though Johnny. I had to. And at the time I enjoyed doing them. You can't be seen as weak in this game or it's all over. I've had fully grown men begging for mercy in front of me son. Crying and pleading and begging and literally shitting themselves all at the same time. That's what got my cock hard back then.'

'So you're full of remorse now Stan? You now wish you hadn't of done all those terrible things?' I asked him.

'Some days I do son. Some days I do.' Stan replied. ' Other days when I look back I give myself a right good tug over them. I guess that's all part and parcel of being a fucking nut job you see Johnny? I've just come to accept each day as it comes. I've suddenly got an urge to listen to Matt Monroe. Do you want to listen to a bit of Matt Monroe Son?'

'I don't know who the fuck that is Stan but it's your gaff so crack on if you like.' I told him.

'The man with the golden voice! Matt Monroe! From Russia with love? My kind of girl?' Stan replied.

'Not a fucking Scooby Stan. Sorry.' I replied, still clueless.

A wave of euphoria suddenly swept over my entire body. I looked over to where Stan was sat on his throne. Even though at first sight, to the uninitiated, he may have appeared to look fucking ridiculous; a seventy something year old man wearing a tight little pair spunk stained golden underpants and socks and shoes, but to me he looked like a god and I was overwhelmed by the love I had for him. I'd never felt anything like it in my life. I got up off the sofa and walked up to him.

'I love you Stan.' I told him.'I really love you with all my heart. I want to hug you. I want to hold you Stan.'

'I love you too Johnny.' He replied. 'I always have and I always will. Come here son.'

And then he got up from his royal seat and we embraced. It was the best feeling I'd ever experienced in my life. Stan then held my face in his hands and we just stared into each other's eyes for what seemed like an eternity. Then we both started to cry. Waves of what I can only describe as elation kept washing over me and I'd never felt such joy to be alive. Then I felt Stan's hand squeeze my balls and he closed his eyes and tried to put his tongue in my mouth so instinctively head-butted him.

'Fuck me Stan you dirty rotter what the fuck mate?' I shouted. 'Well you fucking ruined that didn't you?'

'Fuck me sorry Johnny I got carried away. I thought that was what you wanted!' He replied.

'What?' I asked. 'You really thought that what I wanted at that precise moment, when I'd never felt so loved up in my entire life, and you were the recipient of that love, was to have my bollocks squeezed by a seventy year old nonce while he stuck his tongue down my throat?'

'Well yes Johnny.' Replied Stan. 'I thought that you were up for it after all this time! Helped along by that pill obviously. Even I know that you wouldn't want me straight. But I'm also loved up Johnny! I'm only human son! You're a very sexy boy and half my age! Who wouldn't want to chance his arm? Did I want to suck your cock? Yes. Did I want you to suck mine? Also yes. Did I hope that you'd fall in love with me and we'd be together forever spending our days eating each other's arse holes and sucking each other off and dancing to Matt Monroe? Of course...'

'Stop fucking talking Stan! You're ruining my drugs!' I told him sternly.

Despite old Stan's clumsy and unwarranted advance I was still feeling fucking amazing. I didn't even really blame the daft cunt. He was into teenage boys and I was one and even if I do say so myself, of the more hotter ones, and if the silly cunt felt anything like I did right now then, if I was him I'd have probably done the same thing. And I also couldn't help thinking that if the roles were reversed then I would have been the one to have got head-butted. Plus I took it as a compliment. Plus I was off my fucking nut on love. I loved everyone and every thing. All I wanted to do was hug everyone and tell them that I loved them. And I wanted to dance. But not to whoever the fuck Stan was banging on about.

'It's all good Stan.' I told him. 'I don't blame you for wanting to fuck me. I never have. I've always taken it as a massive compliment. But you need to know that even though I do love you it's not in a physical way. No offence but the thought of you and me being boyfriend and boyfriend makes me want to actually throw up blood... Like proper vomit up blood and bile until I curl up and die. Let's get that straight. I love you like a kid loves his favourite uncle. A normal uncle not one of those touchy feely ones. An uncle that would take you to the park and have a kickabout and then buy you an ice cream without expecting any sexual favours in return. Have you got that Stan? I won't come around any more if you keep trying to fuck me okay?'

'I get it Johnny. I just miss- read the room I guess.' He replied sorrowfully.

'Good. Right then let's move the fuck on and never mention this ever again because I'm in a really good mood and I just want to enjoy this fucking lovely pill.' I told him.

As much as I loved Stan, right now full of fucking beans and I didn't want to waste any more time chatting to the silly cunt. I just wanted to dance. When I was out I always took my personal stereo and a handful of cassettes with me in my rucksack so I immediately started looking through them. The Pogues, Rum Sodomy and the Lash. No. The Smiths, Hatful of Hollow. No. The Jesus and Mary Chain. No. Echo and the Bunny men. No. The Pixies. No. Iggy Pop and the Stooges? No. My hands were shaking and I was sweating. Fuck sake none of them were right for this kind of drug. Soft Cell. Maybe. Closer. Joy Division. No. Depeche Mode? Maybe but still not perfect. I didn't know what I was looking for but I knew that when I found the right one it was going to kick off. I'd looked through them all but they were all too dark and depressing which I usually preferred but now I wanted something light with a beat. A fucking disco beat. My parents used to love to get on the coke and dance to disco. Up until this very second the very idea of that shit was as bad as me hanging out the back of old Stan but now it was all I wanted to do.

  I'd never danced in my whole fucking life but at that moment it was all I wanted to do. Even more than shagging Sally and Pali at the same time. That's how much I wanted to dance. I needed to dance. I couldn't dance for shit though.

'Stan do you like Disco?' I asked him.

'Disco Johnny? Disco dancing?' He replied.

'Yeah mate disco and disco dancing too if you like but what I'm really asking is, do you have any disco records in your collection? That was the seventies wasn't it? Before punk. You got any Donna Summer?' I asked him.

'Donna Summer? Fuck me Johnny I love Donna Summer! And Judy Garland! And Cher! And Shirley Bassey and Barbra Streisand and Cilla Black! I've got them all in there! Did I ever tell you that I was this town's Disco dancing champion from 1976 until 1981? I was a god on the dance floor. Shouted Stan excitedly while pointing to his record collection.

'You? A Disco dancer? Well that's the gayest shit I've ever heard Stan. No offence.' I told him.

'Non taken son. I'm a poofter and proud of it but I'll tell you one thing son, the ladies love a man who can dance! A lady will judge a man's dancing and equate it to how good they are in the bedroom. That's a fact.' Stan replied.

'Do they? Well I've never danced in my life Stan and I've never shagged anyone either. I moaned.

'Don't worry son, you're in good hands. Like anything else we all have to start somewhere. As the Chinese philosopher Lao Tzu said; "The journey of a thousand miles begins with one step."

'Did he Stan? I replied.

'Yes Johnny. He did.' Stan replied. 'So what we are going to do now is take shit loads of drugs and I will teach you all the moves I know, and by the time you leave here you'll be as light on your feet as yours truly.'

'Really? That'll be fantastic Stan! Nice one! Okay let's get started! Do you mind if I was a little gander at your records?' I replied.

Stan told me to help myself and within a few minutes I found what I was looking for; Donna Summer. I Feel Love. Extended Remix. On the B side was Love To love. Fucking bingo. I took it out of its sleeve, gave it a blow and put it on.

'Let's start with this fucker Stan! My mum and dad used to play this when they cared enough to try and hide the noises coming from their bedroom. It's a banger.' I shouted excitedly.

'Hang on a minute Son. I've got a little surprise for you.' He replied. 'If you run your hands under the coffee table in front of you, you'll feel a switch. Click it.' He replied.

I did as he told me, found the switch and clicked it.

I thought that I was tripping because the next thing I knew the blinds came down on the windows and strobe lights began to appear from every direction and Stan's disco balls started turning. He had a disco in his living room! It was magical. The next thing I knew a pole came down from the ceiling. Stan had his own stripper's pole. Of course he did.

'What the fuck is happening Stan?!' I shouted at him in wonderment.

'Good isn't it Johnny?' Stan replied proudly. 'I had this installed years ago. I've held some cracking parties in her over the years. I've had them all in here. I've seen your Wayne's Dorothy slide down that pole more times than I've had hot dinners! Give it a sniff you might recognise the smell!'

'Nah you're okay Stan. I don't want to puke up this pill!' I laughed.

'Let's get at it then son.' Stan replied and we both took to the dance floor.

'Just follow everything I do son!.'

And that's what I did. For eight hours straight we danced and we danced and we danced and Stan showed me all his moves and I did my best to copy him fuelled on by a simple desire to become a proficient disco dancer and thus expert lover. That and a handful of pills and a wrap of speed and forty Marlboro Red and an ounce of weed.

We played those two tunes on repeat for hours and hours and they just got better and better. Then we moved on to Stan's, ''Twenty Disco Classics'' and then dug out his Motown.

Everything sounded like the best thing I'd ever heard as me and Stan danced around his living room Discotheque. We were both drenched in sweat and between us we must have drunk a gallon of water because neither of us felt like alcohol.

  What a mad drug. Up until that moment I'd always fancied a beer. Even while I was drinking a beer I fancied a beer so this was very unusual for me. Before long I'd stripped off my T-shirt and jeans and was dancing in my own underpants. I knew that this was giving Stan all kinds of mucky thoughts but I was fucking roasting and besides, given all the free drugs the free lessons he was providing, as long as he kept his hands to himself, I didn't really give a shit and also felt like it was the least I could do.

  We were both off our nuts but in that time Stan taught me all he knew. The Hustle, the Bus stop, the Point move, the Funky Chicken, the Double arm swing, the Snap, the Hip bump and loads more, and I practised and practised and practised by copying Stan's ever move. I even had a go dry humping the pole and did a few slut drops until my bollocks were all bruised to fuck from hitting the floor.

I'd never been more focused on anything in my life because I wanted women to see me dance and therefore for them to know how amazing I obviously was at the art of love making. As I watched myself dancing in Stan's mirrors for the first time in my life I saw myself for who I truly was. A god. A beautiful, lithe, sweaty god. I was a big wet mess of jet black hair and skin and bones but as that music tore into my soul I started to actually like myself. Eventually I started to relax and soon I was moving in time to those repetitive beats and bass lines and having the time of my fucking life. As the music played I felt like I was in tune with the whole world and I felt loved. I never wanted this feeling to end. I just wanted to stay in Stan's living room and dance in my pants for eternity.

At some point a thought popped into my head. The only thing that could make this feeling feel any better was if I was getting my dick sucked. I looked over to where Stan was now free styling and jigging about like some pilled- up, geriatric half wit and briefly considered letting him have his way with me but luckily even in this state the idea repulsed me so I just kept on dancing.

Eventually Stan said that he was too fucked to continue so we stopped necking pills and sat down and chilled out. 'Take a couple of vallies and have a kip son. That's what I'm going to do.'

'Yeah that sounds like a plan.' I replied. 'I'm fucked too Stan that was fucking brilliant mate!' We are going to make a fortune selling these bad boys!'

'No. You keep them son. It's the least I can do what with trying to seduce you earlier. You take them and sell them and make a tidy sum and put it towards your career.' He replied. 'I don't need any money. I've got enough to last me for three or four life- times. All I ask is that if you ever come across any vulnerable teenage lads who are looking for a place to stay, please send them my way.'

'That sounds like a fair exchange to me Stan.' I replied.

I decided that as I didn't want to be raped by Stan right now, the best thing for me would be to not take any Valium and fuck off home. I also decided that the thing I needed more than anything else right then was a drug fuelled wank. I was going to go home and skin up and then have a lovely long wank about how much I loved the world; and then I'd finish by cumming all over the imaginary face of my darling Sally. Actually I might even knock on her door and invite her round and we can do some more pills and I could try and seduce her like Stan had tried to seduce me. I wished I was the sort of immoral cunt who could do that but frustratingly it seemed like I wasn't. That was kind of cheating anyway. Imagine if she agreed and then we had loads of mind blowing sex and then when the pills wore off she hated me again and it became even more awkward between us? No, fuck that I thought that the best thing to do was neck another pill and leave pronto so by the time I came back up I'd be tucked up safe and sound in my own bed and have the wank of my life. I was drenched in sweat though and my underpants were soaked.

'Stan Can I use your shower please mate?' I asked him.

'Of course you can son, you know where it is.' He replied. Then he looked me up and down and said, 'if you go into my bedroom and look inside the wardrobe on the left you'll find some brand new underwear. Packets of little white cotton briefs of various sizes. I suggest you put a pair on after your shower because you can't go out in the one's you've got on because they are sodden by the looks of them. Just slip them off and toss them in my laundry basket if you like.' Then he licked his lips.

'Cheers Stan that's very kind of you.' I replied. I didn't bother to ask him what the fuck he was doing with all that underwear, of "various sizes" and I didn't want to know either.

I grabbed my clothes, ran up the stairs and into the first bedroom I came across, and looked into the wardrobe. I couldn't see any underwear. All I could see was what looked like loads of his mum's old clothes all hanging neatly on rails and covered in cling film. I looked about the room and saw that this was obviously where his mum used to sleep and it also looked to me like nothing had been touched since she died all those years ago. Everything in the room was covered in clear plastic. It looked like the inside of a gypsy's caravan. Even the floor was covered. I decided to leave the room as quickly and as quietly as I could and not mention it. I stepped onto the landing and tried another door. Success. This one looked like Danny La

Rue's bedroom so I swung open the wardrobe door, found a pair of pants that fitted me and then I skipped back out, and after locking the fucking door I jumped into Stan's shower. I threw my own pants into his laundry basket as instructed because I didn't really want to take them home with me anyway and besides if Stan wanted to eat them or wank off into them then as far as I was concerned he could do what the fuck he wanted with them. It was the least I could do after all he'd done for me. In no time I was washed and dried and dressed and back in Stan's living room which was now all back to normal.

I watched Stan neck a couple of Valium and then said, 'Right then Stan I'm off. I've just remembered I'm meeting our Wayne. I'll be in touch. Cheers for the spliffs and the pills. I won't forget it. But I will forget you squeezing my nuts and trying to seduce me. See you later.'

Stan looked a bit crest fallen.

'Always nice to see you Johnny. Give my regards to your Wayne for me. And his brass.' He replied. 'Don't forget what I said about the vulnerable teenage boys son. I get lonely.'

"Maybe I could ask our Wayne to come round and suck you cock Stan? Then you could suck his.' I asked.

I picture came into my head of Stan choking on our Wayne's enormous cock and I burst out laughing.

'I love the lad Johnny, you know I do, but if I ever say yes to that offer you'll know my head has finally popped and you have my permission to shoot me straight down my urethra and into my ball bag and then put another one in me noggin.' He replied.

'I cannot wait for that day.' I laughed. Then I necked another pill, gave the cunt a hug- while keeping my genitals as far away as I could from his own- and fucked off.

Chapter five

I came out onto the street and into the glaring mid-afternoon sunshine. I'd certainly had worse times than that. That was life changing. I was a bit concerned that something might have changed in my brain permanently and I would stay in this state of euphoria forever though. If that was the case my career as a criminal might well be over before it really began. I didn't want to be a loved- up hippy gangster. I wanted to be a ruthless, heartless mother fucker. I was pretty confident that these pills just released some kind of happy chemical into my brain though and as soon as they wore off I'd be back to my usual cuntish old self. I hoped so anyway. Stan certainly was. The dirty bastard.

Stan was even a nonce on a beautiful thing like an ecstasy pill. I didn't know how you became a nonce, whether it was nature or nurture but I was just glad that I wasn't one. So far anyway. What about if it was genetic? Like losing your hair or being short sighted like the Chinese? Or was it the Japanese? I then started to wonder if each culture had roughly the same amount of kiddy fiddlers and murderers and general wrong-uns in them or was one lot more likely to produce them. Those fucking Germans didn't take much persuading to kill all of the Jews did they? Maybe they always had it in them and that little Hitler cunt just lit the fuse? The Romans were fucking brutal too though and I think a lot of them liked the kiddies as well. I think it was probably only the elite ones though. I suppose the poor had too much on their hands trying to stay alive to bother with any of that kind of behaviour. And the Vikings. Well I don't think they were known for being kiddy fiddlers but they sure did like a scrap. And a pillage. It seemed to me that throughout history, as far as I could tell, the first thing any marauding army did was kill all the men and bang all the decent looking birds. And then nick everything.

I suddenly remembered the time I was in our local library looking for pictures of birds from other countries with their tits out when I accidentally learned that this geezer called Genghis Khan put it about so prolifically that today they reckon that one in two hundred men are direct descendents of the bastard! What a fucking swordsmith he was. Since then I'd wanted to be just like him. I would be such a great fighter and dancer and shagger that all the fit birds would be queuing up to get my little wrigglers inside them. I'd have to be careful after a few years though just in case I accidentally started banging my own daughters but I'd cross that bridge when I came to it.

We lived in a blood thirsty world and we always have by the looks of it. Throughout history the Christians have hated the Muslims and the Muslims have hated the Christians and everyone has hated the Jews. Except the Jews. Because the were apparently the chosen ones so they just seemed to have put up with it as their lot in life. I'd yet to know a religion where their followers weren't the chosen ones though. Most religions that I know of all say that. Typically the priest geezer says, "listen guys we are all fucking amazing and everyone else is a cunt so feel free to rape and pillage anyone who isn't us in our particular God's name. Maybe when I've got a few quid I should start my own religion based around getting off your nut and shagging fit girls. I'd definitely join that myself. I'd have to be the leader so I could have all the best looking ones.

As I walked along the street I thought about the wank I was going to have. I would be a disco dancing sex guru and to get in to my religion birds had to pole dance in front of me while a couple of my lesbian followers snogged each other and sucked me off. A solid foundation. My dick was getting hard and I couldn't wait to get back home. Suddenly I heard someone call my name.

'Johnny! Hey Johnny!'

I didn't recognise the voice so I kept on walking Just in case it was someone I didn't want knowing I was off my tits. What I really didn't need now was having to explain myself to a copper or a social worker or a priest. These fuckers always seemed to know everyone by their first names and they did it to disarm you but they weren't going to trap me. The sneaky bastards. I put my head down, turned up my collar and quickened my pace.

'Johnny you silly cunt!'

'Silly cunt? Maybe it was someone I knew.

'It's me! Michaela! From the cafe! I work for June and Del!' Said the voice.

Oh yeah Michaela! I wondered what the fuck she wanted. I bet she saw me passing and thought she'd give herself a laugh by taking the piss out of me for fingering June or something. She was hot though so I decided to turn around and go back if only to add her to my wank bank.

'Hello Michaela.' I said, wearily. 'What can I do for you?'

'It's not really something you can do for me but something maybe I can do for you.' Michaela replied.

Apart from Stan teaching me how to dance and giving me loads of drugs nobody had ever done anything for me in my entire life so I had to admit to being a bit intrigued.

'What do you mean?' I asked.

I looked at her in the fading sunlight of the day. She was actually hot as fuck and so obviously out of my league I didn't even try and flirt with her. I was evidently shit at flirting anyway and in my experience it had never done me any good so I just stood and gawped at her.

'Listen Johnny, June and Del are away for the day and I'm locking up so why don't we continue this conversation inside so we have some privacy?' She replied. 'I'll get you a drink if you like you look fucking awful if you don't mind me saying?'

I thought that I might as well because apart from my wank I didn't really have many plans, plus she was right, my throat was dryer than my old English teacher's wooden ring piece and I did feel fucked.

'Yeah go on then. I'll have a coke if you've got one. That's very kind of you.' I replied and we went into the cafe.

Michaela walked over to the fridge, opened the door, pulled out a coke, opened it, took a quick swig herself, and then handed it to me. I thanked her and glugged the whole thing down in a few seconds. I'd been dancing non stop for hours and I was very dehydrated it would seem. I tried not to burp but it was impossible not to. Michaela laughed and also burped. Then I burped again and Michaela tried but nothing came out except a kind of half hiccup type sound and we both laughed.

'Why you're a thirsty little boy now aren't you?' She said.

'Yeah I'm thirsty as cu...as anything' I replied.

Michaela laughed and said, 'Listen Johnny, you don't have to put on any airs and graces with me. I'm as common as muck, you cunt.'

And then she winked at me and laughed. Maybe it was the drugs but hers was the most adorable laugh I'd ever heard in my life and as I stood in front of her I saw exactly just how gorgeous she really was. I looked her up and down and my stomach did a cartwheel. The last time I saw her was only briefly as I hurriedly left June and Del's after Del nearly caught me and June at it.

Sometimes I swore I could still smell June's mucky old growler on me fingers. It was days before I could even eat anything because it smelled that bad. It was like a blocked drain that had been blocked for some time with dead fish heads, cheap perfume and bin juice. I still sold the smell to the lads though. Black Clint puked his guts up and Squint said that if that was what bird's fanny hole's smelled like then he was officially coming out as a homosexual. He even went out and bought red trousers. This was before they all started having regular sexual intercourse because of me of course. I still made four quid though.

Me and Michaela stared at each other from across the cafe floor. She was beautiful. In a kind of scrawny, ill looking way. She looked exhausted and pale but some how really fucking sexy. Some people are just sexy as fuck without even trying. Me for example. I couldn't put my finger on why, but there was just something about her that made my heart beat faster and my cock twitch. It could have been all the drugs I'd taken though. Michaela kept looking me up and down clearly deciding what she should do. Then she kind of nodded to herself and slowly sat down on one of the tables, and as she was wearing a very short skirt I got a right good look between her legs. She was wearing little red knickers. Like really tiny ones. They were the complete opposite of June's big mad ones and they looked a lot cleaner too. Even better there were no grey pubic hairs sprouting out from under them. I had never seen anything quite so beautiful in my whole life. My instinct was to take out my cock and just start wanking right there in the cafe and cum all over the cafe floor but I didn't want to appear rude. Michaela then started slowly unbuttoning her blouse and eventually she said,

'I like you Johnny. You're one of my kind... A dirty little council estate, shit- cunt.'

I couldn't argue with that. What the fuck was happening here? I bet I've taken too many drugs and now I'm in some kind of soft porn coma.

'You've got potential Johnny. I've heard a lot of things about you and I like what I hear. I'm looking for a big strong boy to take care of me and treat me like the princess that I was born to be. My mum doesn't have to suck off Eric the rent when we can't pay on time any more because of you and I'd like to show our appreciation.' She said. And then she took off her bra, pushed out her chest and showed me her tits. Her actual tits. Fucking hell. Real tits! Sexy tits! Perky, firm, young woman tits! This was more like it! No veins or hairs growing out of them either! Then she started playing with them. A young woman was actually in front of me right at this moment intentionally showing me her knickers and furthermore she was playing with her own tits! I was definitely in a coma but I didn't care because it was much better than real life so decided to play along.

'Do you like what you see Johnny?' She asked.

'Nah not really.' I replied. I didn't really say that I just nodded and grunted a bit I think. Then I put my hand in my pocket and gave my cock a squeeze.

'You're a good boy Johnny.' She said and then she pouted and batted her eye lashes and said, 'Johnny, will you do me one little favour?'

I would have done anything for her at this stage. I would have literally shot myself in the nuts for her. Michaela was probably about nineteen or twenty and there she was, legs akimbo, sat opposite me on a cafe table actually playing with her own tits like some kind of porn star. If this was what being in a drug induced coma was like then I didn't ever want to wake up.

'I will do absolutely any fucking thing you want.' I replied.

'Good boy. Now then Johnny, I want you to take your cock out. I want you to take out your cock and start wanking it while watching me play with my tits... and my little cunt.' She replied and then she slid one hand into those little red knickers and started playing with herself.

I didn't know if this was some kind of joke or set up or what ever the fuck but my cock was raging and I didn't care what the fuck was going on and I gratefully did what I'd been told. I unzipped my jeans, took out my cock and started pulling it and praying that I wouldn't immediately shoot my load within seconds.

'Ooh, somebody is pleased to see me!' She giggled. 'You're a good boy Johnny. Come closer so I can get a good look at it. Shall I pop it in my mouth? Would you like that Johnny?' She said, and then she licked her lips. 'I need you in my mouth Johnny... and in my cunt. Would you like that Johnny? Sucking and fucking? Fucking and sucking? And licking? Would you like to get on your knees right now and lick out my tight, little, wet, cunt Johnny boy? Hmm?' And as she said those beautiful words she pulled her pants to one side and said, 'Fucking eat me Johnny Capone.'

By now I'd decided that this was all in my imagination because it was most definitely too good to be true. I was just playing out one of my wanking scenarios in my head and in reality I was probably lying in a hospital bed covered in tubes and wires while getting raped by one of the orderlies. Oh well there was nothing I could do so I might as well let the mucky fucker get on with it while I concentrate on what was going on here. I stared at her pussy. It was perfect. It looked exactly like the one's in the pornos. Small and neat and shaved. I couldn't believe it. I was about ten feet away from her and I couldn't even smell it either!

Was this actually happening? I looked down at my cock. It looked like mine. I looked at my hands and my legs and I felt my face. Everything seemed normal. Maybe it was real? Maybe this was all actually happening. Was this it? Was this the moment that I was going to actually have real sexual intercourse. With an actual woman? And not only a woman but a fit one. A really sexy, fit one. I decided to ask.

'Michaela, is this actually happening or are you just part of a wank I'm having? Am I in a coma? You can tell me. I don't mind. I'd rather be lying in a hospital bed getting raped than being in real life if it means I'm also here with you staring at your lovely tits and pussy.'

'You tell me Johnny. Does this little pussy of mine look real to you? Come closer. That's a good boy. That's it, keep wanking you cock. Once you've fucked my mouth and cunt I bet you'd like to spray my pretty little tits with your spunk wouldn't you? Or would you rather empty your nuts in my innocent little face? ... Or maybe down my throat?' She asked.

This was proper porno talk! I didn't think people actually said this kind of thing in real life. Maybe Michaela was an actual porn star? Maybe we were actually making one of those "secret camera" council estate reality pornos! I looked around for cameras and crew hidden about but nothing was obvious. Would I get paid? Or would my payment be giving Michaela one? I didn't mind if that was the case. I decided to play along so if it was a porno I might get asked back to do a sequel. Or maybe a whole series. Maybe I'd be big in the porn industry? Maybe I should become a porn star rather than a criminal overlord? That pill had definitely kicked in now.

'Either or honey! I'm happy to splatter my sweet load anywhere you like!' I replied waving my dick about and thrusting my pelvis sexily while looking around trying to give the audience my best angle.

'Johnny stop! Stop doing all of that!' Michaela cried.' Please don't do that! Ever! What the fuck even was that? Don't ever do or say anything like that ever again or these legs will shut and they will never open again for you. If I wasn't so fucking horny I'd kick you right out of that door. Don't fuck this up because there will be no second chances mate.'

 Fuck it maybe this isn't a porno then? Could this really be happening? Is there really a real life woman... or girl? When does a girl become a woman? Would she become offended if I called her a girl? Or a woman? If this is actually happening I need to stay focused. I gave myself a talking to. Fuck it Johnny you nearly blew it then! Right, you need to concentrate and not get distracted. Please don't blow this opportunity Johnny. This will definitely never happen to you ever again so stay in the game. Do not upset this person. We need to just do as she says. Just follow orders Johnny and we will get through this. We must also stop referring to us in the third person too. We are not that type of sad cunt. Say something to her now and make it something not fucked up or weird. Something from deep down in your soul Johnny. Fuck it. Sorry. Fuck me I was so off my tits. Right, this is really happening! I've got my cock in my hand and I'm wanking in front of this girl, I'm going to stick with girl from now on, and she is pretty much naked and digging herself out right in front of me. This is my reality so I'm going to have to assume that it's all for real. I really need to say something now that's not going to close her legs forever. She does not give second chances so be careful. I took a deep breath.

'Fuck me Michaela I'm sorry.' I told her, ' It's just that you are the sexiest girl I've ever seen in my life and I'm finding it hard to believe all this is for real. I will be your fucking slave. Believe me I've seen a lot of porn and seen a lot of lady's vaginas ...pussies? ... cunts? Whatever, but yours is by far the prettiest and all I want to do is kiss it and lick it and make love to you... and it... and I want to make love to your mouth and put my cock between your tits and I want to cum over every part of you... especially in your hair actually... I want you to lick my sperm off your chin and ... I'm just a boy with his cock in his hand standing in front of a girl with her fingers deep inside her own pussy ... '

'Shush now Johnny.' She told me.'Just shut up! Shush! Don't ever say the word sperm in front of me again please. That was an okay start but you were kind of losing it at the end there. It's better I think if I do all the talking and you just do as you're told. How does that sound?'

I was more than fine with that because I was so off my nut right now I was finding it hard to string a coherent sentence together let alone do a load of sexy chat. It was a fucking minefield. During the act of love making do girls like you calling there genitals their pussy or their cunt or their vagina or their minge or their twat or their fanny or what? I've heard it called a Sacred treasure before now. And what about my bits? Is it sexier to say cock or knob or dick or penis? I was reading a story in a jazz mag once and this bird referred to this guy's cock as a raging root. Should I try and shoe horn that one into the conversation? If I said to her that I wanted to put my penis into her vagina until I ejaculated my semen out of my testiculate sack would she find that arousing? Is the word 'arousing' sexy? I want to make the act of love with you? Is that sexier than I want to fuck your fucking cunt off? "Oh baby I want to rearrange your guts!" Do birds like that kind of thing? Do birds like being called birds? And what about their top bollocks? Is it sexier to say breasts or tits? Bosoms? Titties? Norks? Milkers? Maybe I should use a combination? Or maybe none of the above? And what about underwear? Do I call hers her knickers or her panties or her underpants or her dung hampers or shreddies or skiddies? With all the porn mags I'd read and all the pornos I'd watched over the years I thought that I'd be a natural at this but it seems the opposite was true. I'm well out of my depth here. It's a whole new language and I needed to learn all it but for now I decided that she was right and I was going to keep my mouth firmly closed unless it was to suck her bosoms or lick out her sacred treasure and from here on in I was going to do exactly what I was told or she would never again let my raging root anywhere near here. I was in her hands now and I was happy with that.

'I'm at your command Michaela. I'm just happy to be here. You take the reins' I told her.

'It's for the best Johnny.' Michaela replied. ' Just until I bed you in. Now then, my innocent little baby boy, I need you to give me a jolly good seeing to before that thing in your hand goes off and you lose all your enthusiasm, so, in as few words as you can manage, please can you tell me what you'd like to do to me first and we'll take it from there shall we?

I looked at her, trying my best not to just gawp at her like a spazz. She looked perfect to me. No wonder I was having trouble believing this was actually happening.

'I'm not going to lie to you Michaela, I'm totally out of my depth and I'm a bit overwhelmed. You are so out of my league I feel like I'm not really worthy to be here. I've never seen anything or anyone as awesome as you in my life so I'm a bit disoriented.' I told her and I meant every word.

'I liked that. That felt real. Well done Johnny, that made me wet. I'll tell you what, why don't you decide what you'd like to do while you eat out my little fanny hole? How does that sound?' She said, and then she put two fingers inside herself and then she put the same two fingers under my nose, cocked her head to one side and said, 'You like?'

I'd been here before so I got ready to puke but I didn't need to because, unlike June's and my aunty Joan's, it smelled nice. It smelled fucking incredible. Oh my god thank fuck for that! Not all fannies smelled rank like those other two's! I could eat that no problem. I bent forwards and I licked her fingers. Then I said, 'Yes I fucking do Michaela. Yes I fucking do.'

Michaela then leaned back on the table, spread her legs and said, 'Now we're getting somewhere ...Dinner is served my little Al Capone... my El Capitan... Say hello to my leedle friend.'

It looked so neat and beautiful, like a sugar puff.

'Okay. If you insist.' I replied.

Then I got down on my knees and the first thing I did was to put my nose right up against that wondrous little mound of hers and inhale deeply while furiously wanking my cock. It smelled like fresh, wet, age appropriate pussy.

Finally. It was heaven. I decided there and then that this was the place where I wanted to die.

Michaela then pushed my head back,'Look at me Johnny.' She demanded, 'Look at me please. Now this is very important. I want you to stick two fingers right up inside the entrance of my cunt hole and suck my clit Johnny. Do you understand?'

I nodded a vigorous and enthusiastic yes.

I'd watched enough pornos to know that the clit was somewhere at the top so I put two of my fingers inside her and started sucking in that general area. While I was down there I took a sneaky little peak at her bum hole just to see if it was as swollen and knobbly and generally as fucked up looking as June's. Thank fully it wasn't. It was as neat and as tight as her fanny. And it was pink not brown. I couldn't resist giving it a little lick. It tasted sweet. Score. I didn't think she would have noticed but at the moment she squealed and called me a dirty little bastard.

'Oops sorry! I got carried away and my tongue must have slipped. I'm not exactly an expert at all this.' I replied. Trust me to fuck it all up just when I was about to finally lose my virginity.

'Oi! Don't you be a naughty little tease now!' She giggled. 'I didn't fucking well tell you to stop Johnny! Get that tongue back on my little bum bum!'

And then she slid off the table, pushed me to the floor and sat right onto my face.

'That's it gangster boy! Eat my tight little arse hole! Eat it! Now lick my cunt!' She screamed. 'Eat my fucking cunt out! Don't stop wanking your cock! Did I tell you to stop fucking wanking Johnny Capone? '

I wish I'd had a pencil and note pad because this was proper sex chat! She was using all the rude words! I tried to apologise for stopping licking her bum hole but my words were muffled by the fact that my mouth was buried deep between her bum cheeks as she rode up and down my face. I was struggling for breath. My nose kept jamming itself inside her arse and my mouth was embedded inside her pussy but I didn't care. If I was going to die this way then so be it because there was no way that I was going to selfishly push her off me just in order to save my own life when she was so clearly having a good time.

I wasn't having the worst time either if I was being honest. As she was rocking wildly back and forth and squirming and writhing up and down on my face she started screaming.

'Pull my hair Johnny! Pull my hair and kiss my cunt! Kiss my little wet cunt hole Johnny! That's it! Now lick my arse! Lick it! Lick it! Bite me! Bite my arse! Oh good boy. Now get back on my cunt! Suck it! Suck my clit! Lick it! Just the clit baby boy! Just the clit! Oh that's good! That's so good. Get your fucking tongue inside my fucking arse hole boy! That's it Johnny! That's it you dirty little fucker! That's it fuck boy! That's it! That's it. Lick my cunt! Lick my cunt! Now get back in my arse. Eat it all up you snotty little cunt boy! Eat me Johnny that's it! I'm coming Johnny! I'm fucking coming! Don't you fucking stop now my nasty little gangster cunt boy! I'm coming! Pull my fucking hair!'

As all this was happening I suddenly came to the conclusion that this was by far the best moment of my life. I'd never been happier. This was way better than anything that had ever happened to me before. Kicking the shit out of my parents or setting fire to Butch or kicking Debbie in the cunt were all secondary to me being right here, right now, lying on the floor of June and Del's cafe while Michaela wriggled and squirmed all over my face. I was her dirty little cunt boy! I was her Johnny Capone! I never wanted it to end. I wanted to spend eternity with Michaela sat on my face. But as soon as I had that thought she suddenly leaned forwards and took my cock out of my hand and put it in her mouth. I don't know if it was feeling that sudden warmth as she put my dick inside her gob or the feeling of her tongue flicking around my bell-end, or the way she put all her weight onto my face and ground her cunt onto it, but as soon I felt her lips close around my penis I immediately came down her throat. As I came I couldn't help but buck and rear up like a fucking wild stallion but Michaela stayed on and the next thing I knew she screamed and then she moaned and her body went all limp and her legs buckled and then she pissed all over my face. That's when I must have passed out.

Chapter six

I woke up smiling. I didn't know where I was but it was warm and everything was white. I seemed to be alone but I didn't feel alone. I felt content. I felt happy. I didn't feel the need to go anywhere or do anything. I was just being. Everything made sense. I started to laugh. I was laughing until tears ran down my face. Did I even have a face? Did it matter that I didn't have a face? I didn't need a face. It was so simple. I was happy and warm and everything made sense. Suddenly I heard someone call my name...

Johnny... Johnny... Johnny wake up. The voice became louder. Johnny!... Wake up Johnny! ... Please don't be dead! ... Johnny you must wake up! I don't want you to die! I need you Johnny! Shit! What the fuck am I going to say to June!? Johnny you cannot die! Wake up you little fucker! JOHNNY CAPONE! WAKE THE FUCK UP YOU LITTLE BITCH!

Was that me? Was I Johnny? Yes! That was me. I was Johnny. Not Johnny Capone though. "Little bitch"? I'd heard that voice before. That potty mouth was familiar to be. But where had I heard it? Who would call me Johnny Capone? And a little bitch? Am I Johnny Capone? No I am johnny McQueen. Why was I going back? I didn't want to go back. I wanted to stay here and just be. I was everything here. It was warm and white and I felt loved. Suddenly I saw a group of people in the distance. I didn't recognise them but somehow I knew them from somewhere. Were they dead? I saw heads. Smiling heads. They were telling me to go back. I needed to go back. I wasn't ready to be here just yet. This was an accident. Or was it? I had to go back. I understood. This wasn't my time. I had things to learn about myself. They were smiling. I smiled back. It felt like a smile but I didn't have a face. I heard the voice again. 'Johnny please come back to me. Please don't go! I love you Johnny!' I started falling. I felt like I was falling. Falling back into darkness.

Chapter seven

'JOHNNY WAKE UP!'

I came to. I didn't know where I was but I seemed to be naked and lying in the fetal position. Had I just been born? I could smell piss. I opened my eyes. I looked left and right and up and down. I was lying on my back and I was fully clothed except that my cock was out.

'Fuck me Johnny you silly cunt! You scared the fucking shit out of me!'

I looked up. I knew this person. It was Michaela and she was standing above me. From where I lay I could see right up her skirt. I grinned.

'Hello Michaela. Nice cunt.' I told her.

Michaela's legs gave way and she burst into tears.

'Nice cunt! Nice cunt! Is that all you have to say? Fuck me Johnny I thought you were dead! You were dead! You stopped breathing! I was sat on your face and you came into my mouth and then you went all limp and I thought I'd suffocated you with my cunt!' She screamed.

Michaela loved to say the word cunt and it made my cock hard. I made my d I made a mental note.

'I can smell piss. Did you piss on me?' I replied.

I could definitely smell piss.

'This isn't about whether I pissed on you or not Johnny!' Michaela replied.' This is about you dying on me! How fucking selfish is that? I've known lads to immediately fall asleep after that emptied their balls, but dying? Fuck me Johnny you need to take a good long look at yourself! That's the most egocentric shittery I've ever witnessed!'

'You fucking did piss on me!' I replied, ignoring her words. 'I remember now! I came in your mouth and then you came in my mouth and all over my face and down my chin and then you went all limp and the next thing I know I'm covered in piss! Your piss! I gave you such a good seeing to with my tongue that your legs gave way and you pissed yourself! I am a sex god!'

'Shut up!' Michaela pleaded.

'I don't mind that you pissed on my face Michaela. Honestly I don't.' I told her. ' If that's what you're into then I'm up for that too! It's kinky as fuck but I'm no prude! I made you cum so hard that you couldn't control your fanny muscles or whatever and you accidentally pissed in my face! It was an accident wasn't it? Or did you mean to do it? Oh shit! You drowned me with your piss and I fucking died! That's hilarious!'

I was really enjoying teasing her.

'Of course I didn't mean to piss all over your face Johnny you stupid piss- taking bastard! 'She replied. 'These things happen to us girls sometimes! Listen, it's been a long time since I've had any cock and I just got carried away that's all so you can wind your neck in ! I was just scratching an itch! You could have been anyone! I just opened that fucking door and grabbed the first man, or in your case, boy, that I saw! And before you go patting yourself on the fucking back and telling all your mates what a fucking legend you are you need to know that it was me who did all the work! All you had to do was lie on the fucking floor with your bastard tongue out! I made myself come riding your stupid fucking face! All you were doing was following my directions! I used your tongue and your stupid looking nose as little dildos! And I made you cum! You were wanking that thing for ages but as soon as I put it in my mouth, fucking boom son! That was it! Little Johnny was all done! And I was so good you fucking DIED! So if anyone around here is a fucking sex god it's bastard well me! And I saved your life! You were choking and I got behind you and squeezed your fucking guts until you suddenly gasped and came back to life! I saved your fucking life johnny! God almighty, I'm the actual God around here! I'm the dog's! No, I am the God's! I'm the God's bollocks! And you Johnny Capone are just my little fuck boy. My walking and talking sex toy. You should be grateful that you're lying there covered in my piss! You... you lucky little, council house cunt!'

I was indeed grateful to be covered in her piss. And I did feel lucky. She was amazing. She was fucking incredible. And I was her little fuck boy! I was her Johnny Capone! She was on the back ropes at the moment though and if she ever let me see her again I'd make it up to her but for now I decided to let her have it.

'I heard you say that you wanted me to come back!' I told her gleefully. 'You said, and I quote, "please don't die Johnny" You said that you needed me! I'm not just a sex toy to you! I think you really like me! ... I think you love me! Are you in love with me Michaela ? You are! I knew it! You are so deeply in love with me that you literally piss yourself when I'm around!'

'I will kick kick the fucking shit out of you if you don't stop fucking talking shit Johnny!' She replied. 'If you say one more word I'm going to headbutt you. Do you understand?'

I shrugged.

'Don't you fucking shrug your shoulders at me you cheeky little cunt! What the fuck!' She screamed.

Then I tried sign language but as I didn't know any it just made the situation even more weird.

'Have you gone fucking mental mate? Have you lost your fucking mind?' She asked. Quite rightly really given the circumstances.

This time I tried talking but with my mouth closed hoping that this would be some kind of loophole.

'mmm mmum mm mmu!' I told her.

'Right that's it! I'm going to beat the fucking shit out of you!' She yelled.

Then she ran towards me and was just about to kick me in the stomach before I yelled back, 'you told me not to say anything! You said that you'd kick the shit out of me if I said one more word! So I didn't! But now you're going to kick the shit out of me anyway so I've got nothing to lose! So I'm speaking!'

I said this as fast as I could to try to get it all out before the first blow hit me.

Luckily Michaela stopped in her tracks and said, 'Oh yeah I did say something like that actually. You're right. I do have a bit of a temper. Okay then well in that case it's all good and I'm not going to headbutt you or beat the shit out of you. But for your information, the only reason that I didn't want you to die back then was because I didn't want to have to tell June that the lad who fingered her and shot his load all over her wig or whatever it was that happened the other day, was now dead and lying on her cafe floor with his little cock out... Because then I'd probably lose my job. And I love my job.'

'That's fair enough I guess.' I replied.'And for your information, I pulled off her wig as I got the jester's shoes and her teeth fell out and flew into the bathroom sink! It was her own fault for jamming a finger up my arse!'

'You are fucking joking me! Did she really jam a finger up your arse hole! Why that kinky old bitch. Well that's fucking shocked me that has. She made sandwiches after that too! I think I'm going to puke!' Michaela replied while making fake retching noises.

'Well that's fucking charming' I replied. 'What the fuck is wrong with my arse hole? What do you mean, you think you're going to puke! I should be the one puking! I'm literally covered in your piss and before I died back then I spent a good twenty minutes to half an hour with my tongue rammed right up your arse hole!'

'No way was that half an hour! That was more like fifteen minutes at the most. Twenty minutes tops!' She yelled and then she looked at her watch. 'Fuck me I was sat on your face for over an hour!'

'Fuck! A whole hour!' I replied. 'No wonder it's so sore! I'm not complaining obviously! An hour! Wow! An hour. You sat on my face for an hour. You! Beautiful, amazing you! Beautiful, amazing, incredible, sexy you. I had your pussy in my mouth for an hour! And your bum hole ... Like a delicious genital cocktail.'

'Genital cocktail!' Michaela replied. 'Fucking hell Johnny there you going again! Some things are better left unsaid you know! And stop saying all that out of context! It's embarrassing! I'm not usually like that! I don't even know how that all happened. Oh God you're not like fucking twelve or something are you? Oh fuck I'm a paedo! I'm no better than Myra fucking Hindley! I'm going to get locked up! I'm sexually attracted to children! Scruffy, ill looking, drug addicted psycho murdering, arsonist children!'

'Relax! I'm fifteen! Nearly sixteen!' I told her.

'Fuck me, thank fuck for that!' She replied with a sigh. 'Hey hang on, really? You're nearly sixteen? Really? You're not very sexually experienced for a fifteen year old are you? Are you lying to me to make me feel better?

'No! I wish I was! I'm just a late starter!' I told her. ' I was a weedy little nerd up until very recently! Not even one of those brainy ones either! I'm not even any good at maths or chess or being able to draw intricate buildings from memory! ... I was just a bit of a sad cunt.'

Michaela looked me up and down and said, 'Yes, I can believe that.'

'I'm a ruthless, murdering, psychopath now though and soon I'm going to own this fucking town!' I replied.

Michaela then stood back, crossed her arms and gave me this kind of appraising look and said, 'Have you ever even kissed a girl johnny?'

'What?' I replied.

'You heard me. Have you ever even kissed a girl. On the lips like?' She asked again.

'Well I've been wanked off by June and I've fingered June and my auntie Joan sat on my face, well she's not really my real auntie and it wasn't consensual either in my opinion but it still counts, her fanny does not smell like yours I'll tell you that...' I rambled. '... Your fanny tastes fucking amazing. I want you to know that. You probably already do know that... I bet you've had many compliments regarding the taste of your fanny. And your bum hole. I would never have even thought about eating another person's bum hole until saw yours... Not that I'd consider eating my own obviously. How weird would that be? I have tried sucking my own cock though but I'm still miles away at the moment... Your bum hole is amazing by the way. Very neat. And it tasted sweet. It was actually rather delicious... I would definitely eat that again should the occasion arise. My aunty Joan's actually made me puke! Not her bum hole, her fanny hole! ... Although to be honest it did smell like shit. If I had to describe it I'd say it was like a very unsubtle blend of hot, dead fish, human shit and body odour... and Russian steroids ... I think she headbutted me too actually. Was that her? It's hard to keep up! As you can probably imagine by now I've been headbutted a lot. Oh yeah and I wanked off my tranny mate Andy, also known as Sandy. You might have seen him around. He or should I really say she? Anyway Andy, or should I say Sandy? Anyway the silly cunt likes to dress up like Madonna but he's hung like a horse and he loves to parade it about so he's like Madonna but with a huge cock and balls... Don't get me wrong I'm not homophobic or is it tranny phobic? ... Anyway he or she is a good mate of mine. I've even had a few wanks about him or her... There was this one time I was in class and ... hang on I'm rambling now... Fuck me you should really try these pills! I'll leave you some. My old mate Stan gave me these pills right and ... anyway yeah I wanked him off in those public bogs in the park because he was getting on my fucking tits. His fucking jizz went every where... wave after wave of hot salty man fat all over my hands and some old poofter... and you've sat on my face and gobbled me off...and what else have I done... Andy I mean not Stan. Andy's man fat... that tasted sweet too...'

At that point Michaela cut me off.

'That's enough Johnny!' Stop talking! I'm sure you must be very proud of all of what you've achieved thus far, sexually speaking, but I didn't ask you about that. I asked you if you'd ever kissed a girl. On the mouth. Oh and by the way Johnny, you need to eat more fruit. Try pineapple... and quit the fags because your cum tasted rank. And the term is "transphobic." And it's homophobic to call homosexuals, "poofters." Now answer the fucking question.'

'No. I've never kissed a girl. On the mouth. I've never, ever kissed a girl. Ever.' I replied while lowering my head down and pouting.

'If you'd have asked me for a kiss I would have let you Johnny.' Michaela replied.

Hearing that made me get a bit emotional. It was probably more to do with all the drugs I'd taken but it was becoming very difficult for me not to start blubbing like a little school girl who had dropped her ice cream in the dirt at the same time her new puppy got run over along with her nan.

'I wish I'd had the bottle to have done that. That would have been nice. I guess it's too late now. What with me stinking of piss and all.' I told her

'Yes Johnny. It's too late I'm afraid.' Michaela replied.

Well that was that then. I suddenly felt like I'd been stabbed in the stomach. It was a pain like no pain I'd ever experienced before. Up until this point I was convinced that I was emotionally dead. It seemed now that apparently I wasn't. I felt cold and alone and I wanted to go back to wherever it was I was before I was dragged back here. Life could be so cruel in so many different ways. Just when I thought that my own life was improving a tiny little bit all it was really doing was waiting until I was off-guard and my defences were down just so it could creep up on me, spin me around, and kick me hard in the bollocks wearing steel toe capped boots. That was that then. The end.

I tried to feel grateful for the precious time I'd spent with her which was much more than I could ever have hoped for, but I just felt awful. Why didn't I walk right up to her as soon as we entered the cafe and snogged her face off? I could not imagine how amazing that would have been. I was lying on the floor soaked in her piss and my knob was still out and I'd never felt more ridiculous. Not because I was soaked in her piss and my cock was still out but because I'd dared to hope that she'd want to see me again.

I thought at that moment that I was either going to burst into tears or puke my guts up, probably both, so I decided that the best thing I could do under these circumstances was to get up, put my knob away and get the fuck out. I had to get out of there as fast as I could so I didn't embarrass myself even more.

I still needed to tell her how I felt about her though. Then I was going to go home, have one last wank and then top myself. Or maybe two wanks then top myself. Actually now I came to think about it I now had enough wanking material for ages so I decided to wank my nuts completely flat while thinking about Michaela and her lovely face and tits and fanny and bum hole for as long as it took to get her completely out of my system and then top myself.

Yeah but if I did manage to completely wank her out of my system maybe I wouldn't even have to top myself! Plus after I'd exhausted every possible sexual scenario involving me and her I could add her to my lexicon of previous wanks I'd had over Sally and Pali! I now had a trio of hot, sexy girls to wank over! Imagine if they all met and became lesbians except when I was around! The four of us could move in together and spend the rest of our lives taking drugs and making love! I wonder what Sally's bum hole looked like? And Pali's! I wasn't sure if Pali was the sort of girl who would let a chap lick her bum hole though. Not on the first date anyway. Maybe date three. If that did ever happen we would need to keep it a secret from her dad. Mr Patel would go ballistic if he found out that I was not only sloshing one up his beloved daughter but also licking her bum hole. I then wondered what their fannies might look like. Michaela's was neat as a pin and hairless but that glorious time Sally slipped over in front of me and I got a glimpse of her knickers I could clearly see a few pubes. Maybe that was a political act? Or maybe she really was a lesbian. Fuck knows but one thing was for sure, I now had plenty to think about and I could now see myself wanking off over these three well into the future.

After all that I decided there and then not to kill myself for the foreseeable and I began to cheer up a bit. It was now time to leave because I had a lot of wanking to do. Michaela was amazing and I'd had the best time of my life but I'd been dumped although rather than sulk or act like a little bitch I decided to be honest with her and so I stood up, tucked my cock back into my jeans and said,

'I understand why you never want to see me again completely Michaela. I get it. I'm sorry that I'm such a prick. I keep trying to be less of a prick but I'm beginning to think that I'm just a prick and it's embedded into my genes. My dad is a prick and my mum is a massive prick. Our Wayne isn't though. He's great, although he looks fuck all like me or my parents so he's probably not even my real brother... I bet my dad won him in a card game or something like that. We all make mistakes. I do mad things when I'm horny too... This one time I was stoned and had a wank on the slide in the park and I shot my load all over this cat.... You should have seen the dirty look it gave me. It was weeks before I went back... Can I just say before I go that being here with you was definitely the best time I've ever had... Ever ... Including getting fingered up the shitter by June... You should see how far jizz goes when you cum with a finger shoved up your arse! ... Anyway, that hour that you spent sitting on my face was easily the best hour of my entire life. That was the greatest thing that has ever happened to me actually... I'm not even going to pretend that this kind of thing happens to me on a regular basis because you maybe surprised to here this, but it doesn't. I'm sorry that we never kissed because that would have been the icing on the cake. No, it would have been the cherry on top of the icing on the cake? Is that right? Does that sound right to you? ... I'm not sure, but it's whichever means the best... that's the one I mean... I've just remembered that I have an important meeting and I must be off. Sorry that my cock was out this whole time. ... Hopefully I'll see you around but you probably won't want to see me ever again but I'm just saying if you ever get really horny and desperate you can call me and I'll be more than happy to try and satisfy you sexually. Or we can just chat. I think you're very funny. That's a compliment. I don't have a phone though but I'll get one. ...How easy is it do get a phone installed? Don't answer that. How would you know? I don't mean that in a rude way... I just mean why would you know something as fucking boring as that? God you are so beautiful... I've really had such as great time. Fucking hell I've taken a lot of drugs today and I really need to go home... To my important meeting. The meeting is at my home. I've had such a great time. Can I give you some money...?'

Michaela suddenly put up her hands and cut me off mid flow.

'Hang on. Money? What like I'm a prostitute?' She asked angrily.

'What? Oh my God no! Not like a prostitute! The opposite of that!' I replied getting ready to defend myself once more.

'What is the opposite of a prostitute Johnny?' She asked. 'Anyone who doesn't charge for sex? That makes no sense!'

'No, no, no I meant like some money just because we are friends!' I told her. 'I'm not used to people being nice to me and I have lots of money now. Well not lots and lots but more than I had a few months ago. All the kids at school who were paying protection money to Butch now pay me... Half of what they were paying that greedy cunt... it's just business... if it wasn't me it would be someone even worse... Plus Eric the rent pays me the money Simmer was creaming off the rent collections... Simmer is this ginger nonce cunt... Anyway I didn't mean to be rude it was supposed to be a nice thing. You see what I mean now? I'm just a prick. I can't help it. No wonder you never want to see me again...'

Michaela put her hands up again and said, 'Stop fucking talking Johnny! For fuck's sake I never said that I didn't want to see you again! I DO want to see you again! And not for money! For fucking free! I just can't kiss you today! Calm the fuck down! I do like you!'

'Really? I replied. 'So am I still your dirty little fuck pig?' I asked, relieved as a mother fucker.

'Dirty little fuck boy.' She replied smiling.

'Really?! For real? No take back? I'm still you dirty little fuck boy for real?' I asked her again just to make sure.

'Well let's see how it goes shall we?' Michaela replied. 'You're a crazy and unpredictable, murdering, drug addicted psychopath so I'll have to really get to know you before I fully commit to sitting back down on to your face in any permanent capacity.'

  Fuck me that came as a huge surprise. Imagine if I'd thrown all my toys out of the pram and stropped off and immediately topped myself just to make her feel guilty and now I'd be sat about in the afterlife knowing that it was all some misunderstanding. I'd feel like a right cunt.

'This is definitely the best day of my life!' I shouted. 'What about if I ran upstairs and got some of June's denture powder stuff and swilled my mouth with it? Could I kiss you then? I asked her.

'Absolutely know way Johnny.' She replied crossing her arms.

  I was confused. Why would she have let me kiss her when we first met but not now? Was it the piss? It was her piss. I was actually getting used to it and it wasn't even that bad. In fact I quite liked it. If I'd accidentality pissed on her head I'd still have kissed her. Although my piss didn't smell like hers. My piss was fucking rank. If I'd have pissed on her I'd be home now dead as a dodo. My piss was a deal breaker. There was no coming back from my piss.

'I'm not going to lie to you Michaela I'm a bit confused.' I told her.'If you like me then why won't you kiss me? If you would have let me kiss you before why won't you let me kiss you now?'

'Well Johnny, if you must know, the reason I would have kissed you as soon as you walked through that door, and believe me I wanted to snog your pretty boy face off... and don't ask me why because I don't fucking know why. I mean look at you. No offence. But there's something about you that is driving me fucking crazy. Maybe it's because you look so sad and pathetic and lost and desperate or maybe it's because I've never met anyone as fucking nuts as you, but it's something. Fuck knows, but you get me so fucking wet.' She replied.

'Wet in your panties? Wet in your knickers? Underpants? Bloomers? Dung hampers? Briefs?' I asked her.

 I thought that this would be as good a time as any to clear it all up once and for all.

'What the fucking fuck are you talking about Johnny?' She replied. 'I'm trying to explain something to you here. Are you taking the piss out of me? I will kick the fucking shit out of you mate.'

'Terminology.' I replied. 'Sex terminology! I don't know the right words to say! I want to do loads of sex talk while we're shagging... making love? Fucking? Doing it?

Banging? ...Sloshing one up you? See? There's too many options! Anyway I want to say loads of sex talk like you do but I don't want to spoil the occasion by saying the wrong things you see? Your tits are still out by the way. I don't want you to catch a cold... They are nice tits though and if you want to leave them hanging like that then that's fine by me I'm just trying to do what's right. Tits? Titties? Breasts? Bosoms? Top bollocks? Norks? Jubblies? See what I mean? And what about your toilet parts? Do I say vagina? Or fanny? Or cunt? I think you like cunt actually. Or what about twat? Or minge? Front bottom? Probably not. And is it sexier to say, "oh baby suck my cock?" Or "oh baby suck my knob?" Or "oh baby suck penis?" Or "oh baby suck my red nosed tummy burglar?" Or "get your laughing gear around this mighty mutton dagger."... or "hey baby doll ...'

Michaela cut me off again and said, 'Mate you need to stop! Just stop! And especially stop saying "sex talk" And "oh baby" this and "oh baby" fucking that! You're making me feel sick! Leave that kind of language for when we are actually doing it for fuck's sake! ...Oh God this is so unlike me! I don't even like boys! I don't mean that I'm a lesbian before you start wanking off. I mean I've never met a boy who wasn't an absolute cock-end! Or boring as fuck. What are you doing to me!? I can't believe I sat on your face for over an hour! Oh my poor baby boy does your face hurt? Have you got stubble rash?' She said.

'No I'm fine.' I replied. ' You can sit on my face any time you like. I just want to be perfect for you that's all. I'm new to this and I want to get it right and I don't want you not to like me because I think you're awesome and not just because you're so sexy and hot. It's everything. Everything about you is amazing and awesome.'

'Even the pissing?' She replied' trying to sound coy but with a grin.

'Especially the pissing. It was the pissing that sealed it for me actually.' I told her.

'You're a fucking pervert Johnny McQueen.'

'Kiss me Michaela. Please?' I asked her one more time.

'I won't kiss you today Johnny. Or go anywhere near you. No offence.' She adamantly replied.

'No offence?' I replied. ' No offence!? Well offence taken! What the fuck? Well why not? Just tell me! We are obviously in love with each other! You said yourself that you've never met anyone like me before and you're absolutely obsessed with me so why won't you let me kiss you? Or even come near you now?'

'Well I will tell you. She said, ' but you must promise me that you won't get all sulky and bent out of shape okay?'

'Yes! This is the best day of my life and you're the coolest and funniest and sexiest girl I've ever seen! Why would I get upset?' I told her.

Then she took a deep breath and said, 'because Johnny, when you died back then... well ... I'm pretty sure ... I'm more or less certain... in fact I can almost guarantee you that... you shit your pants!'

'Eh? I did what?' I yelled.'What the fuck!?'

'Yeah. You shit your pants when you died.' Michaela replied. ' I heard you do this big, loud fart and then you sounded like you shit yourself and then when I smelled shit I just put two and two together. And that's why I won't kiss you or come anywhere near you. Because, for one, the smell of shit is not a turn on for me, and two, I want our first kiss to be special. Call me old fashioned but there's too much piss and shit about for that to happen today. Go home and take a shower and I suggest that you throw your underwear away. Probably your jeans too actually. It might be better to throw all your clothes away.

Actually I suggest that you burn them. And then in a couple of days time, when you're all clean and your balls are full again you can take me out to dinner.... and if you play your cards right we can go back to your place, take a couple of your little pills and then you can fuck the living shit out of me. Pardon my French... I'll do my best not to piss everywhere if you try your best not to die and shit yourself. How does that sound?'

   Fuck me that was a lot to take in. I felt around the back of my jeans and sure enough there did indeed seem to be a lot of shit back there. As far as I could tell without taking off all my clothes and having a proper gander I felt like it was about the size of a cricket ball. How the fuck did I manage to produce all of that!? I hadn't eaten for days!

'Fuck me! I have! I've shat myself! Is it shat? Or shitted? I have shit myself. I have shat myself. I have shitted myself. Which sounds better to you?' I asked her.

'None of the above actually Johnny.' Michaela replied. ' None of them sound exactly better than the others ... But I think that now you come to mention it, it's actually, shat. You shat yourself. I shat, you shat, he shat, she shat, they shat ... Johnny Capone shat himself ...'

'Fucking hell Michaela I'm so sorry!' I told her. ' I obviously didn't do it on purpose! I just died! I can't really be held responsible for what I did after I died! Fuck me and you let me take the piss, I didn't mean that as a pun, I mean I was taking the piss out of you all that time about you pissing yourself and the whole time you had that ace up your sleeve and you didn't play it! That's classy. Jesus that's really classy. You are something else. You are unique. I will make all of this up to you! I promise! And you still want to see me again! After I shitted myself! I promise you right now that I'm going to give you so many good memories of us that this particular one will be pushed out of you and you'll forget it! I will treat you like the fucking princess that you were born to be!'

'Listen Johnny, that all sounds amazing and I can't wait but I'm going to tell you now that I'd be very surprised if I ever forget that you died on me while I was sat on your face and then you shittinginging yourself... Or is it shittingingingging .. ing?' Michaela replied.

'I think it's nine 'ings' if it's the present perfect.' I laughed.

Then we both started laughing. God, she was amazing.

Eventually she looked at me and said, 'Go home johnny, you're covered in shit and piss, I'll see you in a couple of days. Do not have a wank about me either. I want it all for me from now on. I will know if you've been pulling on that thing and I won't be happy. I want you to be chomping at the bit for me. I want you to want me so bad that you can hardly fucking concentrate. Do you understand?'

'Fuck me are you sure? That's going to be pretty much impossible. I wank ten times a day!' I told her. ' At least! And that's on a school day! I'm a ferocious wanker! What if between now and when we go out I kill someone or bum a dog!? I will bum a dog Michaela! Dogs will get bummed and it'll be your fault! Come on let me have one last wank! It'll be exclusively about you and today! And then my cock will be in your hands!'

I pleaded and pleaded but she wouldn't have it.

'Stop talking Johnny!' She shouted at me. 'You don't have to say everything that comes into your head you know! Don't you have a filter like normal people? Tell me this, would you rather have ten wanks or fuck me ten times?'

'Fuck you ten times.' I instantly replied.

'Thank fuck for that because I need a big strong boy to fuck my brains out many times in a row and on a regular basis now.' She replied.

Then she put the back of her hand onto her forehead and pretended to swoon and said in what I thought was a very passable impression of Penelope Pitstop, 'Oh my oh my sir would you just kindly leave! My briefs are so wet right now and my toilet parts ache for your red nosed tummy burglar! Lordy Lordy I want you to sperm on my bosoms Johnny! Sperm on my bosoms! But not right now... in a few days... when you're not covered in the good lord's piss and sheeeeeat!'

It was at that exact moment, as I watched her and listened to her carrying on like a loon, I knew deep down inside the pit of my soul that I really did love her and that I always would.

Then she stopped fucking about and looked at me and said, 'Seriously Jonny you really need to fuck off because I need to get the smell of piss and shit out of this cafe. Health and safety and all that.'

As I reluctantly said goodbye and headed towards the door she called me back and as I turned I was just in time to see her wriggle out of her underwear and then throw them at me.

'These are for you,' She laughed, 'you dirty little pervert! You can have one wank into my piss stained bloomers but after that your mutton dagger belongs to me! ... and if you fuck me well enough you can then refer to me as your missus or even better, your royal highness, princess Michaela Capone of June's fucking cafe! Now get your laughing gear around them fuck boy!'

I caught them, sniffed them and put them in my pocket. 'Thank you very much!' I told her delightedly. 'Would you like mine?' and went to undo my jeans.

Michaela gagged and said, ' Nah you're okay cheers. You're a fucking pervert Johnny Capone.'

'I fucking love you Michaela.' I told her.

'You're so full of shit Johnny! And call me by my full name!' She shouted as she theatrically stamped her foot.

'I love you your royal highness princess Michaela Capone of June's fucking cafe.' I replied.

'Good boy.' She replied.' Now fuck off.'

So I did.

Chapter eight

As I walked home, trying my best not to make it too obvious that I'd shat myself, I couldn't help but grin. I actually felt like clicking my heels but I didn't want any shit to fall out. Grinning was new to me. A few short months ago I had nothing to grin about. My life was utter shit back then but I'd definitely started to turn it around. I still had a long way to go but I was more than happy with my progress.

Fuck me I nearly had a girlfriend! All I had to do was take Michaela to dinner and then take her back to my place and give her a good seeing to and if everything went according to plan I was officially allowed to call her my missus. Johnny and Michaela. Michaela and Johnny. Boyfriend and girlfriend. "Hey Johnny! Coming down the club tonight mate?" "Nah, not tonight mate I'm taking my missus out for dinner and then sloshing one up her sacred treasure." I'd never been anywhere near having a girlfriend before and now here I was actually taking one to dinner! She was a hot one too. Michaela was proper blistering and fit as fucking fuck. She'd sat on my face! She literally had my cock inside her mouth! I'd emptied my balls down her throat! I'd licked her out! I'd even licked her ring piece! It was all too fucking amazing! I just wanted to get home and wank off into her bloomers. I wonder if she was taking the piss out of me when she called her knickers her bloomers? Bloomers didn't sound very sexy to me at all. Or the word bosoms. I wouldn't mind if she was taking the piss. I'd love that in fact. She could kick me in the fucking nuts if she wanted to. I was head over heels in love with her because Michaela was the full package. Funny and intelligent but most importantly, sexy as fuck.

   I couldn't wait to tell our Wayne. He was going to be so chuffed for me. Especially if we start going steady and I'm not wanking off into all his t shirts so often. Shit! I suddenly remembered! How the fuck was I going to cope with not wanking off so much for the next few days? I'd been wanking off since I could remember! It was all I did! I was easily the biggest wanker I knew! I was allowed one more wank and then I'd be going cold turkey until I was back with Michaela! She said my balls had to fill back up! My balls had never been full! Fuck! I was literally horny all the time! I was literally horny right after I'd just blown my load. I didn't need a rest in between! Sometimes I'd have two on the bounce! Sometimes three! Typically I'd feel horny, have a wank, cum, feel guilt and shame, for about a minute, and then start thinking about my next one.

   I gave Michaela's bloomers a squeeze. Nah, she must have been taking the piss. I'm not calling them bloomers. I'm just going to call them knickers until I find someone who knows what they're talking about, someone I can trust. One thing I did know for sure though was I knew that I'd have to make this last wank count. I squeezed them again. A real girl's knickers! I was given them too! They weren't even stolen off a washing line or been found by me in the road; I'm not proud of myself any more about this, but there was this one time when I was walking to school one morning and I found a pair of discarded ladies' knickers in the street and before I knew it they were in my school bag and I was running back home. I must have wanked off into them for over a week until they literally disintegrated. I think they'd been shat too actually. I was a changed man now though. I reckoned that these days I could walk right past a soiled pair of discarded underwear without so much as a second look. Well I'd have a quick look into them obviously but I don't think I'd get on the bag and take a week off school like last time. Progress was being made. I was definitely growing up.

   I was a bit worried about me and Michaela's date. I wanted everything to be perfect and that put a lot of pressure on me. I'd never even been to a restaurant before and didn't know how to act. I'd only ever even been to one cafe too for that matter and that was June's and that was by accident. I'd been in loads of pubs though. It was a shame she didn't ask me to take her up the Dolphin. I was very happy in pubs, especially the Dolphin. Everyone knew me in there and if I walked in with Michaela on my arm every bastard would know that I was now the real deal.

   Everyone respects a geezer with a fit bird around here and Michaela was smoking hot. Plus she was probably about five years older than me and that fact was not going to do me any harm either. I would be seen as the fucking Don. At that moment, even considering that my pants were full of shit, I felt on top of the world.

   Just as I was nearly home and thinking that I'd got away without getting spotted by someone I knew I suddenly heard a familiar voice.

'Hey Johnny! Hey Johnny! Why are you walking like you've just shit yourself!'

Oh fuck me it was Sally. I turned around to see her running up behind me. Fuck that shit. I was fucked. There was no way I could talk my way out of having shit my own pants. Michaela seemed to take it all in her stride, which probably said a lot about the calibre of boyfriends she'd had in the past. I couldn't risk Sally knowing that my underpants contained a rapidly hardening ball of shit inside them so I decided to leg it.

'Hello Sally! Goodbye Sally! I've got to run!' I shouted over my shoulder... 'It's Wayne! Yeah it's our Wayne! No I mean it's Wayne's bird! Girlfriend! His fucking lady friend! Dorothy! She's ... she's had a stroke! That's it! She's had a stroke and I've got to get to the hospital pronto before she's gone!' See ya!'

And then I ran. I ran right past my own fucking house and around the corner.

'Oi wait! That's awful! Let me come with you!' Sally yelled.

Fuck it. And fuck that shit. Just my luck. I would have loved that. Me and Sally going off to the hospital to see old Dorothy before she finally pegged it. "Oh Johnny, poor you! You're so caring and thoughtful and that. Please let me suck your cock. It's the least I can do for calling you a cunt the other day!" But no. Unfortunately Dorothy is as fit as a fucking fiddle. The old hag will never die. I was just about to wank bank that particular scenario when I suddenly realised that soon there would be no more wank bank. No more wank bank? Fuck that shit I'd always have a wank bank. I just wouldn't add to it once I'd started making love at Michaela's front bottom.

Michael's front bottom. I'd actually tasted it. That actually happened. It tasted amazing. I was so grateful that not all women's genitals smelled and tasted as bad as June's and aunty Joan's. I decided that Michaela was worth giving up wanking for and also giving up adding to my considerable wank bank. Why would I even need to wank any more anyway? I'd be getting regular sexual intercourse inside my girlfriend's vagina so there would be no need! As long as she let's me give her one ten times a day forever then I didn't see any problem here. I guess it would be like giving up fags and booze and drugs. A bit hard at first but eventually I'd just get used to it. I'd never given up fags or booze or drugs though so I didn't really know.

   But why out of all the days leading up to this day, the only day that I can ever remember shitting myself, had Sally chosen today as the day that she liked me enough to want to come to the hospital to see old Dorothy? That was incredibly bad timing. Imagine if it was today that she suddenly realised that I wasn't a complete and utter cunt and she was going to let me bone her? Or at least lick out her hairy minge. I decided there and then that until I had my final wank I could quite legally and guiltlessly add to my collection of wanking fantasies. Of course I'd have too much respect for Michaela to not make her the actual focus of my last ever wank but I'm sure that leading up to it she wouldn't mind me adding a few extras along the way. Just a few bit part actors who only appeared here and there on the margins and didn't even get a speaking part. I actually thought that I'd owed it to Sally and Pali to involve them and in my opinion it would be doing them a gross injustice not to include them in my final ever act of self- pollution.

   This was going to be the mother of all wanks. I now had a clear conscience. My last ever wank would be a retrospective homage to all the birds I'd ever wanked off to and culminating in a respectful vinegar stroke that involved just me and Michaela. Probably me cumming all over her tits and face. Sorted. The only decision I now had left was whether to either put Michaela's piss stained knickers on my head and sniff them as I came, put them on and parade around my house in them and then wank off into my full length bedroom mirror while still wearing them, or just get on the bag and have a frenetic wank into them, old school. I eventually decided that I'd leave that one until I was actually in a position to even have a wank. All I needed to do now was find some way into my house without Sally spotting me.

   I peaked back around the corner. The coast was clear. She'd obviously fucked off. Thank fuck for that. But just as I was about to sneak back home Sally's fucking mum came out of their gate and headed towards me. She was wearing a short black skirt and thigh high white leather boots. She must have been about forty but she still had great tits and her face wasn't even that ragged considering her lifestyle. She looked like Sally but if Sally had been a heavy drinker and smoker and liked to get on the bag with random men at the weekend and take it up the dirt box. That was a compliment. I cursed myself once again for being covered in shit because I reckoned that for some unknown reason birds suddenly fancied me today and Sally's mum was now making my cock hard. I didn't think it would be being unfaithful to Michaela if I let her suck me off before we were even official; especially if that counted as my last wank. I'd just be doing it into the mouth of Sally's mum rather than into her knickers or onto my big wanking mirror. I could even get her to put on Michaela's knickers so it would be more appropriate and respectful! That might be quite romantic actually. Or I could ask her to nip back to hers and dig out a pair of Sally's from the laundry basket and I could do a compare and contrast as I was getting a nosh.

All these ideas were regrettably irrelevant now though because yes it was patently obvious that I was now clearly irresistible to all women, even I didn't think Sally's mum would suck my cock when it was so close to my shitty arse hole... Or would she?

  I quickly thought about it but decided not to take the chance so fucked off over the wall I'd just hidden behind and after jumping through a few back gardens I came to Big Ron's house.

  Big Ron was a friend of me and our Wayne's. Actually he was the one who'd pretty much introduced our Wayne to his missus. The divine, duchess of death, Dorothy. We were looking for prossies and Big Ron pointed us in her direction. I definitely dodged a bullet when she refused to let me shag her that day I'll tell you that. Unfortunately our Wayne ended up banging her and immediately became cunt struck. They were now inseparable. It's quite revolting to see really but as long as our Wayne was happy that's all I cared about.

  I ran up to Big Ron's kitchen door and gave it a hard knock. I left it a minute but as there was no sign of him I went round to his back bedroom window to see if he might be asleep. He wasn't asleep. He was dressed up like someone's nan and knocking one out on his bed. He was also wearing headphones. That explained why he couldn't hear me. At least he was in. I didn't know whether to bang on his bedroom window or let him finish. I decided that the most polite thing to do was let him finish so I just watched. His eyes were screwed tightly shut and his legs were spread and I couldn't help but notice that he had, what I was fairly sure, was a large thermos flask shoved into his arse hole. What a great idea, I thought to myself. I'd never really thought about putting something up my arse while I was having a Tommy tank. This guy never ceased to amaze me. He was a real maverick when it came to sexual perversion.

Big Ron was a merchant seamen and he's been around the world countless times and on his way round he'd done every mad fucked up thing one could ever dream of. He was the ultimate sexual deviant and he didn't give one flying fuck who knew it. He'd fucked men and women and lady boys and geezer birds and dwarves and circus freaks and everything and everyone in between, and then they'd fucked him. Whatever crazy shit you could think of Big Ron had done it. Twice. He once told me and our Wayne that he'd noshed off every colour and creed of cock and eaten every type of fanny that there ever was. "Black, white, red, yellow and brown and all the colours of the fucking rainbow lads! If I a few quid in my pocket and it had genitals I'd eat them and then I'd lay back and let them eat mine." Big Ron was a free spirit and I loved that about him. Over the years he'd spent every last penny he had on prostitutes and now in his retirement he spent his days sat at home in his council house , dressed as a bird and wanking off to all his memories. He was a hero of mine and an inspiration.

As I watched Big Ron wanking off I wondered what he was listening to. My own musical taste while banging one out often depended on my mood of course. One of my particular go-to favourite wanks to music was to get properly pissed and dance around my bedroom with my cock out, and having an old school Irish punk wank listening to the Pogues. I'd be at one of their gigs and their bassist, Cait O'Riordan would come to the front of the stage and point at me. Then she'd sing, A Man You Don't Meet Everyday, especially for me, and then after the gig a roadie would come and get me and ask me if I wanted to meet the band. I'd say yes obviously and after I met Shane and kissed his feet and told him that he was the greatest living poet and song writer that there ever was and ever would be, I'd spend the rest of the night banging Cait and then the evening would culminate in me cumming in her hair. The next morning the band would ask me to join them but I'd tell them that I wanted to start my own band. Cait would then cry and beg me to stay and be her long term boyfriend but I'd say no because Debbie Harry wanted me to give her one and also that posh bird, Kate Bush. I'd then punch Elvis Costello in the gob and fuck off. Other times I'd switch genres and maybe have a Country and Western wank about Dolly Parton and Tammy Wynette lezzing off for example. It wasn't exactly Shakespeare but it always got the job done.

   After about twenty minutes Big Ron started squirming and lurching about and eventually, after a lot of huffing and puffing, he shot his load. It didn't look very much but he was old as fuck. Then he licked his fingers and nodded. I waited until he'd taken off his headphones and his thermos had slid back out of his arse hole and then I tapped on the window.

'Ron! It's me Johnny! Big Ron! I've shit my pants! Can I come in?' I mouthed through the glass.

Ron slowly sat up, closed his legs, took off his wig and stared at me. He seemed to be off his tits. Suddenly he started shaking his fists at me and shouted, 'Johnny? Jamaican Johnny? Jamaican Johnny from Kingston? I thought I'd killed you years ago ya scurvy dog! Have you come back to haunt me Johnny you blasted old scoundrel! ...After my treasure are ya?! Well you don't scare me Johnny! I'll make you wish you'd stayed in your watery grave boy! Let me get my hands on you, ya scorbutus bastard!' Then he leapt out of bed and headed towards the window.

'No Big Ron you silly cunt!' I shouted at him, 'It's me! Johnny McQueen! From across the road!'

Thankfully this information did the trick and he snapped out of whatever the fuck he was in.

'Oh it's you Johnny!' He replied. ' I thought for a minute that you were a ghost from my past come to drag me to the gates of hell where I'd be consigned to the fiery lake of burning sulphur for all eternity! The second death if you will.'

'Nah, it's only me Big Ron.' I replied. ' I've shit my pants and I can't go back to my house because I've just seen Sally from next door and because I didn't want her knowing that I'd soiled myself I ran away from her before she could smell me! I told her that I was off to see old Dorothy in hospital because she'd had a stroke. So I'm looking for somewhere to stay for a bit and maybe get a change of clothes and have a shower.'

Big Ron sat back down on his bed and started to pour himself a drink from his flask.

'That's okay Johnny. You can stay here.' He told me. ' Do you want a drink? It's fresh coffee. I always like a nice coffee after I've managed an ejaculation.'

'Nah you're alright mate cheers.' I replied.

'All the more for me then. I'll open the window and you can climb in son.' He replied.

'Wouldn't it be easier to let me in the back door Big Ron? I asked.

'Oh yes that would be easier wouldn't it? Sorry Johnny I'm on the opium and I get a bit hazy on it. You ever masturbated on opium Johnny?' He replied.

'I have not. Not so far anyway.' I told him, hoping that he'd give me some to try.

'It's very difficult to ejaculate on opiates Johnny. It really takes it out of you. That's why I need a little pick me up once I've emptied me old sack.' He said. 'Right then let's get you in.'

Big Ron then heaved himself up out of his bed and out of his bedroom. Moments later he was greeting me from his kitchen door.

'Welcome to my humble abode Johnny! Well don't just stand there! Come on in son!' He told me.

   Then as I stepped into his kitchen he said, 'Christ you really have shit yourself haven't you? Now then let's get you out of those clothes before you stink the ruddy place out shall we?'

'Yes please Big Ron. That sounds like a plan.' I replied.

'Now then who do you fancy being? A cheeky school girl? Air hostess? Chambermaid? What about Shirley Temple? Or maybe a dirty little Mud slut?' Big Ron asked me.

'Eh? No I just want a pair of jeans and some clean underpants if you've got anything like that lying around that would be perfect. ' I replied.

'That's a bit boring Johnny. Alright then what about a Baywatch babe then? I've got a lovely little red swimsuit and a blonde wig that would suit you down to the ground!' He continued.

'If it's all the same to you I'd rather not Big Ron. I'd rather just have a shower and get back home. I need to take a pill and have a wank. My last ever wank.' I replied.

'Your last ever wank Johnny?' He replied. 'You dying then son? I'm sorry to hear that. Is that why your face is so red? Scarlet fever is it? How long have you got then? First Dorothy has a stroke and now you dying horribly of the Scarlett fever. I don't know. Where will it all end? They say these things happen in threes. I wonder who will be next. I hope it's that Margaret next door. I hate her Johnny. She called me a lazy tranny the other day! ... A lazy tranny! Well I ask you! A lazy tranny! That's rich coming from her! She looks like a tranny! At least I'm only pretending to look like a woman for sexual gratification! Well sexual gratification and comfort obviously... And I'm doing a far better job of looking like one than her! And she IS a woman! Supposedly. The masculine looking old cunt bag! Just because I didn't bother to shave my legs one time when we went to Tesco's! I told her straight! I said Margaret now you listen to me I said, I said I will never, and I mean NEVER pander to the male gaze! And furthermore I told her, I said, Margaret, I am not just a piece of meat to be gawped at by handsome, young men! I'm an independent woman of colour, I told that absolute slut! And further fucking more I don't need no man to validate me! That was three days ago and I haven't spoken to her since! Lazy tranny indeed! The cheeky fucking cunt. I'm not going round to hers either! If she wants to apologise then that's fine. Water under the bridge, but I'm not making the first move Johnny. She was supposed to be bringing over a Victorian sponge but I haven't seen it! The cunt!'

' I don't blame you Big Ron.' I told him.' Why should you do all the work? Fat, lazy tranny indeed mate. What a cunt.'

'Margaret didn't call me fat Johnny. She's not that much of a hurtful bitch! Do you think I'm fat then son? Don't answer that!' Big Ron laughed. 'No Johnny' He continued, 'I think what she was trying to do was get me to make more of an effort you see son? It's true I have let myself go a bit recently. But what's the ruddy point? Who's going to look at a seventy year old transvestite when there's all these young ones flitting about in the pubs and clubs dressed up to the nines with their young skin and shapely legs and arses and what have you? Nobody son. Not one bugger. It's been weeks since I've had me end away!'

'Weeks!' I replied. 'Only weeks?! Fuck me Ron! '

'Fuck you? Well okay but I'm not rimming you unless you at least give it a bit of a wipe. Big toilet has never been my bag. No offence.' Big Ron laughed.

'No I mean it's cool that you're still getting laid!' I replied. 'Yeah, no, sorry Big Ron you don't look fat at all!' You're big boned I'd say. Like one of those Amazonian women. Powerful. Proper sexy too. I'd definitely slosh one up you if I wasn't going steady with my new bird! Oh yeah and I'm not dying.' ...Scarlet fever? Is my face red then? It does feel quite sore now you mention it. That must because this bird was sat on it for an hour. A whole hour while I was wanking myself off! Then I came in her mouth! It's stubble rash I guess. From her sacred treasure. I've just met this bird you see Big Ron and she's amazing. Her bum hole tastes like sweets. It's mental. Anyway she told me I can only have one more wank until we meet up again in a few days... or was it a couple of days? Is there a difference? Anyway she wants me rampant you see? She wants me chomping at the bit so that when we've had our meal I can take her back to mine and fuck her bandy... Listen Ron, if you don't won't to shave your legs then you don't have to. Especially in the winter months. The lezzers don't anyway. You live your life your way. Do you want me to kill Margaret for you? Or cut her up a bit? I've never had a Victorian sponge. Big Ron can you teach me how to behave in a restaurant?'

'Of course I can son.' Big Ron replied.'I've been to the best restaurants in all the world! I ate a wagyu steak off a Japanese lady's knockers once! No don't kill or cut Margaret... Thank you though Johnny. Bless you for saying that, but no. I think I'll go round tomorrow and we'll have a cup of tea and we'll do a few lines and some mushrooms and sort it all out under the influence of mind bending drugs.'

'Cheers Big Ron.' I replied. 'Fair enough mate. Right then I'm sorry to be rude but this shit in my pants is rapidly drying and it's starting to stick to my pubes. Soon I'm going to need a hammer and chisel to get it off so if you'd be so kind as to direct me to your bathroom I'll go and have a shower if that's okay?'

'Yes! Yes absolutely Johnny!' Big Ron replied. 'You jump in the shower and I'll find you some clothes to put on. I hope I can find you some that fit!'

'Beggars can't be choosers Big Ron and I'll be grateful for anything! I just need something to wear so I can get back home. Whatever you've got lying around will be fine mate.' I told him.

   Mercifully Big Ron finally showed me to his bathroom and I quickly undressed, threw my shitty pants and jeans into a plastic bag and hopped into the shower and after half an hour of frantic scrubbing I was clean again. Big Ron had told me to get changed in his spare room so I hopped across the landing and swung open the door. Lying on the bed all laid out for me was a skirt and a blouse and socks and a pair of huge, white, cotton knickers. There was also a tie. Sexy school girl it was then. Sexy extra large school girl. Fuck me he could of at least tried to hide the spunk stains. I had no option other than to put it all on. At least there was a wig so with any luck anyone who saw me outside would think I was just another fifth year slag bunking off school to go and get fingered by a bus driver or one of the PE teachers. I got dressed and met Big Ron in his living room.

'Well Ron? What do you think?' I asked him.

Big Ron gave me the once over and said, 'Very nice Johnny. Very nice indeed. Now then lift your skirt up and let me see your knickers.'

This sort of thing wasn't even completely mental to me now so I just did what he asked and even did a shy giggle to accompany the act because I didn't have to worry about him bending me over and scuttling me because Big Ron wasn't into teenage boys. That was too much of a cliché after all these years.

He then gave me a playful pat on the bum and told me that I was a very pretty young lady which made me blush.

'You know what Johnny? You could make a lot of money dressing up like that and going to private men's clubs. Old, posh, men will pay top dollar to fuck you hard and mean right in your tight little anus.' He told me.

'Nah you're alright Big Ron that doesn't sound like something I would like. Cheers though.' I replied.

' Just a thought son. Just a thought.' Big Ron said. 'You know what Johnny? I used to sell my arse on the docks when I was your age.' He continued. 'Loved it! That's what got me into dressing up like a woman on a professional level. I was just a kid when I first put on my mother's dresses and paraded about though. It felt natural and right but knowing men will pay you to suck them off while dressed up like a little slut has always given me a certain kind of feeling of empowerment that I've never really had doing the same thing dressed like a fella. It's hard to describe. As soon as I put on women's clothes I feel at home. It comes natural to me. Maybe it's just the thrill of deception? I've never really thought about it much tell you the truth. I just like it. People read too much into these things in my opinion. Live and let live I say. If it feels right and you're not hurting anyone then what harm is it?'

'No harm in being a fucking deviant Big Ron! If you're anything like me it's probably the feeling of silk panties rubbing up against your cock and balls Big Ron.' I told him. 'I had to dress up like a bird once and had a hard-on all the way home. I had a right good wank that night too and I was still dressed like a girl and I loved it I can tell you that. ... It was just something different than banging one out into one of our Wayne's t shirts like normal. I think I came into my own face that time too actually... Just to see if I was the kind of person who liked to have jizz in their face.'

'And were you Johnny?' Big Ron asked.

'I'm still not sure actually. No, yes, maybe, not really. I'm still undecided.' 'I told him. 'I didn't mind the initial splatters but it soon got cold and congealed. It wasn't really for me at the time Big Ron. It tasted awful too, like a bitter combination of fags and chicken nuggets. I think if I did it again I'd change my diet.'

'Fair enough son.' Big Ron replied. 'Well you've got tot try these things. Try everything once. That's my motto. And if you don't like it then at least you know. And if you do like it then you can fill your fucking boots and keep doing it until all your money has gone and they throw you out of the country.'

'Yep. That's a good motto Big Ron.' I agreed.

As I looked at Big Ron as he was chatting away I couldn't help but see Margaret's point. He was a bit of a lazy tranny to be fair. All the other cross dressers I knew, which were Sandy and all the ones I'd watched on Channel four documentaries, seemed to put in a lot more effort than he did. Big Ron was sat on his settee wearing what seemed to me to be an old woman's cardigan that he'd clearly got from the jumble sale, the same grey coloured knee length skirt he'd had on for weeks, a pair of tights that had clearly seen better days and a pair of fluffy slippers. Even his wig was just a blue rinse perm and furthermore he wasn't even wearing it now he was just absent-mindedly stroking it while he was banging on. He wasn't even wearing any make-up.

   I was lead to believe that transvestites all wore sexy mini skirts and high heels and loads of slap and long blonde wigs; like whore versions of real women. That's how I personally preferred my trannies to look too. A classic cross dresser seemed to me to be a hyper real version of a woman but with big hands and feet and no hips. I honestly couldn't have cared less though. Big Ron was a nice person and if he wanted to look like someone's gran then who the fuck was I to think that he looked like a proper cunt. He did have a great set of top bollocks though. I knew they weren't real but they still gave me a bit of a murmur. Big Ron must have read my mind because he suddenly said,

'I know what you're thinking son but not all trannies want to look like Greta Garbo or Katharine Hepburn all the time. No son. Some of us just want to put on a skirt and a cardi and some comfortable shoes. Real women don't always make an effort either do they? I think that I'm more of a genuine cross dresser by actually dressing like real women. You should see those slothful bitches walking around Tesco! Most of them look like they've just got out of bed and put a coat over their pyjamas and still stinking of night farts. It's a pain in the arse dressing up all the time. Men have it easy. They wash, shave, put on a pair of jeans and a shirt and bang! They're ready for the day. The lucky cunts.'

'You're not wrong there' I told him.

I was getting a bit bored by now and just wanted to fuck off for my wank but he wasn't finished.

'A lot of men are poofters you see Johnny.' A lot of men. Respectable men! Working class men, middle class men, upper class men. Men from every realm of society. I've been all around the world and I know for a fact that every race, every culture, every country, regardless of religion or government or whatever, all have a good number of men who like other men. And women who like woman too. A lot of men are poofters Johnny. And I'm aloud to say that because I am one son. Well sometimes me and Margaret do a bit of girl on girl when we're off our nuts on the bag but that's neither here nor there.'

'Are you Big Ron? Are they? Poofters eh? Yes girl on girl.' I replied not really listening any more.

'Yes Johnny.' He continued. 'listen son, this is for your own good, and I'm not trying to lecture you. I'm your pal and I don't find it offensive because I know that your parents were a right couple of Irish bigots, but some people may find your constant use of the term 'poofter', as offensive. Offensive and derogatory ... And not just us poofters either. I'm a poofter so I'm allowed to say it. I fought very hard to gain acceptance as a homosexual and so did a lot of other homosexuals and some were banged up in prison and some even lost their lives. I had a friend who was kicked to death in a public toilet. Kicked to death Johnny. Just for being a homosexual. I know you don't mean any harm but try your best to say homosexual in future.'

Fuck me that was me told. I'd never really given it much thought. I'd always used the term poofter. I didn't know it was offensive until Sally told me that one time. I certainly didn't know it was derogatory either. But that was because I didn't know what derogatory meant. It didn't sound like a good thing though. I didn't mean to be disrespectful to Big Ron so I immediately apologised.

'Fuck me Big Ron.' I told him. ' Sorry mate. I wasn't trying to be a cunt. I didn't even know it was a bad word. Well I did sort of know but I didn't think you cared that much because you were using it and so was Stan the man actually. Do you know Stan the man Big Ron? He's a po.. homosexual too. But he's also a bit fond of the kiddies too if you know what I mean. But anyway that's no excuse, if you're offended then I'll stop saying it. Homosexual it is. Sorry again Big Ron. Actually yeah you're right my parents are a couple of homophobic shit cunts actually. And they're also racists. Fuck me I wish they were dead.'

'That's okay Johnny. Just try and think before you speak that's all. One of my many mantras is, "try not to be a fucking ignorant, uncouth fucking cunt." Replied Big Ron.

'That's a good one! That's good advice actually!' I replied.

I was young and I clearly needed good advice on how to behave it would seem. Growing up in a house with those two fuckers was not doing me any favours now. I was uncouth! And ignorant! And I was definitely a cunt! But I wanted to be a normal person! I just need to learn the language.

'From now on I'm going to think before I speak and remember that mantra!' I told him.

'Good lad Johnny.' Replied Big Ron. ' Oh and finally, I'm sorry to get all preachy again but there's a lot of people who also assume that homosexuals are also paedophiles. Like your friend Stan. You know that that's not a good thing right Johnny? You do know that paedophiles cause a lot of pain and anguish and they should all be castrated and then burned alive right son?

'Yes I do Big Ron. Yes I do.' I replied even though to be honest I'd never really given it that much thought.

'Good boy. At least that's something.' Replied Big Ron. 'Anyway I can assure you Johnny that is certainly not the case! Some gay men are paedophiles but the vast majority aren't. Just like in the heterosexual world. Some women too! Anyway please never make that assumption. I'm a poof but I'm not a nonce Johnny! The little shits! I'd rather shoot a kid than fuck one!'

'Ha! You said nonce when you should have said paedophile!' I corrected him. Pleased as fucking punch.

'Ah yes! Nice try Johnny!' Big Ron replied. 'That means you're getting there already! Thinking! Good lad! Although unfortunately for you though, in their case you are incorrect because they can all fuck off as they are all filthy nonce cunts and you can call them whatever the fuck you like. The absolute rotters!'

'So it's alright to call a paedophile a dirty fucking shit cunt nonce then Big Ron?' I asked him.

'Absolutely Johnny!' He replied.

'Right then let's get back on track,' Big Ron continued. 'In my experience, a good number of these homosexual men seem to be very uncomfortable with the fact that they are sexually attracted to other men. Some are of course and that's great but a lot aren't. But it would appear that if you're sodomising a handsome young lad, such as yourself, but, and here's the difference, you're dressed as a girl, it seems to make them feel a whole lot less guilty about the whole thing.'

'That's great Big Ron but if it's all the same to you I really don't want to be fucked in the arse by old men for money.

Especially not in this because it's too big and my skirt keeps falling down. Plus isn't it a bit noncey? ' I replied.

'Well maybe I guess but it's not like you're a fucking child really are you Johnny? But yes that's that's fair enough son. It's a fine line. I'm just saying that's all. I have always been comfortable with my own sexuality. I knew as soon as my balls dropped that I was sexually attracted to pretty much everyone and every thing and as I never saw the point in hiding it I spent my whole life indulging in every sexual depravity available. Not the kiddies though Johnny. Not the kiddies. I know the Romans did and also the Greeks and a good few cultures now too if the truth be told... Those Afghanistan tribal leaders for one ... look up the term, bacha baz, when you've got a minute. The mucky rotters... and also a lot of public school boys and their teachers and I think the Victorians had a good go too but it was never my thing son. I don't like children Johnny. That's why I never had any of my own. You ever see a happy parent Johnny?'

'No mate I can't say I have.' I told him.

'No me neither. The little cunts. It's a con having kids.'

I just wanted to have a wank. I was glad that Big Ron wasn't a nonce though.

'I remember being in African one summer years ago Johnny.' He began, seemingly out of nowhere.

'Do you Big Ron?' I replied, lighting up a joint.

'Yes son, I was in Kenya on safari with this pigmy lady that I'd won in a card game back in Burundi, anyway as we were driving around looking at all the elephants and lions and what have you, I suddenly spotted this zebra and my penis immediately became extremely hard.'

He had my full attention again.

'A zebra gave you a hard-on Big Ron?' I asked him, somewhat surprised.

'Yes! I suddenly got the hots for this zebra.' Big Ron told me as if it was he most unremarkable thing that anyone had ever said. 'It had lovely long eye lashes and rather shapely legs you see?... And there was also something about its hind quarters that seemed to say to me, "I want you Ronald! Come take me!" It was quite odd actually.'

'It does seem quite odd Big Ron.' I told him. Because it did. Very fucking odd. Even for Big Ron.

'I also noticed that a zebra is very much like a pony in the fact that they are both exactly the right height for a damned good rogering.' Big Ron continued with a far away look in his eyes. 'Unlike a giraffe son. I think a giraffe is one of the few mammals I haven't thought about shagging. No point. You'd never catch one. Too quick you see? They see you approaching with an angry penis in your hand and boom! They're off! Even if you did catch up with it you'd never get your end away because it's genitals are too high. You wouldn't even be able to give it a bit of oral. Did you know that all vaginas taste the same Johnny? Regardless of species?'

'No I did not know that Big Ron.' I replied while toking hard on my joint.

'Yep.' Big Ron replied. 'I can guarantee you that whether it's a human lady, or a dog or a cat or even a mouse or a whale, they will all taste pretty much the same. It's just science and biology really but the government don't want you to know this fact because they don't want everyone going around muff diving all their pets and not getting any work done. It's all about tax Johnny! Paying tax so the illuminati can spend it on guns and tanks and starting wars where they shouldn't be! The ruddy cunts!'

I decided then that Big Ron was definitely mental.

' I don't blame giraffes for doing one when they see a human with his cock out heading towards them Big Ron. No offence.' I told him.

'None taken son.' He replied. ' Anyway I saw this zebra and I managed to sneak up on it from behind and rabbit punch it. With one blow I knocked it out cold and it fell onto its front feet which turned out to be the perfect position for me to scuttle it. And before you ask young Johnny, yes I did lick it out before-hand. A gentleman never goes in dry.'

'Hang on Big Ron, what was this Pygmy bird doing while you were banging it then? Didn't she mind?' I bet if I was shagging a zebra Michaela, my soon to be missus, would get the right arse with me. Animal or not, it's still cheating in my book.' I said to him.

 'No she was fine Johnny! Over there it's a totally different culture you see? A pygmy man can have a handful of wives and also a few goats and cows too if he likes. Probably.' Big Ron replied.

'Can they Big Ron? So over in Africa a man can have as many wives as he likes and he can also bang animals?' I asked.

'Well I don't know the actual in and outs of it Johnny but I do know they have different rules regarding that kind of thing. Probably.' He told me rather unconvincingly.

'Cool. I'll go to the library and read up on it Big Ron.' I replied.

Ron looked a bit nervous but said, 'Yes you do that son. You do that. Anyway Kiki, that was her name, Kiki had the zebra in a headlock just for health and safety reasons you see? Just while I was railing the bugger ... and then, after I'd shot my bolt, I think we went for a Wimpey.'

'They got Wimpey over there then Big Ron?' I asked him.

'Yes Johnny. And Tesco, it's just like over here but hotter and with wild animals.' Big Ron replied.

I didn't know why I was encouraging him but I couldn't help myself.

'So Kiki was quite happy for you to have sexual intercourse with a zebra and then I assume later you gave her one that same evening?' I asked him.

'Well I had a good scrub and brushed me teeth when we got back to our hotel Johnny for goodness sake! What do you take me for? Big Ron replied indignantly.

'Fair enough Big Ron, Fair enough. What happened to Kiki then? She still around?' I asked him.

'No son,' Big Ron replied. 'I set her free after a few months and then I heard she got eaten by a lion.'

'Fuck me that's a shame Big Ron. What about the zebra?' I asked him.

'Fuck knows.' He said. ' We went to see the Maasia warriors the next morning. Plus all zebras look very similar. "Love em and leave em I say." '

'Well I hope you didn't get it pregnant and now there's a load of half zebra, half big Ron's, roaming the plains wearing high heels and boob tubes looking like Bet Lynch! ' I laughed.

   Yes. Big Ron was clearly mentally ill. I liked that about him. There was a lot of it about. Our whole estate was full of absolute nutters and I felt at home in this environment. By now part of me wanted to stay and talk bollocks with Big Ron for the rest of the afternoon while dressed as ropey school girl but I still had a few important things to do. Well one thing to do. My wank. The pills I'd taken at Stan's had worn off by now and I badly needed another one. I was dressed as a sexy school girl and even though I looked ridiculous it was now making me feel horny as fuck. This was going to be the mother of all wanks and I was keeping this kit on while I had it.

'Cheers for lending me all this gear Big Ron.' I told him. 'And thanks for telling me how pretty I look in it too. Sometimes a girl just likes to be told she's pretty.'

 Maybe being a transvestite WAS for me? I did actually feel amazing when I was dressed up like a bird. This was the second time and once again my cock was hard as a rock. Maybe I should just get this wank out of the way and be done with it? Maybe I shouldn't over think it? I briefly wondered that if I asked if I could put my dick in Big Ron's mouth and have a wank into it, would he think that I was a bit gay and thus cooler than I actually was? I didn't fancy him at all obviously I just thought it would be a nice way to thank him for his kindness and it would be a bit classier than just taking out my cock and wanking off over his living room carpet. I'd just be using his warm mouth as a receptacle for my last ever wank as a way to say thanks for being cool about me shitting myself and letting me clean up in his bathroom. I'd take no real pleasure in it either. It would be more medicinal. Just a clinical off-loading of my testicles in order to start afresh as someone who only had sexual intercourse from that moment on.

It wouldn't even be that gay really because I wouldn't be giving a blow job, I'd just getting one. If I lifted Big Ron's skirt up and then pulled down his panties and tights and took his swollen member into my mouth and licked and sucked up and down his shaft while kneading his balls and then eventually ramming a fist inside his arse hole as he shot his salty load right down my throat as he groaned with pleasure and then called me his very own pretty little girl and then burped the words, "thank you daddy bear." that would be gay, but I didn't fancy doing that at all. Furthermore I'd be assuming that he'd say yes to all of this. What if he said no? How embarrassing would that be? That would mean that he would rather bang a zebra than me! The cheeky cunt. I couldn't handle that kind of rejection so in the end I decided it would be more appropriate to buy him some chocolates or nice scarf or something and immediately forgot the whole thing. There was something I could give him immediately though.

'Hey Big Ron, do you want to take an ecstasy pill?' I asked him. 'They make you feel like you love everyone and they also make you want to dance.'

Well long story short he said yes and within no time I was once again sweating and writhing and lurching about with an old man. I showed him some of my new moves and he showed me some of his and when we'd come back down we ended the evening with a bit of role play.

He was a sexy waitress dressed as someone's nan and I was a slutty school girl who for some reason needed to learn all the intricate ins and outs of restaurant etiquette. I'm not going to lie, the plot was weak but I came away from it knowing everything there was to know about not making a complete and utter cunt of myself when it came to fine dining. Eventually I had to say goodbye because my cock was now straining against my white cotton panties and my nuts were bursting to unload their sweet, testicular nectar.

'Cheers for all that Big Ron.' As I got up to leave. ' I'm off now. Don't worry, I've got my shitty gear in this bag and

I'm going to throw it away somewhere outside. Or should I put them through Margaret's door?'

'Hey not so fast Johnny.' Big Ron replied. ' Not so fast son. I'll take them off your hands if you like. I know a few of the lads who'll pay good money for them. The old, ex public school boys go wild for this kind of thing. Not me though. I'm as shocked as you are but shit is one of the few fetishes that unfortunately I never acquired. It's a shame really. How about three hundred quid for the jeans and five for the under crackers?'

'Fucking how much!?' I replied, totally gob smacked.

'Okay okay I'll give you a bag of sand for the pair. I can get double that off one of those old Tories so you'll be doing me a favour.' Big Ron replied.

'No! I mean fucking how much! as in fucking how much?! Like that's a lot of money for beshat jeans and underpants! That's absolutely mental!' I told him.

'There's always been a lot of money to be made from other people's kinks son. Why the things I've done myself just to earn an honest crust back in the day! I could tell you things that would make your hair curl son.' Big Ron replied.

'Fucking a zebra for example' I laughed.

'No that was just for my own pleasure Johnny. The thing with having sex with animals is that you don't have to buy them flowers and chocolates and cuddle them afterwards. It's very cost effective. That's why I've always preferred the company of ladies and gentleman of the night. You pay them and then have your end away and then you're off back down the road no questions asked.' Ron replied.

I really hoped that I wouldn't be the kind of person to end up shagging animals and prossies in order to save a few quid. Zebras were quite pretty though, I had to give him that.

'Listen mate if you want to give me a grand for this bag full of shitty clothes then I'm more than happy to let you. ' I told him.

I'm robbing you really son because if I had the stomach to cut them up and sell it by the ounce I'd be making ten times that!' Shit is not my thing though.' Replied Big Ron.

'Fuck it, it's a deal then. I told him.

 After I'd made him wash his hands, Big Ron gave me a grand in cash and I gave him my shitty clothes and then we shook hands and I said that if I ever died and shit myself again I'd be straight round and then I fucked off.

It took me two minutes to get home and in that time three cars beeped their horns at me and I was wolf whistled at twice. Fucking paedos. It did make me feel nice to be appreciated though. Maybe it was the attention that I enjoyed most about being dressed up like a girl? I didn't know and I didn't care all I did know was that my throbbing dick was burning a hole through Big Ron's old bloomers.

Chapter nine

Finally I was home. What a day. I looked at myself in our hall mirror and liked what I saw. I lifted up my skirt a bit. I had great legs. I flashed my knickers at myself and giggled in what I thought was a girlish way. I was still off my nut. Within minutes I'd balled up a couple of pairs of socks and put them down my blouse to give myself some tits. I decided that now was as good a time as any to bash one out so that I could concentrate on more practical things like practising being in a restaurant so I didn't look like a cunt in front of Michaela and also dry humping one of our pillows in order to practice some of my new sex moves.

   I couldn't wait to clear my head. It would be ground zero. I looked once again at my reflection. I was hot. I'd bang me. All day long. As I stared at myself I put Michaela's sweaty, little, piss- stained knickers over my head and lined up the gusset with my nose. I then lifted up my skirt and pulled down my own, much larger pair of dung hampers which were also piss- stained and sweaty but Ron had done most of that before I'd turned up. As per usual for a stand up wank, I laid out about a metre of bog roll in front of me in order to see which segment it would land on. Segment nine was my record. Here we go then. Possibly my last ever wank! After this one it was all getting sloshed up Michaela's womb entrance. The lucky cow. I was just getting into a steady rhythm and wishing I owned my own thermos flask when the fucking door went.

"Johnny! Knock! Knock! Knock! 'Johnny! You in there you scrawny little cunt!"

   Oh you've got to be fucking kidding me. It was Simmer. "Scrawny little cunt?" Fuck me he was one to talk.

'It's not a good time right now Simmer!' I shouted through the door.

Trust me to get murdered just when it looked like my life was finally on the up. What a load of bollocks. I wasn't prepared for this. I was off my nut and dressed like a sexy school girl for fuck's sake. I wasn't even that sexy if I was being brutally honest. I didn't know whether to carry on wanking and at least die with empty balls or pull Big Ron's panties back up, open the door and accept my fate.

'Listen Simmer I'm a bit tied up at the moment! What do you want? Can it wait?' I asked hopefully.

'No! I want to kill you! Then I need to kill someone else! Not killing you right now will put me way behind! You know how it is Johnny!' Simmer replied.

He had a valid point. He was probably on a very tight schedule.

'Yeah I get that Simmer. I can appreciate that mate but I could really do with you giving me about twenty minutes or so! Could you wait in the car and then I'll give you the signal to come in and kill me? Or you could go and kill that other cunt and then come back and kill me?' I shouted back.

'No I can't do that Johnny! The other cunt is way over the other side of town! That's an hour at least! That'll give you loads of time to prepare to defend yourself and I can't risk that son. Just open the door and let me kill you and then I'll be on my way.' Simmer replied.

'How do you know I'm not already prepared to defend myself Simmer! How do you know that you haven't just fallen into an elaborate trap and now you've only got seconds to live? I'll tell you what Simmer, if you fuck off now and leave me alone we'll call a truce and say nothing more about it? How does that sound mate? You go your way and I'll go mine? Deal?' I offered.

'I can't do that Johnny.' Simmer replied. 'You're a threat to me son. I'm not ready to give it all up and let a little squirt like you take over. I've still got years left. It wasn't like I didn't warn you now was it? Because I know your family and that Stan the man has a soft spot for you I didn't kill you that day in the Dolphin but you're taking the fucking piss now poaching Eric the rent off me. You should have stuck to selling your little Henry's at school son. Come on out and get it over with there's a good lad.'

'Listen Simmer, I'm armed to the teeth in here mate.' I lied.' I'll give you until the count of ten to do one.'

'Don't be a cunt Johnny! Have some self respect! Just open the fucking door!' Simmer shouted back.

'Ten!' I replied.

'Nine!' Shouted Simmer.

'Eh? Nine? Don't say nine! I'm doing the counting!' I replied.

The cheeky bastard.

'Eight! Seven! Six!' Replied Simmer.

'Oi! Stop! That's too fast! Where's your dramatic pause? Call yourself a gangster? I'm starting again and please don't interrupt! ... Right then Ten!' I told the cunt.

'Five! Four ! Three! What are you going to do to son? What are you going to do?' Shouted Simmer through the door.

   Fuck it! There wasn't even enough time for a wank now. The cunt had me on the ropes. Maybe I could burst through the door and try and strangle the prick with my sexy school girl tie? Yes! That was it! First I'll left up my skirt and flash my panties at him and while he's gawping away I'll jump on the cunt and strangle him! It was my only chance. I'd stand a much better chance if I was dressed as a sexy school boy with that nonce cunt but it was all I had.

I looked at myself for the last time in our hall mirror. I'd be in the papers tomorrow laid out on my own front step, dead as a mother fucker, and dressed like a ropey sexy school girl. It wasn't how I wanted to go but there was fuck all I could do about it now. I didn't even have time to run up stairs and put some boy clothes on.

I wanted to be remembered as a legend but it seemed like I was going to be remembered as just another teenage tranny gunned down in the street. I wondered if Michaela would come to my funeral. Would anyone come? I can't imagine Sally or Pali coming once they'd seen photos of me covered in claret and showing my big spaff stained knickers to every Tom and Dick and Harry. "Sex Case Teen Gunned Down in Broad Daylight!" "Headless School Boy Found Dead Wearing Spunk Stained Women's Underpants! (at least five sizes too big!) Full story on pages 13-17." "School boy butchered to death for still being a fucking virgin at fifteen! Was it a mercy killing???" It would be just me and father O'Connor and he's only come for the sex.

I was so close to becoming a criminal mastermind too. It was my own fault and I had nobody to blame but myself. Our Wayne and Dorothy had come round specifically to warn me about Simmer wanting me dead and rather than formulate a plan I just took loads of drugs, died, shit myself and then dressed up like a school kid.

Still looking in the mirror I slowly removed Michaela's knickers from my head and took off the wig in order to at least go out with some form of decency intact. I then lifted my skirt and looked forlornly at my now flaccid little cock. I could still smell Michaela's sacred treasure around my nose. That was something at least. Before accepting my fate I tried one more time with Simmer.

'Stop fucking counting Simmer!' I told him. 'At least let me do the counting! No more counting please! 'Right then before I start again, and it's going to be from ten mate, you're not taking that from me, if I'm going to die, which I'm not because you've fallen into my cunning trap, I'm going to do it on my own terms! I'm going to give you one final chance to leave unscathed. If you leave now I'll let you live mate.'

My plan was to count down from ten then burst out at six with my tie blazing and my skirt tucked into my knickers see what happened from there.

'Right then ten!' I shouted.

'Sweets!' Came the reply.

'Eh?' I replied back.

'Shut up you silly cunt Jeffery!' Shouted Simmer.

'Sweets!'

'Fuck me is that Jeffery?' I shouted through the door. ' The infamous Jeffery! From Stan the man and Big Jeffery fame? How's your mum mate?' I asked.

'Sweets!' came the reply.

The next thing I hear is a loud groan.

'I fucking warned you Jeffery! Now shut up!' Shouted Simmer, presumably at Jeffery.

'Fuck me Simmer how many of you are there out there then? I'm not going to lie to you mate, I've got ten good men in here and they're all armed. To the teeth! And I've got a load more on the roof tops with guns trained on your ugly ginger head.' I lied.

'Johnny, we literally just saw you walk up your path two minutes ago dressed as a school girl and start wanking off in the hallway.' Simmer replied. 'A glass front door is a liability and and a school boy error by the way. You're all alone son. Just come out and let me kill you please.'

I couldn't help but think that if he'd seen me wanking off the least he could have done was let me finish. Especially as he knew it would be my last ever one. He knows I like a wank. The cunt. If it was the other way around I'd have waited until the moment he shot his load then shot him through the door. There was poetry in that. Romance. Simmer was an uncouth, soulless mother fucker though and he didn't have any sense of spectacle or drama.

'Right I'm coming out!' I told him. 'But on the count of one so it's more dramatic!'

'If you don't come out right now I'm going to shoot you through the fucking door! 10,9,8,7,6,5,4,3,2,... One you cunt!' Shouted Simmer, clearly getting upset by all these delaying tactics.

As I was listening to Simmer's countdown I did actually think that I was going to die for the second time that day and even though I was alone I still had the presence of mind to give my refection a double thumbs up and say, "here's looking at you kid," in the style of Humphrey Bogart. I don't know why but at the time it just seemed appropriate. I then hitched up my skirt and gave my cock a final squeeze. Then wrapped my tie around both my wrists ready to wrap it around Simmer's neck if I got the chance, and headed for the front door.

   As I turned the door handle I played my last card. I looked up skywards and said, "Dear Jesus, if you're real prove it by performing a miracle right now and saving my fucking life. Sorry for swearing but I've got a lot going on and I'm also off my nut. Lots of Love Johnny. Amen." Praying was always the last resort but also always worth a punt for a Catholic lad and besides I had fuck all to lose at that point.

   Then it happened. It all happened very quickly. At the exact same I turned the handle of our front door and Simmer shouted ..."one you cunt!" I heard a loud crack. It was the unmistakable sound of gun fire. I looked down at myself and was relieved to find out that whoever fired that shot had thankfully missed. I laughed out loud with relief. Who the fuck misses from that range? They hadn't even smashed the glass in the front door. I was dealing with fucking imbeciles here. Then I looked again at the door. It was covered in claret. And in amongst that claret was the unmistakable shape of a cock and balls sliding slowly down the glass. Someone outside had just had their reproductive organs blown off.

'Fuck me! Fuck me! Oh Fuck me! What the fuck? My cock ! My fucking cock and balls! Oh fuck! Fuck! Somebody ring a fucking ambulance! Jeffery! Jeffery! Scrape off my cock and bollocks from Johnny's door and put them in some fucking ice!!'

Yay! It was Simmer! And if I wasn't very much mistaken, some cunt had just shot Simmer's fucking cock and balls off by the sounds of it. I looked skywards again.

'Fuck me nice job Jesus mate.' I said out loud to my lord and saviour. 'I owe you one. Skills mate. Skills. Amen.'

I was now once more, a believer.

'Sweets!' Shouted Jeffery.

'Listen Jeffery you soppy cunt get me to the fucking car! I need to go to hospital!' Screamed Simmer.

'Sweets!' Shouted Jeffery.

'Johnny! Johnny mate! Phone an ambulance!' Simmer screamed. ' Get me to the hospital Johnny and my empire is all yours! My cock! It's on the floor! Please mate I'm bleeding out here! I don't have much time! Johnny! Open the fucking door mate! Ring 999!'

'Sweets!' I replied.

I then wondered if it was safe to go outside. Maybe whoever shot Simmer would also shoot me? Maybe that shot was for me? I'd only heard one shot. So far. Was that it? Was it all over? What if I walked out and the next thing I knew my genitals were lying next to Simmer's? I couldn't stand here all day though.

'Jeffery are you okay mate? ' I shouted through the door.

'Sweets!' He replied.

'Fuck Jeffery Johnny! I'm dying here! Call 999! I need an ambulance!' Simmer screamed.

'Fucking calm down Simmer you soppy cunt.' I replied.

Fuck that cunt. Moments ago he was just about to kill me and now suddenly he wanted my help just because his bollocks and cock had been blown off. The fickle bastard. I was too curious and couldn't help myself so I opened the door and peaked outside.

'Fuck me Simmer! Jesus fucking Christ mate what a mess!' I shouted as soon as I'd witnessed the carnage laid out before me.

Simmer was sat on my front step covered in blood and holding the place where his sexual organs used to be. Jeffery was hopping from one foot to the other while slapping himself around the head and muttering the word 'sweets' over and over. I looked across the road to where Simmer's car was parked up. The driver had been shot in the head. I breathed a sigh of relief. This was no accident. This was done by a professional assassin. If I was meant to die I would have been dead by now. It was very impressive actually.

Hang on maybe it was actually divine intervention? Maybe I was the new messiah? Maybe I'd been saved this day to go on to do great things in the name of our Lord and Saviour mister Jesus H Christ? Shit. That was a lot of responsibility. I just wanted to be a criminal overlord and take drugs and shag hot chicks. Bollocks. Maybe Jesus didn't want to be Jesus either though.

I wondered if I could back out. No harm done. I looked up towards heaven and said, 'Listen God mate, cheers for saving my life and that and I am grateful obviously but I'm too young to be the new messiah. I'm still a virgin! Can't you let me go and choose someone else? Or even better come back in about twenty years or so? Hopefully during that time even I will have lost my cherry. Kind regards, Johnny. Thanks again. Amen.'

'Who are you fucking talking to Johnny you silly cunt? I'm bleeding to death here!' Shouted Simmer.

'Oi! Language you cunt! I was talking to God. Have some fucking respect.' I replied.

'Have you gone fucking mental son? Please get me an ambulance! And get off my cock! You're standing on my fucking cock! Where are my bollocks? Johnny have you seen my bollocks? They were here a minute ago!' Simmer whimpered.

I looked down and he was right, I was standing on his cock. And also his bollocks as it happened.

'Oops fuck me sorry mate!' I laughed.

I'm not sick in the head I didn't laugh because it was funny I was more laughing out of embarrassment really. I'd stepped on the guy's cock and balls and now they were in an awful two and eight.

'Ooh fuck what's that smell?' I asked to no one in particular. 'Can I smell cat shit? Oh fuck me that's cat shit isn't it? Simmer can you smell cat shit? Some cat has shat on my step and now its all over your cock and balls Simmer! You wait until I catch up with that fucking thing! Don't worry Simmer I'll avenge you mate! I'll kick it right up the arse! Fucking lucky I missed it on the way in hey? Imagine if I'd walked cat shit all through my gaff! I'll skin it alive Simmer! Cats are just cats though really. They are just animals. I'm sure it wasn't done on purpose. Bless its little furry heart eh Simmer? ... I'll tell you what was done on purpose though Simmer shall I? You coming around my house and trying to kill me. That was a mistake wasn't it Simmer? Now look at you bleeding out on my front step with your cock and balls all covered in cat shit.'

'It was a misunderstanding Johnny!' Screamed Simmer. ' I was only going to scare you! I love you son! And all your family! Especially your Wayne! Please let me live and we'll say no more about it. Just get me to hospital son! I'm begging you!'

The cheeky cunt was saying all this with a gun in his hand. I took it off him.

'This gun isn't loaded then Simmer? You were just going to wave it about in front of me and scare me a bit then drive off with me totally unscathed? Was that the plan Simmer?' I asked him.

'Yeah that was the plan Johnny.' Simmer replied.' I couldn't really harm you son. You're family. You're part of the criminal family. Stan would have my guts for garters if I harmed you! He really likes you for some reason Johnny. He always has. And so have I! You know me Johnny I know which side my bread is buttered and I'd never go against Stan. Stan made me what I am today. Please help me Johnny. Please son.'

'You're fucking full of shit Simmer!' I shouted at him. ' Stan made you what you are today? Stan the man made you what you are today? What's that then Simmer? A ginger nonce coming round to a child's house to murder him just for wanting a tiny piece of the fucking pie? You albino looking cunt! We could have worked together Simmer! We could have been massive but no, you wanted it all for yourself. And for that to happen you needed me out of the picture see? But now the tables have turned see? Look ma, I'm on top of the world!'

I rolled my shoulders hoping Simmer would get the reference but I think he had other things on his mind. Not dying being one of them.

'Now look at you Simmer.' I continued, 'you're just another failed gangster bleeding out on the street holding the place where his meat and two veg used to be.' As I said this I picked up his cock off the floor and was just about to eat it for dramatic effect when I caught a whiff of the cat shit and puked up all over him. It was mostly bile but it was still pretty gross. Jeffery had been watching all of this pan out and when he saw me attempt to eat Simmer's cock he puked too.

'Sweets!' He shouted in between bouts of vomiting.

I felt the need to make a bold statement so I took Simmer's cock into our kitchen and swilled it under the tap and then came back out.

'Right then Simmer! Watch me eat your cock!' I told him as I put it back up to my mouth.

'Please don't eat my cock Johnny!' Simmer pleaded.

I opened my mouth but as I lowered his dick into it I couldn't help but gag. Now I looked like a right soppy cunt in front of everyone.

'Sweets!' Shouted Jeffery.

That's it! Sweets! I took Simmer's cock back into our kitchen and dipped it in the bag of sugar I had on the counter. For some reason sugar was one thing we'd always had in the house regardless of how poor we were. Tea bags and sugar. I ran back out with it and waved it about in the air.

'Right then Simmer.' I said.' I'm going to shoot you in the knee and if this gun is empty then I'll believe that you were only here today to put the shits up me and I'll get you help. But if it's loaded you're going to have a hole in your knee and I'm going to eat your cock. I love a bit of theatre I do. You know a lot of folks around here call me the Entertainer actually.'

Before he had chance to try and give me any more bullshit I saw the fear in his eyes so I pulled the trigger and blew his fucking knee cap clean off.

'Ooh you ruddy fibber Simmer! This gun was loaded! How many time were you going to shoot me then?' I asked him and then I pulled the trigger again which resulted in me blowing off his other knee cap.

Simmer looked in a right sorry state by now. I thought of all the times he'd tortured people over the years. Was I getting the same thrill? It was okay I guess and I enjoyed firing the gun but as I looked between my legs I was relieved to find that it wasn't making my cock hard.

'Sweets!' Jeffery was off again.

Oh yeah I had to eat Simmer's fucking cock now didn't I.

'Sweets!' Shouted Jeffery again. He was looking at Simmer's sugar coated penis and he was salivating.

'Sweets!' He shouted as he hoped from one foot to the other.

'You want this Jeffery? You want Simmer's sweet flavoured freckled pecker in your tum tum? Doesn't Simmer give you any sweets mate? He's a bad man isn't he?' I said as I held it aloft and twirled it about. I had to admit that it looked a lot more appetising now than when it was rolling down my front door a few moments ago.

'Sweets!' Replied Jeffery.

'Now Jeffery if I give you Simmer's cock to eat I want you to promise me that you'll stop trying to kill me and go home to your mummy okay? Tell her I'll be paying her rent from now on and every Friday, if you haven't tried to murder me, I'll arrange for you to have a big bag of sweets delivered right to your door! How does that sound?' I asked him.

Jeffery grinned and said, 'sweets!'

'Open wide Jeffery me old mate!' I said and then I threw Simmer's sugar coated cock right up into the air and with a little help from gravity and Jeffery's surprising agility for a big man, it landed, helmet first straight into his eager gob.

'Don't forget to chew Jeffery or you'll give yourself indigestion.' I told him.

'Sweets!' He shouted although this version was a bit more muffled due his mouth being full of Simmer's penis.

 I then scooped up Simmer's bollocks and held them out to Jeffery.

'Would you like these Jeffery? I'll give them a swill under the tap and dip them in sugar if you like? Is it all gone? Have you eaten all of Simmer's little pink ticket?'

Jeffery grinned then opened his mouth wide for me to see. It was empty.

'Sweets!' he shouted proudly.

Jeffery was now having a great time and that was all that mattered to me now. Well that and watching Simmer slowly dying on my front door step obviously. I ran to the kitchen, swilled Simmer's severed ball bag under the tap and then dipped them in the sugar. After deciding that I didn't really want to keep the rest of the sugar I had a great idea and took it out to Jeffery along with the bollocks.

'Look Jeffery! I've made you a sherbet dip!' I told him and I mimed dunking Simmer's bollocks into the bag of sugar and then sucking on them.

'Sweets!' Jeffery shouted in pure ecstasy. And in no time he got the hang of it and was dipping Simmer's bollocks into the sugar and then lifting them out and sucking all the sugar off them and then dunking the fucking things back in and off he went again. It was a very proud moment for me and I was happy that he was happy.

Simmer didn't look very happy though. In fact he looked very unhappy and he didn't look very healthy either. Simmer had always looked a bit ill but having his cock and balls blown off and then his fucking knee caps didn't seem to be doing him any favours at all.

He looked up to me with dying eyes and begged me to save his life. I think that's what he was saying but he was barely breathing to be honest and it was difficult to know exactly what the fuck he was going on about. I think he definitely said, "help me" at one point. That would have made sense actually.

I crouched down beside him and said, 'how many fucking bullets are in this gun Simmer? I'm only asking because I can't help thinking that it would be better for everyone if I just put a bullet in your nut and ended your life. Thoughts?'

I then stuck the gun in his mouth and cocked the trigger and said, 'See ya later alligator!'

It was then Simmer's turn to shit himself. It smelled very similar to when I shat myself earlier. Maybe everyone's last shit smelled the same? Lucky for me Michaela had saved my life and I'd come back but poor old Simmer wasn't going to be so fucking lucky. Simmer's fate lay in my hands so unfortunately for him he was fucked. Or so it seemed because I was just about to pull the trigger and put the soppy cunt out of his misery when a van turned up out of fucking nowhere and came to a halt right outside my house. Two men immediately got out and pulled one of those collapsible stretchers from the back. The next thing I knew they'd picked Simmer up, put him on the trolley and within seconds they were gone.

'Oh you jammy cunt!' I said out loud.

Jeffery was oblivious to all of this because he was so preoccupied with his sugar bollocks.

'Do you know where you are Jeffery?' I asked him.

'Sweets!' He replied.

This wasn't going to be easy.

'Do you know how to get back to your mum's mate?'

'Sweets!' He replied.

Oh for fuck's sake.

    Just then a car pulled up. The windows were all blacked out so I couldn't see who the fuck was in it and for a split second I wondered if I was going to be gunned down too. Fortunately that didn't happen. What did happen was one of the back windows came down and a hand holding a big bag of what looked to me like cola cubes shot out of it.

'Sweets!' Shouted Jeffery and headed towards the hand.

    Just as he got to the car a door opened and Jeffery got in and the car fucked off with him in it. This was all going swimmingly. All that was left was the tricky problem of Simmer's driver and the bullet in his head. I looked across the road to where it was but it had gone. The road was completely empty. What the fuck? When did that go? Oh well there was clearly forces at work here that were a lot bigger than little old Johnny McQueen so I decided to fuck off back in and crack on with the wank I was just about to have before I was so rudely interrupted.

Chapter Ten

And just like that I was stood back in front of our hall mirror. Fuck me what a day. I'd had a lovely visit by my dear brother and his stunning girl friend, I'd got high with Stan the Man and learned to dance, then I had my face sat on by Michaela, then I died and shit myself and then I got high dressed as a sexy school girl with Big Ron and then Simmer and Jeffery came round to murder me! Oh and I think Sally called me a cunt and then later gave me the distinct impression that she wanted me to smash one up her. Well she was nicer to me anyway.

I pulled out Michaela's knickers again and put them over my head. As I stood there staring at myself through the gusset I couldn't help but think that I looked like a complete cunt. If somebody had told me a few months ago that one day I'd be standing in front of our hall mirror dressed like a moody school girl with a pair of soiled panties on my head, just about to have a frenzied wank I'd have totally believed it.

I loved wanking off. I was addicted to it. Wanking was my favourite thing to do. It was my drug of choice! Of course actual drugs were also my drug of choice as well but wanking off was by far my favourite drug. Obviously my favourite actual drugs were ideally a combination of weed and hash and coke and speed and now ecstasy. Opium was also now on my list of drugs I wanted to try too.

Drugs and wanking off had got me through my traumatic childhood. Other kids would have started self- harming or shop lifting or listening to Leonard Cohen to deal with the pain and turmoil of their shitty existence but not me. I chose wanking and drug abuse and I depended on both of them to get through the day. They were my friends. Dependable friends. Loyal friends. Every time anything fucked up happened I'd turn to my old pals and they'd always be there for me; smoothing out the wrinkles of my crappy life. As I stood in front of that mirror I thought to myself, was it now time to let go? Should I now say fair thee well old chums and put away childish things in my pursuit of becoming a man slash criminal overlord?

   Nah. Fuck that shit. I was fifteen for fuck's sake. And a Catholic. Drug abuse and jerking off were two of the bigger sins and we were natural born sinners. We were fucked from the second we came out of our mother's tuna purses so what was the point in giving up the things you loved when you were already doomed? Plus there was plenty of time to repent too. A catholic could sin all to fuck their whole life and then atone on their death bed and all would be forgiven. That was my favourite part of being a Catholic. And besides, giving shit up is more of a Protestant thing. It was a well known fact that Protestants hated nice things.

   Not doing or having nice things was what they were all about as far as I could see. I'd always been told that when the Proddies started up their Mickey mouse religion the first things they did was murder the fuck out of all the Catholics and get rid of anything nice. Say what you like about the Catholics but they love bright colours and nice things. Wine, women and song. That was what we were all about. Especially the Irish ones. Wine, women and song and racism and homophobia to be more precise. Oh and kiddy fiddling. The ones at the top did anyway. The mucky sods.

It was true that, like most religions who want to increase their congregations, they do frown on spilling one's seed on barren ground, which in my case was hopefully going to be right into the gusset of Michaela's knickers where all the good stuff was, but the Catholic church doesn't mind at all if you fuck. They actually want you to. They actively encourage unprotected sexual intercourse. They want all us Catholics to fuck like fuck so that we make more Catholics in order to overtake the populations of other religions, and plus as all Catholics must give ten percent of their earnings to the church or face the wrath of the big man himself, more followers means more money for the Pope to spend on nice things made of gold for his gaff and for paying off all the little kiddies that his priests have fornicated with over the years.

If I was Pope, the first thing |I'd do was to make it mandatory for priests to wank off every morning and evening so that even if they wanted to they wouldn't have the strength to fiddle kids. The catholic church could even provide their own wanking paraphernalia kits too. Wank rags with the face of Christ on them or the Virgin Mary or any of the other hotties from the Bible for example. The same should apply to nuns. Imagine if they all had their own duvets with Jesus printed on them and they were obligated to writhe and lurch all over it until they orgasmed and then calmed the fuck down and thus became less mean and cruel and hateful to everyone who wasn't a nun. Masturbation was the cure for most things in my book and the more wanks you have the closer you were to God. Amen. If that was the case, even if I died tomorrow, I'd definitely be getting a front row seat and more likely I'd be sitting on His lap.

   Eventually I decided that as a compromise for God saving my life earlier I'd swap wanking off for actual sexual intercourse with Michaela but I was still going to do lots of drugs. The way I saw it priests drank whisky and wine which were drugs and many other religions took loads of drugs as part of their ceremonies in order to get closer to God, especially the less established ones that mainly took place in jungles and rain forests and the like. Also, all those mad cults I'd read about seemed to love a drugged fuelled orgy in the name of spiritual enlightenment, so fuck giving up drugs. Religion is also a drug too while we're at it. Didn't some cunt say something about religion being the opium of the people? Yeah well I'd rather have the opium.

   Maybe I should start my own religion. My life had been saved by some kind of higher power earlier today and now I'd seen the light. My religion wouldn't be one of those crap ones where you can't do anything nice though, it would be the opposite. Johnny-ism would be about two things and two things only; drug taking and shagging hot birds. As I would be the leader of course I'd be shagging all the hot female disciples while the men ones went out collecting donations and finding hot chicks for me to enlighten from behind. This was definitely something to consider but not for the moment because right now I needed to focus on becoming a living legend slash crime lord, his royal coolness Johnny Capone.

   My life was now full of potential and I had lots to think about but now more than anything else I desperately needed to empty my bollocks. Within a few short minutes I'd necked another pill, rolled a joint and was sat on our sofa waiting for said pill to take affect. I put Big Ron's wig back on my head and brought our hall mirror into the living room so I could watch myself bang one out. Once again I put Michaela's knickers over my head and inhaled as deeply as I could but disappointingly they'd completely dried out and all the good stuff had gone. It just wasn't the same. Fucking Simmer. If Simmer hadn't have turned up back then to kill me all this would have been over; my balls would have been drained, my mind would have been recalibrated, and I'd now be tucked up in my bed dreaming of having a real girlfriend; a normal one who wasn't really fucking old, mental, practically related to me or a rancid hybrid of all of the above.

    As I sat on that sofa looking at my reflection I suddenly wondered what it would like to be normal. I've often wondered what it would be like to be normal. I sometimes think about how I might have turned out if I'd had a normal childhood and been cared for by normal parents. I imagine two normal parents who loved each other and also loved me and our Wayne. Would I have ended up a psychopath if mummy and daddy had taken us to the park and pushed us on the swings and rad us bed time stories and gave us hugs and cuddles rather than teaching us how to smoke and drink and nick stuff and sell drugs? Fuck knows. It was too late now anyway. The damage was well and truly done. Then the pill kicked in and I lay back and loved everyone and dreamed off my new life hanging out the back of Michaela.

Then I thought about Big Ron and got up and went to the kitchen; there wasn't any thermos flasks about but I did manage to find a rolling pin. Unfortunately even though I smeared it and my arse hole with copious amounts of margarine I just couldn't get it inside me. All this messing about put me right off my stroke and I kept losing my erection so in the end I just went into the bathroom and banged one out into the sink. It wasn't the most monumental of wanks but it got the job done. I then slipped off Big Ron's knickers and mopped up all the jizz with them. As I was cleaning up I caught my refection in the bathroom mirror. Fuck me I looked a right sad cunt but fortunately these days were over now. Just good old normal sexual intercourse like every other fifteen year old boy was having for me now thank fuck.

I then stripped off and had another shower; which was a record for me. Then I went into my room and into my bed and slept like the dead.

Chapter Eleven

The next thing I knew I was awoken by the sound of the fucking front door being banged. Given the volume of the banging it could only be bad news. Many people had knocked on our door that hard over the years and it was seldom for anything but bad news or trouble. The police, probation officers, social workers, debt collectors, rival drug dealers, pissed men wanting to fight my dad, pissed women wanting to fight my mum, pissed people just pissed wanting to fight one of us, they all banged on the door like this so I wasn't expecting any good news.

I went to the window and tentatively looked through the curtains. I couldn't see anyone. Maybe they'd fucked off? Then I heard the loud banging again.

'Johnny you cunt!'

Johnny you cunt. It was always, 'Johnny you cunt.' Nobody ever shouted anything nice. It was never, "Johnny you absolute legend" or "Johnny you handsome fool," it was always, "Johnny you cunt." Oh well at least it was someone I knew.

'Johnny! Yawl need to mosey on down here pilgrim it's your posse!'

Then four voices shouted in unison,"You cunt!"

Good news! The first voice was the unmistakable voice of my good friend Black Clint- Also known recently as 'Just' Clint and also, even more recently, known as Clint, as I now tried to call him but failed to do so so far on every occasion. The other three voices belonged to the rest of the notorious 'Bin boys.' Well they weren't exactly notorious yet, they were just four nerdy weeds but in time I was sure that under my tutelage they'd progress to being at least not just four annoying, sarcastic wankers.

This news came as a blessed relief because those pills had left me with a banging headache and the thought of killing anyone today seemed like a right chore. I open the window and shouted down.

'What do you cunts want? Do you have any idea what the fucking time is?'

'Yes!' Replied Billy, 'it's six o'clock in the evening you soppy cunt!'

Was it really? Had I only been asleep for ten minutes? Apart from the headache I felt incredibly rested.

I shouted down again. ' Tell me boy, what day is it today?'

'Why it's fucking Thursday you absolute virgin!' Replied Squint.

Fuck me had I really been asleep for three whole days?

'Why then I haven't missed it then!' I shouted down again, 'Why I'm as giddy as a mother fucker! Tell me boy is that goose still in the window of the fucking butcher's shop you sad fucks?'

'What the big fat one that looks like your mum you little bitch?' Replied Diamond.

'Yes that's the bastard you little urchin shit cunt! Now run along and buy it then slosh one up it and then eat it you bunch of fucking nonces!' I replied.

Two minutes later they were all in my living room drinking my beer and smoking my weed.

'What can I do for you bunch of mummy's boys then?' I asked them. They all looked at each other until Diamond's cock got hard which broke the spell.

'Well it's a bit awkward really.' Diamond eventually replied.

'Come now don't be so coy lads just get to the fucking point please.' I replied.

I couldn't be doing with any wishy washy bullshit as I'd just realised that because I'd been asleep for three days I hadn't had a wank in three days which was easily my new world record plus I'd be meeting Michaela this very evening and I hadn't planned one fucking thing.

'Well the thing is Johnny. And you're going to love this...' Billy began. 'Actually I think it'll be better off coming from Diamond. Diamond please tell Johnny why we're here.'

'Fuck off Billy you spineless, wet cunt.' Replied Billy.

'Well one of you had better get to the point because, and this isn't even a lie, I've actually got a date tonight.' I replied.

'With your auntie Joan?' Black Clint laughed.

'Or is it that mad old lady from that cafe you were telling us about? The one with the rancid clopper and the Nobby Stiles hanging out of her Derek like a bunch of grapes?

Where are you meeting her? At the Bingo?' Chipped in Squint.

'Or the cemetery? Is she dead then? Are you going to dig her up and give her one Johnny?' Said Billy, all wide eyed and innocent looking. The sarky cunt.

Then Black Clint had a go, 'Now looky here son, is this just really a big ole lie Johnny? You don't have to make up stuff, pilgrim. We're your partners and we know you're a sad and pathetic loser. If you just want us to fuck off so that you can dress up like a liddle ole school girl and have another Tommy tank then just say so, son.'

How the fuck did they know about that? Fuck me you can't keep any secrets around here.

'Nope. None of the above. I've actually got a date with a lovely young lady named Michaela and furthermore we are very much in love.' I told them while trying my best to play it cool.

'Fuck off!' They replied in unison.

'Wait there then you disbelieving wankers.' I told them and then I ran upstairs to my bedroom and came back down clutching Michaela's knickers and waved them under their noses.

'You fucking sick cunt Johnny! Where did you nick them from? Did you break in to your neighbours' again?' Billy asked.

Those cunts. That was just one time and anyway the front door was open and I was just making sure that a sex pest hadn't broken in and was hiding in Sally's bedroom waiting to do unspeakable things to her pert little bottom. Plus the only reason I had a pair of her knickers away was because of their cat Bowie's fucking fur which had made me sneeze so I just grabbed the first thing to hand. It turned out that I'd gone into her mum's room anyway so I can honestly say, hand on heart, that I hadn't actually bashed one out into the gusset of Sally's knickers; because they were her mum's. Actually I think I still had those knickers stashed away somewhere. When this lot had fucked off I might get on the bag and ... fuck! I just remembered that I'd promised Michaela that my jizz was all hers now! Bollocks.

Oh well not long to go now anyway because thankfully I'd slept through most of the time I had to wait between my last wank and her little wet fanny hole or up to and including, her gob... Or her little bum hole. If she was Catholic then she might be saving her virginity until after she was married; in which case her bum hole was traditionally the 'loop' hole. I was a gentleman and would obviously let her decide which hole my sperm would end up in anyway, or we could decide as a couple.

'You cheeky cunts!' I shouted at them,'my new missus gave them to me! She told me that I was allowed one more wank while I ether sniffed them or wanked off into them and after that my cock and balls belonged to her! Look into that gusset! It's covered in stale piss and fanny batter! She was sat on my face and when I came in her mouth she had such a massively intense orgasm she lost control of her bladder and pissed all over me!'

Diamond then grabbed them out of my hand, held them up to his nose and inhaled them.

'That's real pussy all right!' He said earnestly. 'And piss and sweat and fanny batter if I'm not mistaken. The stain in the gusset suggests to me that they belong to a female of around nineteen to twenty five. White with her own hair and teeth... These are not the dung hampers of an old woman.'

Before I had chance to react he then threw them to Billy. Billy immediately put them over his head and then his hands down his jeans.

'Yes lads, that's the unmistakable smell of cunt! Good cunt too. Top notch cunt. I will give you twenty English pounds for them. Cash.' He said.

For fuck's sake give me back my bird's bloomers!' I shouted.

'Bloomers? Bloomers you cunt? Who the fuck calls bird's knickers fucking bloomers you soppy bastard?' Diamond shouted as they all curled up laughing on the sofa.

'You may laugh but Michaela has been teaching me all the right sex words to say so I don't make a cunt of myself tonight while I'm ponding her sacred treasure.' I told them.

'Well you're already making a right cunt of yourself by calling her knickers fucking bloomers for a start mate!' Replied Squint. 'Hang on, what else did she say?'

'Well she said that girls like their vaginas not to be called vaginas or pussies but to be called their sacred treasures and rather than saying tits or top bollocks you have to say bosoms ...'

Before I could say anything else they all burst out laughing again.

'This bird of yours, if she's real, sounds like a right laugh Johnny!' Cried Squint.

I had to admit that was a real funny fucking thing she'd done to me there and it actually made me love her even more.

'Hey pilgrim, pass those liddle ole bloomers over her so I can have a good ole sniff too I'll thank yawl kindly.' Said Black Clint to Billy.

Billy threw them to Black Clint and he too put them up to his nose and inhaled.

'Why that there be a mighty fine scent of cowgirl snatch adoodledoooo! I do declare!... And no mistake! Yeeeehaw!' He shouted and spun them around his head like a lasso.

Then Billy grabbed them off of Black Clint and did the same.

'Yummy! Fuck knows where you got these Johnny but whoever they belong to certainly has a lovely smelling sacred treasure that's for sure. I'll give you thirty two quid for the fuckers.' He said.

Then Billy inexplicably sucked on the gusset and said, 'Well I've just had the best of that stink away so I'm dropping my offer to fifteen quid.'

'For fuck's sake stop sniffing my girlfriend's knickers!' I told them. 'It was mostly all gone before and now thanks to you sick bastards there won't be anything left in them at all at this rate and if it all goes tits up later they'll be the only thing I'll have left to remember her by! Plus it's disrespectful! Now you all know what her cunt smells like!When you meet her I want you all to promise not to tell her that you all know what her sacred ... what her pussy smells like!'

Then Billy said, 'Johnny mate, we know you. You're a sexual deviant and a massive pervert. We all were once but what you've done is probably a serious offence! Breaking into some bird's house and riffling through her soiled laundry and then actually having a pair of her knickers away is not what normal people do!'

'Yeah didn't your Wayne get community service for something similar a while back?' Asked Squint.

'No that was totally different.' I replied.'He just had a wank in Pound world's lingerie section. Apparently he was found sat in the middle of a huge pile of knickers writhing and lurching and generally being a fucking pervert. He only got a warning but they did have to throw most of their stock away.'

'Because of all the spunk he produces?' Asked Black Clint.

'Yeah it went fucking everywhere apparently. The security guard slipped in it and broke his collar bone by all accounts. The silly cunt.' I replied.

'What your Wayne's?' Asked Billy.

'My Wayne's what?' I replied.

'Your Wayne's fucking collar bone!' Billy replied.

'Eh? Fuck me of course not you cunt! The security guard broke his own collar bone when he slipped on our Wayne's Harry monk!' I replied.

'Oh yeah that makes more sense. Fuck me this is good weed Johnny. I can hardly think straight.' Replied Billy.

The Squint said, 'Your Wayne has had a lot of warnings hasn't he Johnny?'

'Yeah I think my mum was fucking some of the coppers back then. She's a cunt but I think her deep throat skills have kept our Wayne from going to jail over the years.' I replied. When I said those words, I felt for the first time in my while life, a tiny amount of something for her but I didn't know what it was. Maybe it was sympathy or pity or was it love? Fuck knows.

'Your mum is certainly no oil painting but she does look like she'd give you a good nosh.' Said Diamond and we all nodded our heads in agreement.

I was rather chuffed at this revelation. We all wanted to fuck Billy's mum of course and Diamond's too for that matter but nobody had ever mentioned my own mum as being someone who was anything other than sexually repellent. Billy's sister was hot as fuck too actually and we all wanted to give her one but up until now nobody wanted to fuck anyone in my family.

Nobody wanted to slosh one up Black Clint's mum either obviously because she was old as fuck, his adopted mum anyway. Nobody knew what his real mum looked like or anything about her. Apparently he was found all wrapped up in a blanket and left outside a church like in some fucking Dickensian novel and eventually after being in a series of care homes he was adopted by Doris and Roy aka mister and misses Black Clint. Nobody in their right minds would want to fuck my mum but hearing that they all felt like she'd give a good blow job filled me with pride.

'I bet she likes it up the shitter too!' Shouted Squint.

'Fuck me alright! Alright! Enough is enough. Blow jobs are one thing but taking it up the Gary is going to far! That woman raised me!' I shouted.

There was a moments silence before we all burst out laughing again.

'Right then chaps, as much as I'd love to sit here all night and discuss our mothers' sexual proficiency I really do have a date tonight so if you'd kindly tell me what the fuck you want that would be great.' I asked them again.

'Tell us where you got those knickers from first Johnny!' Diamond replied.

'Fuck me Diamond have you got a hard-on you sick cunt?' I asked him even though it was clear for every cunt to see that he fucking well did. And it was Michaela's knickers that had given it to him.

'I do indeed young man.' Diamond replied proudly, ' I do indeed. But before you go all psycho and nail me to a park bench and brutally sodomising me, I feel duty bound to report that tis not only I sporting a rather proud erection at this particular juncture but alas, all of us. All of us bar you Johnny.'

I looked at all their crotches and found Diamonds words to be true. Those filthy animals.

'Johnny, how about if you put your imaginary girlfriend's knickers on that coffee table and we all have a bit of a wank and the first one to shoot their load gets to keep them? Asked Billy.

'Ten quid each and you all clean up afterwards.' I replied.

'Deal!' They all shouted.

And that's what happened. I left the room and let them get on with it because as I wasn't joining in it would have been a tad awkward just watching. Five minutes later it was all over. I walked back in armed with a load of our

Wayne's t shirts for them to mop up with to find Diamond gleefully stuffing Michaela's knickers into his coat pocket.

'Now then, to business.' I said.

'Well to be honest it's a little bit embarrassing Johnny.' Replied Diamond.

'Oh fuck me just spit it out lads!' I told them. 'How fucking bad can it be? You've all just wanked off over my girlfriend's dung hampers and my last wank was while dressed as a fucking school girl for fuck's sake so I don't think any of us have anything else to feel embarrassed about right now!'

'And not even a sexy school gal by all accounts... pardner.' Said Black Clint.

"Pardner." Is that it? You just tacked the word pardner onto the end of your sentence and that'll do now is it. "Pardner" You're getting lazy mate. I'm not even sure that's even a real word. "Pardner." Fuck off.' I replied.

'Yeah well sometimes I can't rightly be fucking arsed with it all Johnny.' Replied Black Clint flatly.

'That's fair enough mate. Why not try something else out? Mexican or maybe Chinese? We could call you Black Pedro or Black Jacky Chan?' Said Squint.

'Or how about you all go fuck yourselves and just call me by my real name guys? How about fucking that?' Black Clint replied.

There was another moment of silence before Diamond asked the question we all wanted to know the answer to.

'What actually is your real name then Black Clint?'

'You cunts have known me since primary school.' Black Clint replied coldly.

'Is it Clint?' Asked Billy.

'Of course it's not fucking Clint you absolute bell-end!' I replied. Billy was a decent looking lad but he was fucking thick as shit sometimes.

'Well then why does everyone call him Black Clint then?' Billy asked.

'Are you fucking kidding me Billy? You've known the cunt longer than me!' I replied.

'He's fucking called black Clint because he's black and he talks and dresses like a fucking cowboy!' Shouted Diamond.

'Ah I see!' replied Billy.

I could tell by his gormless fucking expression that he didn't really see at all though.

'Do you really see Billy? Do you really mate? Explain it to us then. Just explain to us why Black Clint is called Black Clint and I'll give you fifty quid.' I told him.

'Well it's obvious isn't it? He's called Black Clint because he's black and he's called Clint because he dresses like a cowboy!' Billy replied.

'Okay, but why Clint? Why Clint Billy? I asked him, knowing full well that my fifty quid was safe as fucking houses.

Silence from Billy.

'Come on Billy!' Shouted Squint. 'You've got this! You must know why we call him Black Clint! You're half way there mate! We call him black because he's black and we call him Clint because...?'

'Because ... well because ... we call him Clint because ... well I always thought we call him Clint because it rhymes with Squint!' He replied.

That fucking idiot.

'So you thought that even though the silly cunt has dressed like a fucking cowboy since the day he was found outside that church all wrapped up in fucking rhinestones and denim and wearing a fucking fun sized Stetson, that his name just happened to fucking well rhyme with Squint and it was just all one big fucking coincidence? Is that right Billy?' I asked him. Dismayed as a mother fucker.

'Yes.' He confidently replied. Then he grinned and stuck out his hand and said, 'fifty quid please Johnny. Two twenties and a ten would be ideal.'

'No Billy! No! What you need to do right now is to go and fucking fuck yourself in the fucking arse because you have not won the fucking bet you absolute moron! No fifty quid for you! Bad boy! No Billy! In your basket and no biscuits!' I told him.

What a fucking plank. I should have fucking shot him in the head right there and then really. Then Diamond tried to explain.

'Billy mate, we call him Black Clint because, one, he is indeed black and, two, because there's a very famous actor who has starred in some very famous cowboy films. Does that give you a bit of a clue? Do you know any famous actors who play cowboys in cowboy films whose first name is Clint?'

I thought he'd worded that rather well and I was now sure that Billy would finally see the light.

Billy looked to be deep in thought for a good five minutes before saying, 'John Wayne?'

I was just about to head-butt him when Black Clint suddenly shouted, 'My fucking real name is Brian! Brian Jenkins! I've known you cunts all my life and you've never even fucking asked me what my real name is! Well that's my adopted name anyway! That's the fucking name I was given at the fucking first care home I was taken to! Fuck knows what my real name is! I probably didn't even have one!'

Silence prevailed once more. It was just getting really awkward before Billy suddenly piped up and said;

'So let's call you Black Brian from now on then! Or BB! That's kind of cool! Like BB King. He's cool as fuck! And he's black! Maybe your dad is BB King! I bet he's fucked loads of birds and got loads of them pregnant and then just fucked off! Maybe he fucked your mum, got her pregnant and she was all like, "BB baby I'm pregnant!" And BB King was all like, "fuck that shit babe I'm off back to the good ole USA! See ya later bitch!" And your real mum was all like, "fuck that shit I'm giving BB junior to the church!" Are you any good at the guitar Black Brian?'

That was when Black Brian head-butted Billy.

I fetched Billy a tea towel and he put it on his nose to try and stem the flow of blood and after a while he was fine. I'd been head-butted a lot over the years and I knew what to do in such a circumstance. I gave him a shot of whiskey and rolled him a joint.

'Drink that and smoke this and you'll be fine Billy. It's good to get head-butted at least once in your life. It's character building. Now apologise to Brian for assuming his real mum was some kind of blues, groupie, slag that got knocked up and abandoned please and we can all move on.' I told him.

To give Billy his due he didn't sulk his socks off like I thought he would and did what I'd asked him.

'Sorry for saying your real mum was a slack bitch Brian. I'm sure she was hot as fuck and well shaggable and I bet she's out there looking for you right now too mate.'

'That's okay Billy, you can't help being thick as fucking pig shit and ignorant as a cunt mate.' Replied Brian.

Then Diamond said something about us all having a wank over Brian's real mum at the next opportunity and everything was settled.

'Now then for the love of God please tell me what the fuck you are doing here.' I asked them one more time.

'Well Johnny, the thing is.' Said Squint, 'You see the thing is, well the thing is that basically our birds have given us the boot because they were only going out with us because we know you and since you haven't been around lately they've kind of, well they've all kind of fucked off.'

'That's fucking brilliant!' I replied gleefully. 'That's definitely the best news I've ever fucking heard in my entire life! That's fucking hilarious! Fuck me I might have a wank about that! After I've had a wank about your real mum Brian mate, obviously.'

'Cheers Johnny.' Replied Brian.

'Actually how about this for a scenario lads.' I said, 'Brian's real mum knocks on Billy's door trying to locate Brain and Billy's mum answers the door and as she's just stepped out of the shower she's only wearing a skimpy towel around her and as she's talking to Brian's mum the towel 'accidentally on purpose' slips off and the next thing you know they're fucking at it! Right in the fucking doorway! Brian's mum has massive great tits and Billy's mum is playing with them and fingering her and she's just about to start eating her out when Billy's sister comes in and catches them at it! But check this out lads! ...Rather than getting all mad and sticky about it ... she joins in and the next thing you know the three of them are dildoing the fuck out of each other and then my bird turns up and starts pissing all over them until they are all squirting and cumming all over the gaff! Then I turn up and they all tell me to eat their bum holes and pussies... bird's bum holes are a lot cleaner than ours by the way and Michaela's tastes like sweets so if you ever get another chance I suggest you have a go at that... Oh yeah and then they demand that after I'd railed the fuck out of the four of them I cum all over their faces and Brian's mum's huge fucking tits! ...Then they all lick it up and lezz off while I sit watching and smoking weed until it all kicks off again.'

I glanced around and I was delighted to see that even though they'd all bashed one out less than half an hour ago they were all trying to hide their stiff cocks. Even Billy and Brian which told me just how fucking hot that particular scenario was. It was a crying shame that I wasn't allowed to have any more wanks until I met up with Michaela later because my own cock was raging and I was bursting for a wank and I already going through severe withdrawal symptoms.

'I bet your real mum's pussy tastes fucking lovely Brian mate.' Said Diamond.

''Ah cheers Diamond. That means a lot. Just to let you know that I've had loads of wanks about giving your mum one. And yours Billy. And also your sister too obviously.' Replied Brian solemnly.

'Cheers mate.' Replied Billy.

'Right then can we all please stop patting each other on the dicks now and get back to the bit about all your birds fucking off please?' I told them.

'Yeah we need a way to get them back or at least get some new ones because I already miss having regular sexual intercourse with real life girls.' Said Brian.

'I'm assuming that you've given up talking like a fucking cowboy then Brain?' I asked him.

'Yeah fuck that shit. It was exhausting trying to keep that going. I still like country and western music but as soon as I get home all this clobber is going in the bin.' Brian replied.

'Well thank fuck for that mate because I'm not going to lie, you sounded like a right cunt. I'll have your hat and those boots off you though because I think Michaela would look hot as fuck in them on the right occasion. And that occasion will be while she's sat on my face.' I replied.

'Not a fucking problem pilgrim.' Replied Brain and he threw me his once beloved Stetson.

'Ladies and gentlemen I'd like you to meet Brian, formally known as Black Clint.' I said to the rest of them.

'Howdy Brian!' They all replied, which considering how fucking stupid they usually were was quite impressive to be honest.

'Right then,' I said, 'the way I see it is that most birds want a fella to be able to take care of them. They want to feel protected and they want things like jewellery and clothes and makeup and all kinds of shit like that. And we men, we just want sex and blow jobs.'

'And drugs!' Replied Squint.

'And money!' Said Brain.

'And power!' Said Diamond.

'And clothes!' Shouted Billy. 'Birds like a fella to be dressed well.'

'Yeah, that's true actually Billy. Clothes maketh the man as they say.' I replied. 'Right then birds want makeup and protection and men want sex and money and drugs and power and clothes.'

'And alcohol!' Chimed in Billy.

'Well yeah but I think that comes under drugs. Like fags. Alcohol is a drug like fags and weed and coke and pills and food too really. Some food is addictive as fuck. Like sugar for example.' I told them.

'What the fuck is your point then Johnny?' Asked Diamond.

We were all very stoned now and I was finding it difficult to concentrate and stay focused.

'I can't remember.' I replied. 'What were we talking about?'

There was a few minutes silence while we all tried to remember what the fucking point was and then Brian shouted, 'I think we were talking about my real mum's big, fucking tits!'

'Oh yeah!' Shouted Squint. 'Brian's real mum went round Billy's looking for you and ended up licking out Billy's mum and sister while Johnny's pretend bird pissed on everyone!'

'My bird is real Squint you cunt!' I replied.

The cheeky bastard. I couldn't really blame him though because ever since we'd all known each other we'd all been making up fictitious girlfriends and sexual exploits that were, in real life, absolute bollocks.

'No!' Shouted Diamond. 'It's what birds want! We were talking about what birds want and how to keep them happy so they don't fuck off!'

'Oh Yeah!' I replied. 'And what was it?'

There was another few minutes of silence before Billy piped up again.

'Blow jobs!'

'Blow jobs?' Enquired Brian.' So the best way to a girl's heart is to give her blowjobs? In order to keep a bird, the most important thing to do is to suck her cock? Right. Dually noted Billy.'

Brian then pretended to write that information down on an invisible note pad.

This whole situation was hopeless and we were now running around in circles nobody really knowing what the fuck was going on so I was left with no option but to put an end to all this floundering.

'Right then who wants a fucking line?' I asked.

'Fuck me a line Johnny?' replied Diamond. 'Yes please mate!'

'And me please Johnny!' Replied Billy.

Nobody in my experience has ever said no to a line and before long we had the mirror out and snorting back big fat ones.

'Birds want things! And us lads want sex!' Shouted Diamond.

'And money!' Shouted Brian.

'And drugs!' I said as I snorted a big line.

'And power!' Shouted Squint.

  Our heads were now clear and we were back on track so finally I could give them their orders.

'Right then this what you lot are going to do. First we are going round to see a friend of mine and get loads of drugs and weapons. Then you will all be given a big bag of drugs each and your job will be to sell them. It's not a competition obviously but whoever sells the most and makes the biggest profit gets a nice reward.'

'What's the reward then Johnny?' Asked Diamond.

'Fuck knows I haven't really got that far yet I just want to gauge what you lot are like as drug dealers.' I replied.

'What do you mean, 'weapons' Johnny?' asked Squint.

'Well you know Squint. Things that you fuck people up with. Guns, knives, swords, bombs, you know, just weapons. Surely you're familiar with the concept of weapons' I replied.

'Fuck me Johnny, Bombs? Are you serious?' Gasped Brian.

'I'm Deadly serious Brian.' I told him, 'you don't get to be a criminal overlord by using cuddles and hugs now do you? Being a criminal is a dangerous game and being a member of a gang involves more than you cunts getting laid just because you know me. Or did get laid any how. Your former girlfriends thought they'd look cool if they were going out with gang bangers but they soon realised that you were just a bunch of little weeds so they quite rightly fucked off. For a brief moment in time you three wank socks were somebodies, even if it was through association, but you all need to prove yourselves worthy of being in my gang or everyone will think you're all a bunch of wet little poofters. No not poofters, I promised Big Ron I wouldn't use that word, so pansies, people will soon find out that you're all a bunch of little pansy boys and that's no good for my reputation or indeed yours. The Bin Boys' mission is to take control of this town and then we expand until one of us, or all of us, gets a bullet in the head and some other little cunt takes my place. That's the nature of the game but until that time comes we are going to have the fucking time of our lives.'

They all looked like they were about to shit themselves because the reality of their situation just hit home.

'Obviously,' I continued, ' If you want you can leave. Nobody is forcing you to stay. But if you do go, you're no longer under my protection, and the likely hood is that sooner or later you're going to get fucked up one way or another... People know we are all mates so the chances are if some cunt wants to get to me they might do it by fucking one of you up. Or all of you... You know to make me sad or angry or whatever. I think we've all seen enough films to know how these things pan out.'

'So basically we are fucking fucked either way then Johnny.' Said Diamond.

'Yes.'I replied. 'So in my opinion I think that the best thing that you can do under the circumstances is to try and enjoy the ride.'

   None of them looked at all well. They were just ordinary boys who, up until now, had had ordinary lives. Brian was the hardest out of them because he'd been in loads of care homes before being plucked to safety by his adopted parents but he was still soft as shit really. Billy was handsome, a bit thick and certainly not a fighter. He took

Brian's headbutt quite well though which was encouraging. Squint was just your run of the mill kid except for the fact that having one eye looking at you and the other one looking for you had given him a certain degree of resilience and a thick skin. Diamond was my best friend and the most intelligent of them all but definitely not the bravest. He, like me, loved drugs and girls and music and having a good time, and the good news was that he knew that if he wanted that life then he had to do a few shady things to maintain it. They all had strengths and weaknesses but the main thing we all had in common was loyalty to each other. We were all misfits and outsiders, we'd been bullied and beaten up on a daily basis because we were seen as vulnerable and easy prey for life's predictors. Up until very recently we were just another bunch of losers, we were the meek but soon, if I had any say in the matter, we were going to inherit the fucking earth.

    I got up from my dad's old chair, stretched and said, 'Right then men let's fucking do this! First stop, Stan the man! You're going to love him. He's a real hoot! He will try to fuck you all though, especially you Billy so keep your wits about you at all times. Let me do all the talking and try not to appear vulnerable or flirtatious. If anyone accidentally or on purpose finds themselves being both vulnerable and flirtatious then I'm afraid you're going to be on your own because once Stan senses any kind of weakness he'll be on you like ... um ... Brian on a plate of beans and grits or whatever it was cowboys used to eat.'

'Yeah but Brian isn't a cowboy any more Johnny.' Replied Billy.

'Oh yeah that's true. Okay how about, he'll be on you like me on your mum's pussy as soon as I pull out of your sister's bum hole?' I replied.

'Yeah that makes much more sense Johnny. Cheers.' Billy replied.

'Fuck me I'd love to come in your mum's face Billy.' Said Brian.

'Yeah me too Billy... then watch your sister lick it all off!' Said Squint.

'And which eye would you use for that then Squint?' Replied Billy nonchalantly.

'Who said that?' Replied Squint, and we all laughed.

Then Diamond said to Billy, 'When I'm fucking minted do you think your mum would let me give her one if I paid her?'

'Yeah probably mate.' Billy replied.

'Really?' Asked Diamond.

'No you soppy cunt of course not. She's happily married to my dad.' Billy replied.

Everyone except Billy and Billy's sister Nicky and Billy's dad, if he was really Billy's dad, knew that Billy's mum was a bit of a slag.

Billy's mum was hot as fuck and she knew it and good on her and why not? If I was a bird and hot as fuck I'd be getting as much cock as I could get down me too. If she was a man she's be called a stud but as she was a woman she was regarded as being a bit of a slapper. Double standards but that was the way of the world around here and there was fuck all that anyone could do about that. I actually admired her but I think that was because I fancied her all to fuck like everyone else.

I really fancied Michaela but there and then decided that if for some reason it didn't work out then I'd do my best to try and bang Billy's mum, and Billy's sister. Then I immediately had a word with myself and decided that I would never do that. It would be disloyal to Billy; unless he gave me his consent of course, which he never would. He loved his mum and dad and as he was blissfully unaware that she put it about a bit who the fuck was I to spoil that illusion for the soppy cunt?

'Enough of this bollocks you all have work to do!' I told them and we all fucked off to Stan's gaff.

Chapter Twelve

I rang on Stan's doorbell, looked up to where his security camera was positioned and waved.

'Yoohoo Stan! It's me!' I told him, 'I've bought the boys around for your appraisal!'

A few moments later we heard a tinny voice coming from the little intercom, 'Come on in lads! Let's have a look at you all!'

I turned towards the Bin Boys and grinned. They all looked like they'd just shat themselves.

'Fucking chill the fuck out!' I told them, ' we're just going in, saying a quick hello, getting the drugs and a few weapons and then fucking off again. We'll be two minutes max. Unless he tries to rape one of you. And by 'one of you' I obviously mean you Billy. Do not turn your back on him at any point.'

'For fuck's sake Johnny! Can't I stay out here and keep guard or something?' Billy pleaded.

'I'm afraid not mate. I want Stan to see you and fancy you so that he wants to protect you. He loves a bit of vulnerability you see? If he wants to fuck you it's in his interest to keep you alive until that day comes.' I replied.

'What the fuck do you mean, "until that day comes" ? That fucking day ain't ever fucking coming mate!' Billy replied.

'Oh calm down,' I told the silly bastard, ' It's just a figure of speech! There's no way I'd lure you here to give Stan the green light to scuttle you just so we can get more drugs and guns and an added incentive to keep us all alive! What sort of friend do you think I am? You're a cheeky bastard Billy. Although as you've brought up the subject, what I will say is that Stan is a very attractive man for his age and if you two take a shine to each other I for one will not stand in the way of love. Back door love. And, furthermore, if Stan shows his appreciation to me for bringing you two together then I for one will not dishonour him by not accepting any financial or material gifts that he may bestow upon me.'

'Get fucked Johnny.' Billy replied.

'Charming Billy, and also rather apt given the circumstances.' I replied.

'We should have invited that little Kev cunt. He's a little bender ain't he? We could have fed him to this Stan cunt rather than giving up one of our own.' Said Diamond.

'Fuck me Diamond your language is fucking appalling mate. And apparently these days you can't call someone a bender unless you are yourself a bender so stop saying it. Unless you secretly are a bender in which case I guess you can fill your boots.' I told him.

'Yeah I am a bit of an uncouth kind of cunt but a lot of birds find it both cute and charming I'll have you know. And no, so far anyway, I am not a bender. Or should I say homosexual? Although to be honest it might be worth sucking a few cocks just in the name of freedom of speech.' He replied.

'Well now is not the time for politics but your luck might be in with regards to that last bit sunshine' I told him as I pushed them all into Stan's hallway before any of them could back out.

We all bundled through the entrance to find Stan the man stood in the doorway dressed in a two piece gold Lame track suit. The top part was completely unzipped exposing a large, gold medallion around his neck. He was also wearing a pair of those photosensitive glasses that made the wearer look even more of a sex case than they normally did; which in Stan's case was pretty much always anyway.

I looked at Stan and then looked at the Bin Boys. Stan was grinning from ear to ear and licking his lips while sizing them all up; while my boys looked fucking petrified. It was hilarious.

'Now then, what can I do for all you lovely lot then?' Said Stan the man.

'We've come for the drugs and weapons Stan.' I told him, 'Oh yeah and Billy here wants to suck your cock.'

There was a moments silence which seemed to hang in the air for an eternity. Then me and Stan fucking pissed ourselves laughing.

'You should see your fucking face Billy! Oh fuck me that was priceless!' I laughed through my tears of merriment.

Billy replied by calling me a cunt which I thought was a reasonable response.

Stan the man then stuck out his hand and said, 'My name is Stan and I'm very pleased to make your acquaintance lads.'

They all shook his hand in turn and introduced themselves.

'Right then boys,' said Stan, 'If you'd all like to bend over that table in my living room and pull down your jeans and underwear I can get on with the business of the day, namely, giving you all a jolly good seeing to up the council gritter.'

This was followed by another long pause before once again me and Stan absolutely pissed ourselves laughing.

'Right that's it now lads. That was just our little joke to test you mettle and break the ice, and have a laugh at your expense too obviously.' I told them.

Billy was shaking like a fucking leaf which did make me feel a bit guilty but, the way I saw it, if they were going to be notorious gangsters, they'd all have to toughen the fuck up.

'Down to business then Lads!' Said Stan, 'Right then let's have your cocks out so I can give them all a nice suck!'

We all burst out laughing this time. Everyone except Stan that was.

'What the fuck are you all little no mark cunts laughing at then eh? Get you fucking cocks out! NOW!' He yelled.

He looked angry as fuck and even I was getting a bit perturbed, especially when he reached inside his joggers. Mercifully, rather than his own cock he pulled out a pistol, which he immediately put to Billy's head.

'Right then cunts, if you don't want me to blow pretty boy's fucking head off I suggest you all strip and start FUCKING each other!' Stan shouted at us all.

'Eh? What even me Stan?' I asked him.

This wasn't part of the gag at all.

'Yes even you Johnny! Especially you son. You think you can muscle in on my territory and shoot up my best mate Simmer and I'll just let you off Scot- Free? I'm going to fuck you all and I'm going to start with you Johnny! Then I'm going to butcher the fucking lot of you!' Screamed Stan, and then he stuck the pistol right into poor Billy's mouth.

For fuck's sake. Just my luck to get fucked and killed literally hours before I lost my virginity. Was that irony? Although would getting fucked by Stan count as really losing my cherry? At least I won't die a virgin. It wouldn't be the same though. I wanted it to be romantic and with a girl and I wanted to be the one doing the fucking not the one getting fucked.

It was a difficult one really because in my mind I couldn't help but think that if it was me doing the fucking then it would definitely count but if I was getting fucked then that was a grey area. Yes I'd had the odd wank about Sandy and even wanked him off that time but there was no way I was one hundred percent gay because I'd had hundreds of wanks about girls so I reckoned I was about eighty percent straight and getting bummed against my will was not my idea of a good time.

   Although as I looked on as Billy was being forced to nosh Stan's pistol that percentage did rise a bit higher. Billy looked so handsome in a defenseless and petrified way as he stood there shaking like a shitting dog and I know it was shameful but the whole scene did start to give me a bit of a hard-on.

'Right! You with the squint! What was your name again!' Demanded Stan.

'Squint.' Replied Squint.

'Really?' Replied Stan. 'Is that a fucking coincidence or is that a nick name son?'

'It's a nick name. Because of my lazy eye.' Replied Squint.

'Yes that makes sense actually.' replied Stan.

'Right then Squint I want you to pull down your black friend's trousers and pants and start sucking his cock or I'll blow this little cunt's head clean off.'

'Nah.' Replied Squint.

   Stan cocked the trigger on his pistol and pushed it further into Billy's mouth and said,'nah? Fucking nah, you cunt? Do you think I won't pull this trigger and splatter your mate's brains all over the fucking place?'

'Fuck knows. Maybe you will and maybe you won't but one thing is for sure is that I won't be sucking Brian's cock. Or anyone else's cock for that matter.' Replied Squint with a coolness that shocked the fucking shit out of me to be honest.

'Yeah and that goes for the rest of us.' Said Brian.' If you pull that trigger I'll guarantee you right now that me and the rest of the Bin Boys are going to jump on you and kick the living shit out of you and then I'm personally going to take that pistol from your cold dead hand and shove it right up your fucking arse hole, you old, nonce cunt.'

I wondered whether to suggest Billy sucking me off as some kind of a compromise but decided against it. I hadn't gone three days without a wank since I'd learned how to do it and I was getting desperate but Billy was a mate and I couldn't help but think that using this situation and his mouth, however pretty and inviting it was, as a kind of loop hole with regards to the promise I'd made to Michaela was probably inappropriate.

Then inexplicably Diamond joined in with this bravado.

'Listen Stan, we get it, you're a big time gangster, and we love that about you, but if you blow Billy's head off then we are going to chop you into little pieces and scatter them all over town and I'm personally going to write, "nonce" on your front door using your own fucking entrails so I suggest that you put the fucking gun down... Bitch.'

Fuck knows where all this fucking bravery had come from but I was extremely proud of them at that moment. Of course we were all going to be killed but at least they were going out with some kind of dignity. Nobody had even shit themselves yet. Not even Billy. They were good lads and I'd miss them.

Stan wasn't having any of it though.

'There's six bullets in this gun lads and there's only five of you and I'm as quick on the draw as Clint fucking Eastwood himself so I'll have plenty of time to put one in each of you before you're anywhere near me, so get down on your fucking knees and start sucking cock!'

'Ah! Glint Gleswood!' mumbled Billy as best he could with a gun stuck down his throat. At least he'll die finally knowing where Brian got his fucking nick name, I thought to myself.

'Come on Stan mate, put that fucking gun down. Billy would have probably sucked your dick for a few hundred quid anyway if you'd asked. Nobody has to die today.' I told him.

 I think Billy then gave me a dirty look look but it was hard to tell.

'Just put the fucking gun down Stan,' I said, 'and then we can all discuss this like gentleman. It wasn't me that shot Simmer either, I'll have you know. He came round to my gaff to kill me and some cunt shot him while we were chatting. I didn't see who it was but it wasn't me. I was going to strangle the cunt but he got shot before I could do it ...'I'll tell you what Stan, as a gesture of goodwill I'll let you watch while Billy sucks me off and Squint and Brian and Diamond could all kiss each other while you wank off and then we can grab the drugs and guns and be on our way no harm done. How does that sound?'

'No Johnny, how about this. You suck off all your mates then me and then I'll shoot you in the back of the head as I cum down your throat, then I'll shoot everyone else. How does that sound?' Stan replied.

'No deal Stan. What about I leave and go and get our friend Kev and you can have him as your sex slave? He's gay so it won't even be that big a deal for him. Then we grab the drugs and the guns and be on our way, no harm done?' I countered.

'Fuck off Johnny! You're not leaving us here with this cunt!' Shouted Brian, 'and you ain't going to give him Kev either. He's had enough on his plate what with his dad fucking off and leaving them skint ... and just because he's gay it doesn't mean that he'll enjoy being this cunt's sex slave you fucking cave man!'

'How hot is this Kev lad Johnny?' enquired Stan.

'Well he's no Billy but you'd definitely shag him. He looks kind of pale and vulnerable and a bit sad these days. Weedy little cunt with big eyes. Right up your street I'd say.' I replied.

'You ain't leaving us here Johnny.' Shouted Squint. ' This cunt will have bummed and killed us long before you get back. I say we just rush him and kick him to death and if we die then at least we died trying. Sorry Billy.'

Billy mumbled something but we couldn't make it out.

'Okay what about this Stan.' I asked him, 'Billy sucks me off. Squint sucks off Brian and you suck off Diamond? Then we all sit down and do a couple of pills and then we take the drugs and guns and that and leave. No harm done? What say you?'

'What about me and Billy?' Said Stan.

'What about you and Billy Stan?' I replied.

'Well it seems like everyone is getting sucked off apart from me and poor Billy here. I think that if anyone should be getting noshed off then it's got to be Billy because he's the one who's had my gun rammed down his throat all this time... Plus, as I'm the only cunt in the room with a shooter then it's also only fair that I get a nosh too.' Stan replied.

'Yeah that is actually a good point Stan. Right then does anybody want to nosh of either Billy or Stan?' I asked.

'I'll suck off Billy!' Shouted Squint.

'Fuck me Squint give it some thought for fuck's sake.' I told him.

Squint blushed. 'Well only to save his fucking life! It's not like I lay awake at night dreaming of his engorged member beating and battering my tonsils like a speed ball before emptying his load down my eager throat for fuck's sake!' He replied indignantly.

'I think you should suck off Stan Johnny.' Said Diamond. 'You're the cunt who got us into this situation so I think that the least you can do under the circumstances is suck our way out of it for us.'

'Agreed!' Said Squint and Brian at the same time.

Those cheeky bastards. After all I'd done for them. I was fucking livid to say the least.

'Listen guys.' I told them, 'how the fuck did I know that Stan was going to pull a stunt like this? I've known him all my fucking life and yeah he's a bit of a nonce but he's never tried to bum me before... well he has a bit but up until now he's always taken no for an answer. I'm as surprised as you lot! I thought that we were going to come here, grab the fucking drugs and weapons, then I'd give the fucking drugs to you cunts to sell and by now be on my way to pick up Michaela from the cafe before taking her for a meal and then losing my fucking virginity inside her tight little wet sacred fucking treasure! At least you sad cunts have nothing better to do! I was this fucking close to losing my virginity before my fucking sixteenth birthday and now that's all fucked. I'm more than happy to suck off Billy but I'm not sucking off Stan. That would just be too weird. That would be like sucking off a member of my own family. I'd rather take a bullet to the head if it's all the same to you cunts.'

'I say no cunt sucks off any cunt and we rush the cunt then.' Said Diamond. 'I'm sorry Billy but you're just going to have to take one for the gang. You'll be remembered as a hero and your family will be taken care of. Especially your mum and sister.'

Billy mumbled something but once again nobody could tell what it was. He didn't look too happy though.

'What about if Billy sucks us all off?' I asked.

There was a good few minutes of silence as they all considered this one.

'Nah that'll take too long. Hang on what about this then,' said Brian. 'Johnny sucks off Stan, that's a given because it's his fucking fault that we're in this situation. I'll suck off Billy because I think I'd be the best at it and it's only fair

Billy gets a good one as he's the one whose had a gun down his gob all this time plus if I'm going to suck a cock it's going to be one from a boy that is the most girly looking out of us all. No offence Billy.'

Billy nodded as best he could and I think out of all the scenarios that had been offered up so far he liked this one the best which was a bit hurtful to be honest.

'Yeah so Johnny sucks off Stan. I suck off Billy and Diamond and Squint suck each other off.' Continued Brian.

'Hang on a fucking minute!' I shouted. 'Fuck that shit! Who the fuck is going to suck me off then? Everyone gets a nosh but fucking me! Well that's fucking charming that is. That's fucking typical of my luck that is.'

   What a load of bullshit that was. If I got sucked off I'd have empty balls to go and meet Michaela and I'd be all relaxed and if she got the arse I'd just tell her the truth and say one of my mates was held hostage by this town's biggest and best gangster and he made us all suck each other off and it wouldn't even be a lie. I might even get some sympathy. But no. Nobody wanted to suck me off did they? The cunts. I gave them one more chance.

'Hang on. What about this then.' I asked them, 'we all do a pill, take our clothes off and put on some nice music and then we all have a bit of an orgy? That way we all get sucked off but without any pressure. We wait until the pills kick in and then we will all want to fuck each other organically... And I promise you lads after one of these pills you will all want to suck me off one hundred percent. Then we we grab the drugs and the weapons and be on our way. No harm done?'

'Oh fuck me Johnny I forgot about your date!' Said Stan. 'She sounds like a lovely girl too. Right then lads I won't waste any more of your time!' Then he emptied his pistol into Billy's mouth.

'No Stan!' I shouted.

Click! Click! Click! Click! Click! Click!

   Then Stan pulled the gun out of Billy's mouth and started laughing. What the fuck just happened? Billy was still alive.

'Sorry I had to put you through that Billy son. I'll go and get you a drink. You must be parched.' Said Stan and he sauntered off to the kitchen.

'Anyone like a beverage?' He shouted.

'Um I'll have a stiff one if you don't mind Stan.' I replied.

'Lads? Does anyone want a stiff one?'

'I'll have a stiff one.' Replied Diamond.

'Yeah me too actually. A stiff one would be great thanks.' Said Squint.

'Brian? Stiff one mate?' I asked him.

'Yes please. I'd like a large stiff one if that's okay.' Brian replied.

   I followed Stan into his kitchen and said. 'We'd all like big stiff ones if that's okay by you Stan. Oh and by the way, what the fucking fuck just happened back there? I thought you were going to sodomise and kill us all.'

'Don't be bloody daft Johnny! Why on earth would you think that?' He replied calm as a mother fucker.

'Well because that's what you said you were going to do Stan' I replied. 'You put a gun in Billy's mouth and pulled the trigger! Fuck knows how he didn't shit his pants.'

'That was just a test son. I had to make sure that if I was going to hand over my empire that it was going to remain in good hands. I didn't want you and your gang to ruin my legacy by being a bunch of namby pamby little fairy cakes now did I?'

'Fuck me you're a very good actor Stan! At one point there I thought I was a goner and I'm sure all the lads did too. Fuck me Stan well played sir. Look at my hands I'm still shaking. Although that may be because I haven't had any drugs or alcohol for over an hour' I laughed.

Stan poured me a large whiskey and said, ' There you go son. You deserve that. You were all very brave. Especially Billy. No wonder you all want to suck his cock.'

'What? Fuck off! No Stan we didn't really want to suck his cock! Well I didn't anyway. I think Brian did though. And Diamond. And Squint too to be brutally honest but I was just playing along.' I protested.

'Listen son,' Said Stan, 'There's nothing wrong with wanting to suck off your mates. I've sucked off loads of mine. Especially when I was in the nick. That was a great time. It's not poofy if it's prison love. Although I am a poof obviously and I would have done it anyway but a lot of straight lads will suck a cock if there's no birds around. Plus you haven't lived unless you've been sucked off by someone who knows what they're doing. That's why being a poofter is so much better than being straight. I can go out right now, get me cock sucked and be back here within twenty minutes and there would be no need for any kissing or cuddles or would there be any tears or tantrums or asking me to ring them four or five times a day or buy them jewellery just because they've let me cum in their mouths. It's perfect. Sometimes you can go swallow a chap's load and then go for a pint and a game of pool with them and never see them again afterwards.'

  That did sound quite good actually. I wasn't sure about the cock sucking but getting a nosh off a guy who knew what he was doing sounded okay. If push came to shove I'd suck off Sandy and probably Billy too but but not Brian or Diamond or Squint. Well maybe Diamond. Brian's cock was quite a specimen though and I've definitely put worse things in my mouth. And if I was being brutally honest with myself, sometimes Squint's lazy eye gave me a soft lob.

  Maybe all those years we spent not having any girlfriends we should have been wanking each other off? Prison love. Imagine if we'd all taken turns to dress up like birds and then got scuttled by everyone else? How good would we'd be at sex by now? I still wasn't sure about swallowing a load though. If everyone else's tasted like mine then I wasn't sure if I could keep it down. Fuck knows how women did it. Men's cocks were pretty much all ugly as fuck too. I had lots to think about but now wasn't the time.

   Stan handed me a tray of drinks and I brought it into his living room where the Bin Boys were sat about all ashen faced and discombobulated to say the least.

'Here you go lads! And thoroughly deserved too! You passed the test!' I told them.

'What fucking test' said Billy as he immediately grabbed a drink and wolfed it down in one.

'Well apparently all that back in the hall, the gun in your mouth and Stan saying he was going to kill us and then rape us...' I began.

''He didn't say that, he said he was going to rape us then kill us and shoot you in the back of the head as he came in your mouth.' Replied Billy.

'Yeah that was it. Anyway all that was a test! And we passed it!' I continued.

'When he said that my first thought was whether he'd shoot off his own cock.' Said Squint as he grabbed a drink and also drank it in one go.

'Eh?' I replied.

'You know,' Replied Squint,'when Stan said he was going to shoot you in the back of the head as he came down your throat, my immediate thought was, "I wonder if he'll shoot off his own cock." I mean the bullet could have gone right through your brain and into your mouth and he'd have shot his own cock off and if that was the case, depending on when he did it, that could have been a chance for the rest of us to have escaped.'

'Yes! I thought the same thing!' Shouted Brian.

'And me!' Billy Chimed in. ' I thought to myself, "if Stan starts off by forcing Johnny to suck him off then accidentally shoots off his own cock then that would be our chance to run because he can't have his gun in my mouth and pointed at the back of your head at the same time!"'

'So you were all praying that I'd be the first to be executed so that you could all fuck off while poor old Stan was sorting through my brain to find his blown off cock? Well

I've heard it all now. I was well proud of you back there too but not after hearing that. I'm not even angry, I'm just disappointed.' I told them.

'Well it was your fault that we were in that situation Johnny. We weren't to know that it was some kind of test! It was all a bit gay though wasn't it?' Said Billy.

'Yeah and I couldn't help but notice that your cock was getting hard while poor Billy had a gun shoved down his throat too Johnny.' Quipped Squint.

'Fuck off! ' I replied. '... And anyway if I did get a bit of a twitch it was because I haven't had a wank in three days and after that amount of time even you would give me a hard-on Squint. You ugly cunt. No offence.' I protested while going bright red.

'Fucking offence taken johnny! What the fuck mate!' replied Squint.

'Oh fuck me Squint I was joking mate! Your gammy eye makes you look cute! I said back there that I'd suck you off didn't I?' I told the needy cunt.

'I'll be fucked if I can remember to be honest. I was shitting myself and didn't really know what the fuck was happening. I do remember you wanting to suck off Billy though. In fact you were quite persistent if my memory serves me well.' Replied squint.

'Yeah but to be fair to Johnny you all wanted to suck me off!' Said Billy. 'I was quite moved to be fair! Even Brian! I thought to myself, "well even if I do get my head blown off at least I know that I was the hottest out of the Bin Boys."'

  I was happy to hear them refer to themselves as the Bin Boys finally. It had been quite an arduous and cheeky little test that Stan had put us through but at least we all knew that we had each other's backs now and that when the chips were down we all wouldn't mind sucking off Billy. There was something bugging me though and I needed to clear a few things up.

'Hang on a minute!' I said, 'there was no way Stan was going to blow his load in my mouth first and then shoot me in the back of the head! What would be the point of that? Once he'd shot his bolt, if he's anything like me, he would have gone off the idea of anything else sexy... like making you lot snog each other or whatever and just shot you all and then had a nap. So if you all thought that was your only chance of escape then you'd all have been sadly mistaken. And dead.'

'How would you have done it then Johnny? Hypothetically speaking like. If you were Stan.' Asked Diamond.

'That's a very good question Diamond... But do you mean, "what would do I think would have been your best chance of escape" or "if I were a raging nonce what order what I have put us all in in order for the sexiest time to have been had?"' I replied.

'Fuck knows to be honest.' Replied Diamond. 'Hey do you think Stan could make us another drink because I think I'm still in shock to be fair.'

'Right then, I began, 'seeing as though you asked, if I was Stan, first of all I'd make Billy suck me off but very slowly as I watched Brian and Squint sucking each other off. Then when they'd both ejaculated into each other's mouths I would have shot them in the head. Game over. Then I'd make "me" as in "me" give Billy one up the arse while getting sucked off by "him" as in "me" and getting my own arse eaten by Diamond as in "Diamond" while he wanked off. Then once I'd come inside of Billy, "I", as in "Stan"would have shot us both and then made Diamond wank off into "my" aka "Stan's" face while I wanked off and then I would have shot Diamond in the head as I came. Or should I say as "Stan" came.'

'No that's complete bollocks!' Shouted Brian. If I was Stan the first thing I would have done was to make Billy suck my cock and as I came into his mouth I would have shot you Johnny right between the eyes. Then I would have made Squint and Diamond snog each other while wanking each other off and fingering each other's arse holes because that would be so awkward to watch and also hilarious...'

'No you silly cunt! You've made Stan shoot his load too early again! And what the fuck? I don't even get to suck anyone off or be sucked off just like in the fucking real scenario! I just get shot in the the fucking face! I'm not having that! I'm at least sucking off Billy!' I complained.

Just then Stan the man walked into the room with a suitcase which he placed delicately on the coffee table. Then he went out and came back in with a holdall.

'Right then lads. Sorry for all that business back there. It had to be done unfortunately but the good news is that I was very pleased with what I saw. And not just the parts where you all seemed to be desperate to suck young Billy's penis.' Said Stan. Then he turned to Billy and said, 'You're a good looking lad Billy and if Johnny is correct in assuming you'd suck my old cock for a few hundred quid I'd be more than happy to pay you to.'

'Um no you're alright Stan. But thanks all the same.' Replied Billy.

'Well if you ever change your mind you know where it is son.' replied Stan while pointing to his dick and then giving it a squeeze.

'Yep. Will do Stan, cheers.' Replied Billy.

'Now then, unless any of you other lads want to suck my cock for free or for money we might as well press on because young Johnny has a date to keep.' Stan continued.

   We all shook our heads and Stan laughed out loud and said, 'I'm only joking you daft buggers! You're all too old for me anyway!'

Then we all laughed out loud with relief.

'Right then, down to serious business.' Said Stan in a serious tone. ' In that case you'll find, weed, and hash and amphetamine and coke. Its all bagged up and ready to go. All you need to do is find someone to buy it off you. The prices are also in the case. I could give you all some leads but I want you to do all the ground work yourselves. That way you'll learn quicker. Inside that holdall are five sawn off shotguns, five pistols and five hand grenades. There's also a couple of swords and a handful of knuckle dusters, Stanley knives and a few other bits and bobs. If anyone tries to tread on your toes you mention my name and if they're still being a pest then shoot off a knee or a foot. Don't try and argue with anyone just shoot them.'

   Then he opened them both up and we all stared wide-eyed at all the drugs and armoury. I could feel my dick getting hard again. I looked over to where Diamond was sat and was relieved to see he was also sporting a raging boner. Then I noticed Brian put a hand down his pants to free his own erection. Squint and Billy were also sitting rather uncomfortably.

'Fucking beautiful isn't it lads? Even I'm getting worked up and I've been doing this for over sixty years. It never ceases to make my cock hard. Drugs and weapons. Weapons and drugs. There's nothing on God's green earth quite as fucking sexy as a case full of drugs and a bag full of fucking weapons.' Said Stan, pulling out a sawn- off shot gun and waving it about.

'Now then let's have you all bent over that table over there shall we?' He shouted at us.

Then he laughed his fucking head off and after we realised he was joking again so did we.

'Listen lads its really getting late and as Stan said, I have a very important date to keep, so if you don't mind I'm just going to take a few pills and a few grams of coke and some weed and a bit of hash and this little pistol here and a few of these bullets, and this Stanley, and leave you in his capable hands.' I told them.

They all looked terrified again so I made Stan promise not to make any more jokes about raping them and fucked off.

Chapter thirteen

I shot back to mine, had a shower, got dressed in my finest clobber; black jeans, black shirt, black socks, black ten- hole Doctor Marten boots and my black leather jacket, slicked my hair back in a homage to my style guru, Joe Strummer, and was back out the door again within fifteen minutes. Boom! Just enough time to pick up my gal from her work and then court the living shit out of her.

   Just as I was about to slip on my Walkman I heard a familiar voice.

'Hello Johnny! Golly gosh you scrub up well! The last time I saw you, you were dressed up like a big school girl! ...And the time before that you looked like you'd just shit yourself and were trying to hide it!'

   Fuck me it was Sally from next door. It took me less than a fucking minute to go from Big Ron's to mine yet it seems like the whole world witnessed it. You cannot keep secrets on a council estate that's a fucking fact. I wanted these cunts to know me as the Entertainer; I'd specifically murdered my enemies in theatrical and fucking entertaining ways just so I'd get to be called the fucking Entertainer but at this rate I was going to be called, "Tranny Boy Shitty Pants" or something similar.

   Sally could fuck off anyway because I'd moved on from her so I decided to play it cool and detached. That was until I saw her. She looked so utterly amazing for a moment I couldn't speak at all and just stared at her. I wasn't even trying to perv over her I was just transfixed and dumbfounded.

'I said hello Johnny. Are you deaf? Cat got your tongue? Are you too cool to speak to me now you're channelling Johnny Cash? Hello! Johnny are you in there?' Sally mocked as she waved a hand in front of my face trying to get my attention.

I couldn't move my legs and my face felt numb.

'Listen Johnny I'm just off into town maybe we can walk together? Apparently you're hard as nails these days so you can be my body guard if we're going the same way.' Sally continued.

At first I was petrified that my cock would get hard like all the other times I saw her and she'd get all outraged and knee me in the nuts or headbutt me or kick the shit out of me like all the other times and then I'd be useless to Michaela and then she'd get the arse and do the same but then my feelings got a lot deeper and I was finding myself trying not to fall even more deeply in love with her. I was awe struck like all the other times. Fucking hell here we go again.

Like every other time I marvelled at her pale Irish skin and green eyes and her cheek bones and the dimples and the shape of her jaw and her long black hair and her slim waste and huge tits and her tight little bum cheeks and her skinny little legs but rather than just wanting to take out my cock and wank off and come all over her like I normally did, I felt more like I wanted to just hold her in my arms and kiss her face and her eyes and tell her that I loved her over and over again and wanted to tell her that I would protect her and keep her save from harm and cherish her and bring her roses every day and write her poems. If Sally had asked me to die for her at that moment I would have gladly done so.

'Johnny! Johnny! Hello! Earth to Johnny! Is anybody home?' Sally was talking again.

   Suddenly I came to. Sally was waving her hand in my face to get my attention again and as it moved about so did her tits. I was back in the room.

Sally grinned and said, 'Ah Johnny there you are! Finally he's back on Terra Firma!'

 She seemed to be overjoyed that I was still spellbound over her.

'I thought I'd lost you for a moment then. You seemed to be transfixed for some reason.' She continued with a glint in her eye.

Then she said, 'Johnny can I ask you two serious questions?'

It took all my wits but I finally managed a nod.

'I'll take that as a yes.' Sally told me. ' Well the first question is, do you like my new jeans?'

As she said this she turned around and threw out her hips giving me a perfect view of her perfect bum.

Sally's jeans were very tight and left nothing to the imagination. Why was she doing this? What the fuck was happening? Why was Sally being nice to me? Was she actually flirting with me? I was no expert in these matters and I didn't dare hope but surely if a girl basically asked you to have a look at her arse then, unless she's related to you, or it's on fire or something, then surely that's got to be a bit flirtatious.

Maybe it was a trap? Maybe if I said her jeans made her arse look so fucking sexy and edible that I wanted to put my tongue right inside her bum hole and stay like that until the day I died, she'd say I was a male chauvinist pig who was objectifying her and then knock me the fuck out and I'd miss my date and then when Michaela asked me where the fuck I'd been I'd have to say that I got knocked sparko for telling my next door neighbour that I wanted to eat out her Derek and then Michaela would fucking stab me to death or something. Well fuck that I wasn't going to fall for it. I was going to play it safe.

'Yes they look good. Well done.' I told her.

'Good? Fucking good? Well done? Is that it?' Well... fucking... done?' Sally replied, 'I show you my lovely, pert arse and you tell me that my jeans look "good"? "Well done?" This from the boy who admits to wanking off about me since the day he first set eyes on me? You need to stop hanging around with the trans community sunshine because you're fucking changing mate!' Tell me Johnny do you know what a Bulgarian split squat is ?'

  I didn't but I did know that I wanted nothing more in this world than for her to squat on my fucking face and empty her bladder all bastard over it. I really needed a wank and seeing Sally all dressed up was driving me insane. At that moment in time if she had crouched down and shat on the floor and then told me to eat it I would not have hesitated.

I then wondered if I should go back inside and have a quick wank just so I didn't do anything stupid and embarrass myself before I met up with Michaela.

"Hey Johnny please tell me why your breath tastes like human faeces."

"Well Michaela it's a funny story actually, you see I was just coming out of my house, on my way to meet up with you, when I bumped into my neighbour Sally and as my balls were so fucking full, thanks to you, when she pulled down her jeans and pants and crouped down onto my path and took a shit and then asked me to eat it I didn't fucking waver"

I prayed with all my might that Sally would calm the fuck down and I could just be on my way.

'...For your information', Sally continued, 'a Bulgarian split squat is a particular type of squat that makes one's bottom look fucking amazing if you do enough of them and I've been doing fucking loads in my college gym recently so the least you can do is tell me that you want to eat the fucking thing... What is fucking wrong with you lately? Do not fucking tell me that you wouldn't like rip off my jeans and pants, bend me over and then bury your fucking head between these pert little cheeks of mine before fucking my bastard brains out Johnny or I will fucking headbutt you right fucking here and now!'

Fuck me if this was some kind of trap then it was elaborate as a mother fucker and it seemed like I was going to get headbutted either way.

Sally then looked me up and down and then with a disgusted face she then said, 'which brings me to my second question Johnny ...why isn't your little cock hard? I look like this and you don't even have the fucking decency to have an erection? ...You're a fucking rude boy Johnny.'

Then she paused and then eventually she kind of nodded to herself and said, 'Yes, I think I'm going to kick the living shit out of you now. You little bender.'

I took my chance and grabbed it with both hands.

'Little bender?' I cried with mock horror. ' Fuck me that's double standards right there Sally! You said if wasn't allowed to say derogatory words for homosexuals unless I was one and only doing it politically to reclaim its power! But now you're doing it! You're not reclaiming its power or being political! You're just being horrible because I was being aloof about your lovely bum! Even if you were a lezbot you still can't call me a bender! Well I'm outraged Sally! I know lots of homosexuals and when I tell them what you've said you'll no longer be welcome in their community! ...And we both know that gay men throw the best parties.'

'Yeah well I was being ironic you little cunt!' Sally shouted back in defence. 'You're far too ugly to be gay! And you can't say lezbot unless you are one, which you probably are you fucking freak! You're just as bad as me! So you Do think I have a lovely bum! I fucking knew it! I'm still going to kick the shit out of you though. You've just got one of those faces that makes me want to punch it.'

Then she expertly tied back her hair into a bun and said, 'But first, a headbutt.'

   Le sigh. What was not to love about her? There was a part of me that would have head-butted me just so I could wank off while looking at the bruise it would have made but right then I didn't have the time to have fully appreciate it so I decided to tell her exactly what had occurred right up until that very moment and hopefully she'd understand and save my beating until a more mutually favourable day.

'No! Please don't headbutt me Sally!' I pleaded,'I still fancy the fucking fuck out of you obviously! In different circumstances there would be nothing I'd like more than to have you do one of your Belgian split squats right onto my face and then piss all over me while I wanked off!'

'Bulgarian. It's a Bulgarian split squat but please continue.' Sally told me.

'Oh is it? Okay cool, anyway you need to know that on a different day if you took a shit right here on this path and asked me to eat it I gladly would of course but I don't have the time right now!' I continued.

'Fuck me Johnny don't be going too far the other way. I won't be shitting on this path for you or anyone else. And as for you eating it that's a whole new world of depravity ... although I am starting to feel a bit better.' Said Sally.

' Yeah well the shit thing is more of a metaphor. Or is it hypothetical? Hypothetically if you were to shit on the path and ask me to eat it then, hypothetically, I would, anyway fuck knows if that's correct or not but what I mean is that's how much I'm into you! Especially with my bollocks being so full right now!'

'It might be an analogy actually. I don't know, I was always shit at English. Full of fucking ponces. Hang on why are your little balls full then Johnny?' Sally asked,'have you joined the priesthood? Or are you a monk now? Is that why you don't want to rail the fuck out of me and spray your sticky load over these big firm tits of mine? ... Because you've suddenly found religion?'

'Oh fuck me please stop saying things like that Sally I'm fucking bursting!' I replied.' I'm literally on my way to lose my virginity...'

'Wow you're still a virgin! I would never have guessed!' Sally laughed.

'You can make fun of me as much as you like but there's nothing that's going to stop me from meeting up with my new girlfriend and breaking my duck before I'm sixteen!' I told her.

'New girlfriend? You mean you've had a girlfriend before Johnny? Or are you referring to your auntie Joan or maybe that old woman who put her finger up your arse hole that time ... and you came in her wig? The one with the false teeth.' Sally replied gleefully.

'Oh come on Sally!' I pleaded, ' I don't have time for this! My balls are just about to burst their banks! I want to at least see Michaela before they explode. She made me promise not to wank off until our date you see and that was nearly four days ago and as you can imagine that's been quite a commitment...'

'Fucking hell Johnny congratulations! That must have been difficult as fuck for such a prolific wanker such as your good self!' Sally replied with hilarity.

'Yes it was and it's not over yet! I can't even think straight!' I replied.

'So if I started to play with my lovely... big... firm... bresticles and then dipped my fingers inside my... tight ...little... silk... panties and then started to play with my soft... wet... freshly shaved... cunt, you might be in danger of creaming those jeans? That wouldn't do at all would it Johnny? Not at all.' Sally theatrically moaned as she pushed out her tits and slowly ran her hands up and down her thighs. 'I wouldn't like to be responsible for spoiling your date ... or would you rather fuck it off and just lay down on the ground right now and watch as I slip down my jeans and knickers then lower myself onto that handsome face of yours? ...Would you rather go on your silly date or wank off as you licked my little pussy cat? Maybe, as you lapped at my tight, wet cunt I could bend forwards and slowly take your big, swollen cock into my soft... warm...'

Just as I was about to cum in my pants I was rescued from a saviour from above.

'Sally you horrible little bitch! Stop teasing the boy! You know what he's like! He'll probably murder us now! Or nail us to a park bench and bum us both! No offence son.'

'None taken Missus Holmes!' I shouted back.

It was Sally's mum, shouting from their upstairs bedroom.

'Oh fuck off mum! He was just about to shoot his fucking load!' Sally screamed back angrily.

She was fucking right too. One more word from those lips and it would have been goodnight Vienna. If I hadn't have had the presence of mind to think about my dead nan, on my mum's side, the whole time, I'd be back in the shower right now with empty pods and ruined jeans and I only had one good pair that went with this outfit. It was a lucky escape and I could explain the pre-cum in my pants to Michaela later by saying that she'd been responsible because she was so fucking hot. Phew. Hang on, " you know what he's like? He'll probably murder us now or nail us to a park bench and bum us"? Oh for fuck's sake here we go again.

Sally mum hadn't finish yet though.

'What have I told you about reading those mucky magazines Sally! The whole ruddy street can hear you! What will the ruddy neighbour's think! They'll think I'm a bad mother that's what! And they'll think you're a bloody scrubber too! Soft, wet, freshly shaved cunt indeed! Filth! It's nothing but raw filth! You're an embarrassment!' A living endorsement!'

'Living endorsement? What does that even mean? Stop calling me things you've heard on Top of the Pops! Oh come on mum I was just having a bit of fun with Johnny! He's always up for a laugh aren't you Johnny? No harm done eh?' Sally replied while winking at me.

Fuck, I hope the whole street didn't hear me tell Sally I'd eat her shit. Fuck it. What if that got back to Michaela! Maybe I should murder them both? And then the whole street. No that was too mental, even for me. I could never murder Sally anyway. And her mum had saved me from cumming into my pants so I'd feel bad about killing her too.

'...And for your information Johnny, Sally does not have a "soft, wet, freshly shaven cunt." It's hairy! And it's not fresh either because even though I told her to she couldn't be bothered to have a shower! ...Even though she was going out! It wouldn't have happened in my day I'll tell you that! ...If we were going out we'd make sure our genitals were freshly laundered just in case we got some cock! No respectable man wants to be eating something that's been hanging around all day in a pair of sweaty pyjamas I'll tell you that for nothing! She saw you coming up the road and quickly got dressed up and even put on makeup, which isn't like her at all, because even though she'll tell you it's because she's a feminist lesbian it's really because she's a ruddy lazy little bitch who'd rather lay around reading her filthy magazines with her bedroom door closed! ...And she's still a virgin Johnny so don't you go worrying about that! Well she'd ruddy well better be! I brought her up to keep her hands on her purse until she meets the right fella! So now you're all square! Oh and while I'm here son thanks for sorting out Eric the rent for us. He's a mucky sod that one and I'll be eternally grateful for what you've done and continue to do. ...If Sally won't suck your little cock then I will! And gladly too! And so will everyone else around here! You're a lovely looking lad and it'll be a pleasure now that you've obviously started giving it a bit of a swill around the sink! Not like that Eric's! His ruddy stank! Stank it did! It was a job not to puke up my ruddy ring piece most of the time! Oh yes and please don't murder us Johnny!' Bellowed Sally mum.

Sally was no longer laughing or winking. She was now bright red.

'Don't listen to her Johnny. She's off her nut on the vallies! I've done it loads of times! With loads of lads actually. Bum stuff too so... And some lezzy stuff so ... Hang on mum what the fuck do you mean '' feminist lesbian''? Oh for fuck's sake. My fanny isn't that hairy either so ... Those magazines are actually art anyway so ... and they're not even mine ...' Sally rambled incoherently.

Apart from the other day when I got sucked off and pissed on and died this was turning out to be the best day of my life. Seeing Sally lose all her composure was so much fun to see and now it was my turn to be gleeful. She'd been laid bare by her own mum and I'd never loved her more. I was still going on my date though so I didn't really have much time to gloat. Time was now of the essence.

I shouted back up to Sally's mum.'Thank you for your kind words Mrs Holmes! It was indeed a pleasure to hear all that! Eric the rent is a cunt, oops excuse my language! Eric the rent is a cad and a bounder and he won't be bothering you or anyone else for illicit blow jobs any more, that's for ruddy sure! I'm also sure your Sally's vagina is absolutely succulent whether it be freshly shaved or resembling a gorilla's salad! I hope to dine upon it one day but alas not this one for I have a prior engagement with another young lady! Oh and furthermore you need not worry about me murdering you or your daughter as I hold you both in high regard! I wish you a very pleasant evening Mrs Holmes and now I shall bid thee fair well and be on my way to lose my virginity forthwith! Oh and thanks for the offer to suck my dick! I'll get back to you on that depending on how this evening pans out! Ciao Bella!'

And with a theatrical bow and a foppish wave of my hand I fucked off down my path and out into the street.

'See you later Sally! You virgin!' I laughed.

'Cunt!' Replied Sally. This made me laugh even more. What a prize.

As I sauntered down our road feeling like a million dollars, even the sensation of the pre-cum that I could feel congealing around my helmet couldn't dampen my sense of euphoria. Suddenly I heard, once again, the unmistakable, dulcet tones of my beautiful albeit, genitally hirsute, neighbour coming up fast along the rails.

'Oi! Hang on cunt!' Sally shouted.

'Alright virgin? What can I do for you? Would you like me to unlock your sacred treasure? Well you'll have to wait.' I replied cool as fuck.

Sally threw a right jab towards my head but as she'd thrown so many at me before I knew it was coming and managed to expertly move out of the way.

'I will stab you to death if you tell anyone what my mum just said back there.' Sally threatened.

'No you won't Sally.' I replied nonchalantly.

Sally then lunged towards me and put both her hands around my neck and snarled, 'Yes I fucking will Johnny! I'm a mad, dangerous bitch!'

She was so close to me I could smell her breath. It smelled like sweets. My face was less than an inch from hers and even at that close range she was flawless. I looked straight into those emerald eyes of hers and said, 'You are fucking beautiful Sally Holmes.'

She looked at me and I looked at her and she knew full well that I was smitten by her and always would be. It took all my will power not to plant a kiss on those full, delicate, pale, chapped lips of hers and then tongue fuck her mouth. I was trembling being this close to the object of all my adolescent fantasies. I must have shot my load a thousand times over her and here we were, as close as two people could be without actually touching. Apart from her hands throttling me obviously. I could smell her perfume. It was cheap and horrible and it made my eyes water but it was a small price to pay for such intimate proximity to this council estate goddess. I suddenly remembered that her mum had told me that she hadn't showered today so I surreptitiously took a long deep breath hoping that I might be able to get a whiff of her fanny like that cunt Eric the rent did the other day. Unfortunately she must have guessed what I was thinking because she then kneed me in the bollocks and I hit the floor.

 'You are a dirty bastard Johnny McQueen.' She told me.

'Guilty as charged Sally. I've never claimed to be anything more than a simple murdering psychopath and a sexual deviant.' I replied. 'Any red blooded man in my position would have done the same. And a good few of you lezzers too I'll wager. If I hadn't at least tried to get an idea of what your your pussy might taste like then I would have regretted it. Maybe not today and maybe not tomorrow but one day and for the rest of my life.' and then I grinned.

'You're full of fucking shit Johnny and that doesn't even make any sense and stop saying ''lezzer'' and ''lezbot'' it's ''lesbian'' ''...and a good few 'lesbians' too I'll wager.'' ...saying lezzer and lezbot is disrespectful. You will never learn will you?' Sally scolded.

'Fuck me you are full of contradictions! I'll tell you what I'll stop saying lezzer if you stop saying bender because my gay mates find it offensive and I'm sure the lezzers do too. Deal?'

'Fuck off Johnny you wet lezzer.' Sally replied.

'I'll take that as a yes. I'm a horrible mother fucker and ignorant as a cunt but I'm trying to be a nicer person to people that like me or I respect. Now I've got sore bollocks. I hope you're happy. I know that was sabotage by the way. You had your chance Sally. Please just move on and let me find happiness with someone else I beg you.' I teased.

My bollocks did ache a bit but I'd been kicked in them so many times they had stop registering any real pain a long time ago.

'I'm very happy for you Johnny. I'm sure she's a lovely girl. Blind is she? And deaf so she doesn't have to listen to the bollocks that's constantly coming out of your mouth? No sense of smell hopefully either. I can literally smell your cock from here. She a goth is she then? Is that why you're all dressed in black? I bet she's a moody cow. I bet she writes dark poetry and self- harms and I bet her cunt stinks too! It's a well known fact that all goth girls are fat and their cunts stink like fuck so good luck on your stupid fucking date Johnny.' Sally replied scornfully.

   Talk about mix signals. The last time I saw Sally she hated me and now she's clearly jealous as fuck for some reason. There was no time to stand around trying to figure out what the fuck was going on though. I looked at my watch and told her that I needed to fuck off.

'I really need to go now Sally so if you'd kindly take your hands from my throat that would be great. I will say that she's not a goth and she's not fat and actually she does look a lot like you. And also, for your information, I'll have you know that her cunt tastes fantastic and furthermore her bum hole tastes like your breath. Which is sweets before you hit me again... I'm flattered that you popped a sweet in your mouth before getting all up close and personal with me back then although I wouldn't have minded if your breath did smell like a bum hole. As long as it was yours. Or my bird's.'

'Is that supposed to be some kind of compliment you sick little prick?' She replied.

'Yes.' I told her.

Then I said, 'I'd love to stay here and chat but in all seriousness I do not want to be late for my date so I'm going to have to love you and leave you I'm afraid.'

'That's fine by me I'm going clubbing anyway and I'm also in a rush so see you later and good luck and I really, sincerely, hand on heart, hope your date goes really shit.' Sally said and then laughed. 'I'm joking Johnny have a super evening together and you can tell me all about it next time. Good luck with losing your virginity.'

'Thank you Sally and who knows maybe you'll meet a nice young man tonight and he'll fuck the living shit out of you and you'll come home limping.' I replied.

'That's a lovely thought Johnny.' Sally replied.'Thank you for those kind words. Oh and before you go I've got a little parting gift for you.'

Then Sally grabbed me by the head, forced it between her legs and said, 'If you wanted to smell my cunt you only had to ask Johnny! Now then let me show you what you could have won! And Bully's star prize...My tiny, weeny, little mouse's ear of a wet cunt! That's it Johnny take a good few deep breaths because that's the first and last time you're ever going to be near it! That's a good boy

Johnny take it all in! Good boy! That'll give you something to think about on your shitty little date!'

I didn't know if this was some kind of punishment or reward and neither did I give a shit either way because I was just happy to be down there and eagerly did as I was told. It smelled of, in no particular order, piss and sweat and the unmistakable aroma of what I now knew to be teenage pussy and if I'd been shot in the head right there and then I would have died a very happy boy. I was inhaling so deeply that I was in danger of passing out but I didn't care.

Before I could help myself or really know what I was doing I opened my mouth and started sucking at her crotch. It wasn't the classiest thing to have done under the circumstances but Sally herself had told me that this was going to be the first and last time I'd be anywhere near it again so I took the opportunity to fill my fucking boots. Moments later Sally must have felt the sudden warmth between her legs or something because I immediately felt a rabbit punch to the back of my head and she pushed me away.

'That's your lot you greedy little boy. Now fuck off and have your date. You might want to wipe your face before you kiss the slag though. ' Sally said and then she gave me the double Vs before skipping joyfully up the road.

'Tell your mum it wasn't me that bummed Kenneth on that park bench please Sally!' I shouted at her.

It was good to know that I'd made her wet. Although it might have been wet anyway, the dirt bird. I was going to claim it though. My eyes followed her little arse wiggling away until she turned the corner and out of sight. I then looked at my crotch to see if I'd inadvertently cum in my pants but thankfully I hadn't. Part of me wanted to go home and wank my fucking socks off but I'd made it this far and wasn't about to fuck it up at this late stage so I headed towards June's cafe to where my date would hopefully be waiting expectantly for me.

Chapter fourteen

After doing my utmost to commit the smell of Sally's genital secretions into my long term memory I reluctantly popped into our local public toilets to wash my face. I was no expert in these matters but I couldn't help but think that turning up on a first date smelling of another girl's vagina was not the most chic way for it to begin.

In my experience public toilets always have an air of seediness about them. The men's anyway. I'd never been in the women's but I'm sure that they can't be as sexually charged as ours. It almost seems to be intentional. They're always dark and gloomy and smell of a heady and intoxicating potion of bleach and piss. I'd had quite a few dealings with piss recently and to be honest I didn't find it all that bad; depending on from whom it came out of obviously. Bleach too actually. When me and our Wayne kicked the shit out of our parents and turfed them out of our house I'd bleached the fuck out of the place in order to exorcise it from those two demons.

Maybe it was for these reasons that I felt so at home at that moment. I also loved the acoustics. All those tiles on the walls gave off a great sound and as I walked in to this shit house I'd always felt compelled to have a bit of a sing song and this time was no exception.

As I headed towards the row of sinks and mirrors I went through the scales as a warm up and then did a bit of Elvis and then had a bit of a croon. My parents were absolute gob shites but I had to admit that they did have great taste in music between them. I was only fifteen but I already knew hundreds of songs off by heart. From Country and Western, Rock and Roll and Blues, and Motown to the Irish rebels songs and folk to heavy metal and punk to New Wave and Indie and also all the shit pop songs they played on radio one, my lexicon of music genres was large and broad.

'Do, Re, Me, Fah, Sol,La, Ti Do! Do, Ti, La, Sol, Fah, Me, Re, Do! Are you lonesome tonight? Do you miss meat tonight? Well that's alright mama, that's all right for you... I came in for a piss but now I need a poo but that's alright ... Strangers in my tights ... exchanging fluids... Thank you very much ladies and gentleman! Johnny has left the building!' I sang as I washed off the smell of Sally's delicious fanny from my face and then fixed my hair.

  So Sally thinks I'm handsome eh? Well that's good to know, I thought to myself as I combed my hair into a perfect quiff while gyrating my hips like the King.

'That's a lovely voice you've got there young man.' Said a voice from behind me.

Well I was in a world of my own up until that point and to say that voice, seemingly coming out of fucking nowhere startled me, was an understatement to say the least, and I jumped out of my fucking skin. I instinctively span around and reached for my pistol like a cowboy but couldn't see anyone.

'Fuck me sideways mate!' I shouted. ' Where the fuck did you spring from? Hello? Where are you? Show yourself or I'll blow your fucking head off!'

'Ooh you're a spiritedly little imp now aren't you! Beautiful too! Has anyone ever told you that you look like a young Paul McCartney? The Berlin years?' Said the voice.

The voice was coming from the direction of the cubicles.

'Come out and show yourself before I come in there and drag you out!' I replied; although I was still fucking shaking and a tad terrified too if I was being honest. What if it was one of Simmer's boys bent on revenge? I was clocking up enemies at an alarming rate these days and I had to be constantly vigilant and it was already starting to destroy my nerves.

'Oh such a butch young man! Well I'm certainly not coming out if you're going to harm me now am I?' Replied the voice. 'You come in deary!'

'Fuck off! I'm not going in there! How do I know it's not a trap? How to I know there's not loads of you in there with knives and guns just waiting to murder me? To death!' I replied, trying to sound menacing but failing miserably.

'Oh don't be daft! Little old me? A murderer? I wouldn't hurt a fly, I wouldn't! Well that's just the most ridiculous thing a girl has ever heard!' Replied the voice.

  For fuck's sake yet another obstacle in the way of me sloshing one up Michaela and finally losing my virginity.

'Okay,' I replied, 'What about if you come out with your hands up and I'll promise not to blow your head off when I see that you're not a cut throat, murdering bastard bent on revenge? ...Once you've shown yourself I'll put my gun away and then fuck off. How does that sound?'

'Oh my, that sounds adorable! Have you really got a gun then ducky? Ooh show me it! I've never seen a real gun! Are you a gangster then? Well you've got the cheekbones for it I'll tell you that for nothing. You could shoot me any day of the week!' Replied the voice.

I didn't know who this cunt was but he was certainly good for my ego. First Sally now this fucker. What a day so far.

'Mate, that's really kind of you to say but you need to come out now and show yourself because I have a date to keep and she'll be furious if I'm late!' I replied.

'Oh a date is it? With a girl? Oh how disappointing. You're far too pretty to be a straight boy. I was beautiful once too you know but this game hardens you.' Replied the voice.

'I'm sure you're a very handsome man and if you come out I'll be able to see that for myself so if you don't mind please step out of the cubicle so I can see that you're unarmed and not a threat to me.' I replied as I cocked the hammer praying that I didn't have to pull the trigger.

'Okay I'm coming out but don't shoot! Unless it's your load into my face!' The voice giggled.

I aimed the gun at the cubicle door just in case but my instincts told me that this person was not going to do me any harm. The next thing I knew the door burst open and out stepped a man of about thirty with long blonde hair wearing flared jeans and a cheese cloth shirt knotted at his waste. He was also wearing lipstick and mascara and that red stuff birds sometimes put on their cheeks. He clearly knew what he was doing and the whole look worked rather well in my opinion. Unlike Big Ron whose look could be seen as being a bit too obvious and somewhat gaudy, this cunt was a lot more subtle and my first thought was that he could give Big Ron a good few tips on how to dress like a proper bird. It was none of my business how either of them dressed though and I decided there and then to try and be less of a judgemental cunt.

'Ta-da!' Here I am! In all my glory! Feast your eyes on this little bitch!' He yelled.

   Then he slid down the cubicle door frame until he'd literally done the splits.

'Fuck me mate I wouldn't do the splits in here it's fucking filthy!' I told him.

'Oh I don't mind a bit of filth here and there you gorgeous creature, He giggled, 'it's good for your immune system! And besides if you've seen some of the things that I've had in my mouth today you wouldn't have bothered saying that!' Then he let out a loud shriek of delight.

   I liked this cunt. He was hilarious and like me he clearly didn't give one flying fuck about what people thought about him. He then sashayed slowly towards me and stuck out a bony white hand.

'Hello sailor. My name is Julien and I'm very pleased to meet you.' He purred.

He then slowly looked me up and down and said, 'Oh my you really are quite exquisite aren't you? Would you like a blow job? On the house?' Then the cheeky cunt had the audacity to squeeze my b.

  Now I'm not going to lie, if it had been any other occasion and I wasn't so pressed for time I would gladly have let Julian suck me off, especially for free, but time was now of the essence. I took his hand and shook it. It was pale and cold and clammy and soft as a baby's arse.

 'Hello Julien. My name is Johnny. Johnny McQueen. Also known as, The Entertainer.' I replied; well there was no harm in starting the ball rolling with regards to my new moniker. 'Pleased to meet you. It's a polite no to the blow job but that's not to say that I'm not flattered. On another occasion I may well take you up on your kind offer. Especially if this date goes tits up... Listen Julian, I don't mean to be rude but can you please take your hand off my bollocks because I haven't had a wank in nearly four days and I'm just about to pop and these are the only jeans that go with this outfit and I can't risk saturating them in spunk. Yours or mine.' I told him.

Julien gave my balls one last squeeze and then with a sudden look of recognition he cocked one eye brow and said, 'Johnny McQueen? THE Johnny McQueen?'

I bowed and replied, 'The one and only sir.'

'THE Johnny McQueen who nailed that boy to that park bench and brutally sodomised him?' Julian gasped.

'No! Not that one for fuck's sake Julien! I mean yes I am the same guy but for the love of God it wasn't me that scuttled the little bastard!' I told him. '...It was my brother Wayne! It was our Wayne not me! Fuck me gently Julien mate, will you do me one small favour and as you go about your business would you tell all your punters that it wasn't me who fucked Kenny but our Wayne and then ask them to tell all their family and friends because this is getting beyond a joke right now and it's really starting to piss me off.'

'Well I wish I'd nailed the horrible little shit to a park bench and fucked him in the arse with a fucking chainsaw deary because he's a horrible little boy! He's not even a boy! He's the same age as me for goodness sake! We went to the same school! We were in the same class! Why he's always hanging around the park with teenagers one can only speculate but I have my suspicions I'll tell you that!' Replied Julien, 'he was always coming in here with his horrible friends and calling me all kinds of hurtful names and then having the brass neck to wait until his gang had left before asking me to suck his little cock for free! Oh the ruddy irony of it! He's only got a little tiddler too! It smelled bigger than it looked! I think that was why he was so angry all the time Johnny! And of course he was also in denial! The closet poofters are the worse if you ask me! That lot will cum in your mouth then give you a hiding because they feel so guilty about being a poofter! They hate themselves and take it all out on the likes of me! I've had it time after time I have! ... You can't fight nature you see Johnny! If you're born a poof you're a poof for life! You can get married and have kids but the cock will keep on calling you and calling you until you give in to it or you go mad Johnny! I've seen it happen! It'll drive you mad if you try and deny your true nature! They can run but they can't hide! Or can they hide but they can't run? Either way sooner or later the truth will out! The truth will out

Johnny! You can't run from the truth! Yes that's it I think. Gets them all angry and twisted up Johnny! Beat me black and blue over the years they have! Not until they've shot their bolts though! Oh no! They wait until I've got a belly full of their wrigglers then they bash me about! I've been plastered all over this lavatory over the years. The rotters. All of them. Bloody fuckers Johnny that's what they are! And that's swearing!'

  Poor bastard reminded me of myself and so many of my friends to such an extent that I was compelled to throw the cunt a bone and help him out.

'Listen Julien', I told him,'as I said, I'm a bit pressed for time at the moment but I'll tell you what, if you like you can work for me from now on. That way you'll be under my protection and if anyone harms you they'll have to deal with me... I can either put a bouncer on the door or you can just mention my name and hopefully that'll be enough for them to leave you the fuck alone. You can keep all the money you're making sucking cocks and getting bummed and what have you but I'll give you some drugs to sell to your mates and any of the punters who come in here and I'll give you a percentage. How does that sound?'

'What? Really? You'd do that for me? But we've only just met! Really? Hang on what's the catch? I suppose you want free blow jobs for life eh? I bet you heard I give the best ones in town! No gag reflex you see dear... I wore it away over the years... Ah so I get it now! You thought you could stroll in here with your tight jeans and pretty face and get the goodies for free is that it? Well let's get those jeans down and I'll pop you into my mouth then because I accept the deal! Finger up the bum dear?' Replied Julien and he got down on his knees and reached for my belt buckle.

I pulled away.

'Nah you're alright Julien mate.' I told him, 'It's just good business. Hopefully it'll work out well for both of us. You don't have to suck my cock. Not today anyway. Right then I'm off. I'll be in touch okay.'

I then took one last look at myself in the mirror and my surroundings and said,'Actually maybe I'll get the painters in and give this place a bit of a spruce up? Maybe you'll get a better class of clientele and you can raise your prices? We'll leave the smell of piss and bleach though because for some reason it gives me an enormous sense of well being. Know what I mean?'

'I do indeed. I do indeed... You're a good boy Johnny McQueen. Replied Julien, 'and you've got a big heart too dear. I'll tell you now that as long as I've got a mouth you'll always have somewhere to put your cock. And another thing, thank you for not calling me a poof or a poofter or a bender or a fairy or any of those other horrible names. I pretend I don't care but deep down I do. We all do. That means the world to me dear. We're just like you, you know, but we just like men that's the only difference between us... Although I think you've got a little bit of sugar in you too if you don't mind me saying... God bless you dear now you go and enjoy your date. She's a very lucky girl... but if it all goes pear shaped you know where I'll be. Cubicle two. The one with the glitter on the seat.'

'That's very sweet of you to say Julien. Yeah I'm slowly trying to be less of an ignorant cunt. From now on if anyone gives you any trouble they're dead.' I replied.

I then pulled out my bag of Es and shouted, 'close your eyes and open your mouth! ...But don't close your eyes!'

Then I threw one in the general direction of Julien's gob and surprising it went straight in.

'Have you got a boyfriend Julien? I asked him.

'Ooh you are a terrible flirt Johnny McQueen! Oh go on then I accept! Now kiss me you fool!' Julien replied gleefully.

'Yeah in your dreams! You know I mean.' I replied.

'I'm only teasing Johnny, yes I do. I do indeed' He replied proudly.

   I then threw another pill at him and said, 'well brush your teeth and go and met him and tell him to get that down his neck. Then I suggest you hit every gay bar in town and dance until dawn... You'll probably want to give your mum a ring too and tell her that you love her.'

Julien clapped his hands together and said, 'Ooh you're a veritable angel Johnny McQueen! Thank you my darling. Now fly my little beauty! Spread your wings and fly!'

Then I had another little idea.

' Say hello to my leedle friend!' I said in a very unconvincing Cuban accent as I pulled out my bag of coke.

Me and Julien then did a quick line each off his glittery bog seat and then I went back to the mirror to check my nose, looked around one last time and inhaled deeply. Fuck me I loved the smell of piss and bleach.

Julien then ran up to me and said, 'Oh Johnny you're a real heart breaker! I think I'm falling in love!' and he kissed me gently on the cheek.

'Well you're only human Julien.' I replied and kissed him back. And then I fucked off.

Chapter fifteen

I ran out of the bogs, sprinted across the park and glancing at my watch I found that I still had around fifteen minutes to get to June's cafe before it closed which was plenty of time.

Once I'd left the park I slowed my pace so I wouldn't be all sweaty and slipped on my Walkman. I was two streets away now and with James Brown coming through my ears I was on top of the fucking world. Sally had let slip that she thought that I was handsome and clearly wanted me to give her one and so did her mum by the sounds of it and now Julien had not only offered me free blow jobs for life but more importantly he said that I had a big heart!

Nobody had ever said that about me before. Up until then I'd naturally assumed that most people thought I was a massive cunt. I was a massive cunt though. I was trying to change my ways but it wasn't easy. I couldn't change fifteen years of living and behaving like an animal overnight and it was going to be a long journey but at least I was becoming aware of just how fucking horrible I'd been.

Julien was over the moon that I hadn't called him any derogatory names even in fun. I tried to imagine his whole life of being bullied and beaten up just because he was different. I could definitely identify with that. People were fucking horrible to anyone who wasn't just like them.

I didn't know why but that did seem to always be the case. I wondered if it was a working class thing. It certainly didn't do to stand out from the crowd where I came from that was for sure. Around my way if you were a lad you went to school and left as soon as you legally could and then you went out to work and any spare time was spent getting off your nut and then you'd get a bird pregnant and that was that. Game over.

After that you lived for the weekend and then eventually you'd split up from your first bird because you were both bored shitless and then you'd try again with someone else, preferably ten years younger and then sooner or later die of lung cancer or chlorosis of the liver or some other poor person's disease.

Yeah well fuck that for a game of soldiers. I had bigger plans. They would still involve me getting off my nut though because I loved taking drugs. Drugs made everything better.

Thanks to that cheeky little livener coupled with the funky jazz fusion of mister James Brown I actually arrived a bit early. I peered through the window of June's cafe and there she was; wiping tables. That sight made me feel sad but if our date went well and my business started to take off it wouldn't be long before she could stop serving egg and chips and mugs of tea to those miserable fuckers sat in there and become a lady of leisure.

In my experience people who ate in cafes were usually wretched mother fuckers who only left their houses in order to make everyone they bumped into as unhappy as they were. Cafes always seemed to be occupied by the same kind of miserable fuckers. As I watched the condensation drip down the inside of that cafe window; while making sure not to be spotted by my soon to be lover, I saw the same old usual suspects. In the corner was a lonely old man wearing a worn out suit and a flat cap nursing a mug of tea while reading the cafe's copy of the Sun and nodding away to its bigoted opinions. His ashtray was full of tiny ends of roll-ups that he'd smoked down to the very last possible string of tobacco. Even from where I was standing I could see his yellow, nicotine stained fingers. They looked just like mine.

   On the next table were two fat teenage mums. They were also smoking fags and one of them was idly pushing a pram back and forth while chatting away to her friend. I could hear their conversation through the glass and tuned in for a minute or so even though I knew that it was going to be the same shit that working class council estate girls have been saying since cave man times.

'He's a fucking two timing cunt Tracy!'

'Well I tried to fucking warn you Nicky didn't I? '

'Yeah. You did Tray.'

'But you've always been attracted to bad boys haven't you?'

'Yeah.'

'As soon as that scaffolding was going up you was out there flirting away like the dirty little mud slut you are!

'Yeah. I was to be fair Tray.'

'My dear old nan always used to say to me, never trust a man with a tattoo on his neck! '

'Yeah. That's good advice actually Tray.'

'They only want one thing, She'd say.'

'I fucking loved your nan Tray. She used to let me smoke fags round hers when I bunked off school didn't she?'

'Yeah she was a fucking Diamond that lady. A real princess.'

'Brought me and my brothers up she did Tray. Single-handedly. All on her own! We didn't have a pot to piss in but we never went without!'

'How long as she been in the nick now then Tray?'

'It must be nearly three years by now Nick.'

'Three fucking years. Fuck me. When is she due for parole then Tray?'

'Fuck knows babe. Fucking ages I think. They threw the fucking book at the silly old bitch. Fucking criminal it was! A real miscarriage of justice in my opinion!'

'She did shoot that fella in the face though didn't she Tray? Emptied both barrels into the poor cunt by all accounts. That's what it said in the papers anyway.'

'Yeah but like the defence said, it just went off in her hands! It was an accident! That shooter was moody as fuck and if anyone should be in the nick it should be the fucking pikey who sold it to here! The slag. He's going to get it I'll tell you that. Plus she told the soppy cunt not to try anything silly but you always get one cunt who wants to be a hero.'

'Yeah you always get one Tray.'

'Shit his pants apparently did he? Fucking awful smell by all accounts... You having another cup of tea babe?'

'Yeah we'll have one more and a couple of fags but then I've got to fuck off because Darren is coming round and I need to swill out my minge.'

'I thought you said he was a two timing cunt?'

'Well he is but when he's on the bag he'll eat me out for forty fucking minutes straight and besides I've been shagging his brother behind his back for months anyway!'

Then they both cackled which led to a synchronised coughing fit until they both spat up what looked like blood into their respective mugs and then started cackling again.

  I couldn't wait to get away from that life although I would have definitely shagged the one with the tattoos on her hands. Cafes were also refuges for mental people. Since so many of the nut houses had been closed down in favour of what they called, 'care in the community' more and more loonies were walking the streets and sooner or later they'd end up in the local cafes for a bit of warmth and a hot cheap drink.

  I was literally hiding behind one so Michaela wouldn't spot me. She was old and haggard wearing a dirty rain coat and I knew she'd smell like piss and not the sexy kind either. It wasn't her fault obviously. You can't expect to open the doors of the asylums and just expect the patients to just crack on in the outside world. These poor fuckers had been institutionalised and then thrown to the wolves to save a few quid. It was fucking appalling.

My parents were cunts but they were socialist cunts and even though they didn't exactly practice what they preached and neither did I until very recently, somehow they'd managed to installed in me a sense of right and wrong and also a sense of community. I think it's an Irish thing and was practised just to spite the Brits.

Individualism was anathema to me and I had evidence of how it would have fucked me in the arse hole because If I had tried to go it alone in my quest to become a criminal overlord I would have fallen at the first hurdle. Luckily I had my brother's stinging fists to help me along the way and now I had the beginnings of a gang and I was picking up waifs and strays from all over. Slowly but surely I was getting to where I wanted to be and I knew that in order to make these gains I needed the help of others.

I looked at my watch and saw that it was two minutes to eight. In two minutes Michaela would clock off and then she would be all mine. At least for the evening. I was now crouched behind the mad old lady and when I tentatively poked my head up and looked inside I could see Michaela keep nervously glancing towards the door. When she'd asked me to take her out she hadn't been specific she'd just said, " Take me out in a few days" and a few days had now elapsed and here I was all shiny and clean and most definitely chomping at the bit, just as she'd asked.

   Maybe she was looking nervous because she thought that I'd try and play it cool and keep her waiting but that wasn't my style. Any girl that was desperate enough to want to be taken out by me was going to get five star treatment all the way. I was no player. I was too pathetically grateful for any kind of attention for that kind of behaviour. Plus she was awesome and I couldn't wait to spend more time with her.

   As I watched her and saw her anxious face it was at that moment that I realised that even if she'd changed her mind and didn't want me to "fuck the living shit out of her" or words to that affect, like she'd told me the last time we were together, I would not have cared. I just wanted to be in her company.

   Across from the cafe the local florist was just closing up so I ran over.

'Hello babe. Please can I purchase one single red rose? It's for my date.' I said proudly.

'So you're the infamous Johnny McQueen then... Finally.' Said the lady who presumably ran it.

"The infamous Johnny McQueen!" I loved that.

'Wow! I see my reputation proceeds me! Yes! You stand correct! It is indeed I! The infamous Johnny McQueen! The man, the myth, the legend. The scarlet pimpernel! They seek him here, they seek him there, they seek the silly cunt everywhere!' I babbled.

To be fair to me I'd taken a lot of drugs and after that line and the fact that I was just about to meet up with Michaela, I was bouncing off the walls.

'Yes we all know you Johnny. The lady replied.'You're the lad who bummed that horrible little Kenneth boy. And burned down half your school and murdered two school boys and put your parents in hospital along with a load of other misdemeanours. Where the hell have you been son?'

I took a deep breath and relied,'Fuck me here we go again. Right then, well for one it wasn't me that bummed

Kenny. Although I did nail the little nonce to the bench... and I'll have you know he's not a little boy at all he's a fully grown man who hangs around the park with teenagers and tries to get his cock sucked for free ... And two, I didn't exactly murder those two school boys. I'd argue it was manslaughter and self defence. Three, guilty as charged over kicking the shit out of my parents and Mickey and Benny and Kenny and Debbie and Mattie. I kicked the fuck out of my headmaster too because he was also a noncey cunt. Excuse my language... It'll be a good while before he's spanking any more little boy's bottoms I'll tell you that ... now then what else was there? I'm sure that there was more...'

'Well I heard you also killed two men in the Dolphin and shot off Simmer's legs and murdered his driver while dressed as as school girl.' The lady replied. 'Oh and didn't you shove a watch up your uncle's arse hole?'

'Oh yeah that's right!' I replied. 'I'd completely forgotten about the Dolphin! Yeah that was fun. No, someone else shot Simmer and his driver. Fuck knows who that was. But yes I did shove a watch up my uncle Sean's Derek. I don't like families taking sides. Especially when they've chosen the wrong side. I'm on the side of righteousness you see lady? Sorry, I didn't ask you your name... I don't mean to be rude but I'm a bit over excited you see because I'm just about to take out the girl of my dreams.'

'Janet. My name is Janet. Like it says above my shop. See? "Janet's flowers." Replied Janet while pointing up to her sign. I looked up at it and couldn't help myself.

'Well I'm very pleased to meet you Janet but what that sign actually says is, "Janets" Flowers. There's no apostrophe after the T you see Janet? I'll get a pen later and sort it out for you. Free of charge, because now I've seen it it's going to do my fucking head in until it's fixed.' I told her.

'Really? No apostrophe? That sign cost me nearly seventy fucking quid! No apostrophe indeed! What a swizz! The cheeky cunt!' Replied Janet.

'Don't worry I'll sort it out tomorrow. I can't now because of my date and I don't want to take the piss by being late.' I replied.

'Well you're already late.' Replied Janet crossly.

'Eh? What do you mean?' I asked her, while looking at my watch, 'I've still got about thirty seconds. I'm right on the nail Janet.'

'You should have been here yesterday son. You broke that poor girl's heart you did. She was waiting for you outside that cafe until gone ten last night. Shivering with the cold she was. I told her to go home but she wouldn't have it. She said that you'd obviously got caught up and that sooner or later you'd come for her. But you didn't and I had to watch that girl waiting at the bus stop freezing cold and crying her eyes out.' Janet replied.

'But she said, pick me up in a few days! A few days! A few days is a few days! Like three days! Or even four! If I'd have come yesterday that would have been a couple of days! Not a few! I would have come yesterday! I would have preferred to have come yesterday Janet! I would have preferred not to have never left her in the first place! I would have preferred it if she'd said to me, "Johnny take me out now and never leave my side until our last day on this earth!" I'm in love with her Janet! Oh shit she's going to hate me! I have to get over there!' I said as I got out my wallet and handed her ten quid. 'Can you please just give me a red rose Janet! No! Give me all your roses! Yes! Please give me all your roses!'

 'Oh for fuck's sake calm down Johnny. You're a day late so a few more minutes isn't going to make any difference. I believe you son but you've got a lot of making up up to do. Here, take these roses, there on the house. You're a good boy I can see that, now run over there and treat that girl like she deserves to be treated.' Janet replied handing me a big bunch of red roses.

'Thank you Janet but I must insist on buying them otherwise it wouldn't be right.'

  I then gave her fifty quid and said, ' Can I take these as well? And these? And these?' As I started to randomly grab different bunches of flowers in my arms until I couldn't hold any more.

'Take the bloody lot if you like son and keep your money! I won't take it! Now go! Go and meet her before you do any more harm! And promise me you're stand her up again! Janet told me sternly.

'For fuck's sake I have not done that girl any intentional harm Janet!' I protested.

'That's your problem to sort out. So go. And have a lovely time. She's a sweet- heart Johnny and if you hurt that girl I don't give a fuck who you are and you can murder me if you like but I'll have your guts for garters son!' Janet replied.

  I briefly thought about shooting her in the mouth but there was no time for that so I just fucked off with my flowers. I bounded across the road and up to the glass front door of June's cafe and peeked in. It was still fucking packed and noisy as fuck. I'd assumed that it would have been pretty much empty by now as it was just about to close but it was heaving.

  I didn't want to make a big entrance so I put my collar up and my head down and slowly opened the door. My plan was to try to sneak up to her unseen and then shout, "boo!" And as she turned around I'd grin and then present her with her flowers and then she'd smile shyly and be overwhelmed and then she'd jump into my arms and I'd feel her pubic bone rubbing up and down my cock and then if I'd shot my load it would be okay because she'd know I'd kept my promise by the amount of jizz that was seeping out of my jeans and then she'd tell me she was in love with me and then she'd get her coat and then we'd fuck off.

   As I slowly opened the door the whole place went quiet. Deathly quiet. Fuck it. Everyone was staring at me so my plan about sneaking in and surprising Michaela was fucked from the get go. Then someone threw a glass at me. My first thought was that maybe it was just an unfortunate coincidence but then another one came flying at me. Luckily my instincts kicked in and I managed to shield myself using the flowers. Then a plate of what looked like bubble and squeak came flying towards me and this was quickly followed by a plate of liver and onions and then a cheese burger and a strawberry milkshake. Who would have thought that June's cafe had such a wide and varied menu?

   It was when I was hit in the face by a piping hot jug of custard that the penny finally started to drop. These items were being thrown at me on purpose! Then I got hit on the head by a large plate of Alphabetti spaghetti and all thoughts then turned to survival.

   I was soon getting barraged by the whole fucking clientele and it was absolute fucking mayhem. Maybe they were holding a wake for some cunt I'd recently killed? Or maybe I'd inadvertently gate-crashed the annual loony tunes' works meal? But then, above the sound of breaking plates and glasses, I heard someone shout, 'we'll teach you not to mess with our Michaela you disrespectful little cunt!'

Ah now it makes sense! Well that cheered me right up because I knew, hand on heart, that I was not guilty of this particular crime. I was now crouched in a fetal position by June's front door trying my best to protect myself the best I could with the rapidly diminishing flowers I'd recently purchased from Janet and I was thanking my lucky stars that I'd been so generous because if it had been one single red rose I was holding when I'd entered that cafe I'd have surely been dead by now.

I grabbed a table cloth from the nearest table and waved it about shouting, 'I surrender! I surrender! Please let me explain! It was a miscommunication! It was a miscommunication!'

For a minute all was silent then the bird with the tattooed hands shouted, 'Fuck off you lying cunt!' And all hell broke lose again.

Plates and cups and glasses began smashing behind me and before long all I had to protect me was a tiny piece of cellophane and a few twigs.

'I'm not lying guys!' Ask Janet from the flower shop! She believes me! I'd never do anything to harm Michaela! I love her!' I shouted as best I could through the fucking havoc.

There was another brief hiatus before tattoo piped up again.

'He's in love with Janet! The two timing cunt! Kill him!'

'Oh fuck off Nicky! I shouted back.' You know I didn't mean that you soppy cunt! Of course I'm not in love with fucking Janet! She's fucking fatter than you! ...Which is no bad thing obviously! I love a bird with a healthy appetite! And I'll tell you what, if you lost a few stone you'd be beautiful! I was only thinking about that when I was staring at you through the window a minuter ago!'

Another moment of silence followed before her mate shouted, ' He's a peeping Tom!' and then Nicky shouted the worst insult you could ever throw at anyone from where I'm from.

'Fucking nonce cunt!' And it all kicked off again.

   Well that was the final straw for me. I've been called all the names under the sun over the years but being called, ''a fucking nonce cunt'' was crossing a line. Everyone knew that. If you got called a fucking nonce cunt then it was on. And it was definitely now on. I decided that what was needed then was a bold statement.

'Right! That's fucking it!' I shouted across the room. 'Enough is enough! Nobody calls me a fucking nonce cunt and gets away with it! I'm Johnny McQueen! I'm Johnny Capone! I'm the fucking Entertainer!' And with that I stood up, pulled out my gun and put two bullets into the ceiling.

That did the trick. I let the screams and shouts die down and then shouted at those fuckers, 'Everyone needs to shut up now! Enough is enough!'

Then there was silence. Dead silence.

'Right then if any cunt throws one more thing at me, one more mug or one more glass or plate of fucking food and especially one more fucking jug of bastard scolding hot custard, I am going to shot some cunt in the face!' I bellowed.

Then I strolled over to Nicky and Tracy and put the gun inside the pram and said, 'If anyone tries anything fucking heroic I'm going to shoot this fucking baby! That is how fucking mental I am and also that is how much I do not like being called a fucking ... nonce... cunt! Right, now I've got your attention I want to explain just what happened and why, in your eyes, I appear to be a day late for my date with Michaela. Actually where is she? Where are you baby?'

'I'm here Johnny! Said a voice. 'I'm hiding behind the counter! Please don't shoot me!'

 'Fuck me Michaela I'm hardly going to shot you am I?' I told her, 'apart from coming here smelling like another girl's genitals, shooting you would be the worse start to a date ever!'

   Then Nicky's hand went up. What the fuck did she want? I pointed my gun at her head and after all the screaming died down I asked her what the fuck was more important than me explaining to my date why, in her eyes, I was late.

'That's not a baby.' Nicky replied.

'What do you mean Nicky? Sorry. Can I call you Nicky?' I asked her.

'I couldn't give a fuck what you call me mate.' Nicky replied.'The thing in the pram. That's not a baby.'

'What does that mean? That's not a baby? What? In the pram? That's not your baby in the pram? I replied.

Then Nicky's mate Tracy said, 'Are you fucking special needs son?'

For some reason everyone seemed to find that highly amusing.

'Right that's fucking it! Have you not heard about me you pair of absolute fucking scrubbers! I will fucking shoot you both and then I'll shoot whatever the fuck is in this fucking pram!' I screamed.

   Fuck me I was livid now. Fucking special fucking needs indeed. Those cheeky slags. Then I pointed the gun inside the pram again and pulled back the cover. It was an old dog. One of those shitty little tiny ones with the breathing difficulties.

'That's Dave.' Said Nicky like that was the most normal thing to say and in not anyway fucking insane.

'Are you sure that's not your kid Nicky because it fucking looks like you!' I quipped, expecting a big laugh but not getting one.

'I'm joking Nicky!' I continued, 'this dog has got a lot less hair on its face!'

Still not even a ripple so I plodded on.

'Why is there a dog in this pram Nicky?' I asked her.

'Well he's fucking old as fuck ain't he? And he's too fucked to walk these days so I carry the little cunt around in a pram. He likes it.' Nicky replied.

'I'm sure he fucking does! I'd love to be carried around all day in a fucking pram too!' I replied.

I don't know why I said that it just seemed appropriate at the time but I could see by everyone's faces that I was only adding fuel to the fucking nonce cunt accusation.

'Why do you call him Dave then?' I asked.

'Because that's his fucking name mate!' Replied Nicky and everyone pissed themselves laughing again. I even heard Michaela giggle from behind the counter.

'No sarky bollocks I mean why is he called Dave and not fucking Rex or Fido or fucking, I don't know...'

'Sabre?' Someone offered.

'Eh?' I asked, turning around in order to see the face of the voice who'd said this. It was the mad bird with the dirty rain coat.

'Sabre. Sabre is a good name for a dog. My grandad had an Alsatian called Sabre.'

'What about Lassie then?' Came another voice.

'What about Lassie?' I replied, really getting annoyed now.

'Well Lassie is a good, strong, traditional name for a dog. Who remembers Lassie off the telly then?' said the voice.

This was then followed by a general conversation about lassie the fucking dog detective or whatever it was and then someone started banging on about Champion the bastard wonder horse and then telly in general and how it was all repeats these days and how good Benny Hill was compared to all these new so-called comedians.

Everyone now seemed to be having the time of their lives and totally ignoring the fact that I was waving a gun around so I walked up to the counter and after promising not to shoot her Michaela stood up and then I said "boo!"

and grinned and then presented her with a couple of twigs.

'In my defence I thought that a few days meant at least three.' I told her. 'surely a few days means three at least baby? Oh and by the way, you look drop dead gorgeous.'

   Michaela took the twigs from me and said, 'Oh Johnny they're beautiful. Thank you! I thought we agreed on a "couple" of days? Oh well it doesn't matter anyway now because you're here. I was just getting myself at it. I've been let down so many times in the past and I really didn't want you to be like all the others and I just couldn't wait to see you and when you didn't turn up yesterday I thought you'd stood me up and when June found out she got really angry at you and then all the regulars found out and then they got angry too because we're all family to each other in here and then when you came through that door they obviously thought that you thought that turning up a day late with a bunch of flowers would be enough to win me over, which they probably thought was fucking cheeky as fuck and taking the fucking piss actually, so they decided to let you fucking have it.'

'No you definitely said "a few days." I replied, ' I think so anyway. If you'd have said a couple of days then I would have been here yesterday with bells on. I would have loved to have taken you out the night I died and shat myself but I was covered in shit and piss and it wouldn't have been right. That's more date three stuff. Either way I'm here now and you look amazing and beautiful and sexy as hell and it's killing me that I, however inadvertently, upset you, so why don't you grab your coat and let me start making amends?'

Before Michaela could reply there was a loud scream. It was Nicky.

'Dave! Dave is having a fit! Somebody do something!' She yelled.

Michaela grabbed me by the arm and shouted, 'Johnny do something! Dave is having a seizure! Go and help Nicky!'

  Fuck Nicky. Nicky called me a fucking nonce cunt. I couldn't say no to Michaela though because then her vagina would be off the table because birds love animals, even scruffy half-dead, ratty looking little fuckers like Dave but what the fuck was I supposed to do? I wasn't a vet! I had a quick think and came to the conclusion that I could do one of three things. I could give it an ecstasy pill or give it some coke or shoot it in the fucking head.

'Should I shoot it in the head? I asked her.

'No!' Screamed Michaela.

I wished I could have put a bullet in Nicky's head just so she'd stop fucking screaming. I could have shot her then the fucking dog then all would be quiet again and I could have proceeded with our date but life isn't always that easy it seemed. Instead, with all eyes on me, I felt obliged to walk over to the pram and tentatively I peered in. Dave was indeed looking very distressed. His eyes were bulging out of its sockets and it was staring up at me pathetically while foaming at the mouth and its little legs were frantically going nineteen to the dozen. Bizarrely this wasn't the first time I'd seen a dog do this and I knew immediately that poor little Dave was choking to death.

The same thing had happened to our old dog Satan a few years previously. On that occasion I came downstairs to find the poor cunt lying on its back fitting out while trying unsuccessfully to puke so I picked the fucking thing up and whacked it on the back like I'd seen in some film and after a couple of minutes it threw up a pair of my dad's shitty underpants and after a while was right as rain. Apart from the nightmares obviously.

'Right everyone fucking stand back! I need some room! I shouted, while roughly shoving Nicky out of the way and just hoping that she'd call me a nonce again so that I had an excuse to put a bullet in her so she'd have something to actually scream about.

I then swiftly took Dave out of his pram, turned the little bastard upside down and then gave him two sharp whacks on the back. Dave immediately stopped shaking because I'd accidental killed it. I'd killed the soppy little cunt and it hung there in my hand, swingy gently in the breeze that was coming from June's cafe's extractor fan. We were all transfixed for what seemed like a good long while until the inevitable happened.

'Oh My God you've killed my baby!' Screamed Nicky.

'Listen Nicky if you don't stop fucking screaming I'm going to put a bullet right in your skull! How can I think straight with you fucking screaming at every tiny incident that's happening!? Dave ain't your fucking baby either. Although the resemblance is striking!' I screamed back but still no laughter came from those miserable cafe cunts.

'Dave is old as fuck and besides the cunt was choking to death! I did what I could! I saved my own dog's life doing exactly what I tried to do to Dave but it seems like his little heart couldn't take it, and by the looks of him, also his little spine. He's in doggy heaven now. Come on Michaela let's go babe. I did all I could.'

'No Johnny! Give it another go! Hit the cunt again!' Michaela shouted back.

Oh for fuck sake. Well the way I saw it as the poor little dick head was already dead I had nothing to lose so I gave it another whack but it just swung about all limp and lifeless. Then I had a brain wave and started to swing Dave around my head hoping that centrifugal force might dislodge whatever it was stuck in his throat but after a good few revolutions it was clear that this wasn't working either.

It was quite quite good fun though because as I was swinging him around everyone was ducking just in case I accidentally let him go. I was just thinking that maybe if I did let Dave go and he slammed into the wall, the impact might free the obstruction in his throat when Michaela shouted, ' It's not working |Johnny! You'll have to give him mouth to mouth!'

Oh You've got to be fucking kidding me. Mouth to fucking mouth? To a dead dog? Fuck that. But then the rest of them joined in.

'It's Dave's only chance! Give him CPR son!' The lonely bigoted man shouted.

'CPR? You a doctor then?' I asked the silly old bastard. 'Maybe you should give this old bag of bollocks CP fucking R?'

Fucking CPR these pricks had watched too many American TV shows. Fucking CPR indeed.

'Please Johnny! It's his last chance!' Pleaded Michaela.

Birds fucking loved animals. All birds wanted to be vets when they were kids and spend all their days combing their Barbie's hair and riding ponies and feeding rabbits and guinea pigs and putting dogs in prams and pretending they were their babies.

I did love that Michaela cared so much about Dave though. I was a cold hearted psychopath but I didn't want to date one. I was left with no choice so I took off my jacket and rolled up my sleeves. I'd also seen a few medical dramas over the years so I reckoned I could blag it until everyone got bored and started chatting about immigration and ration books and powdered egg and Vera fucking Lynn again.

'Okay you two move out of the way and give me some room please! I'm trying to save a life here!' I shouted at two bored looking teenage girls who really didn't look like they gave a shit either way.

'Oi don't push me you nonce cunt!' Said the one nearest to me so I stuck my gun right inside her fucking mouth and cocked the trigger.

'Fucking move out of the fucking way you scruffy cunt or I'll splatter your brains all over this cafe and make your fucking mate clean it up!' I screamed in her ear and she replied by letting out a huge, high pitched fart.

 Then Michaela leaped over the counter, bounded over and proceeded to headbutt the pair of them before dragging them away.

 Swoon. That's my gal. I could feel that my cock was getting hard but I had to try and bat it away just in case everybody thought it was the idea of giving Dave the kiss of life that was causing the lump in the front of my jeans. I then pushed all their shit off the table and lay Dave on his back. He did not look at all well.

'Right then Dave. Brace yourself mate.' I told him.

I then started to gently push down just below his little ribcage while saying, "one! Two! Three!" "One ! Two! Three!" "Stay with me Dave! Don't you dare die on me!" Like I'd seen those fit birds in the TV soap opera, Young Doctors do. Finally all that wanking over fit Australian nurses in tight fitting little white nurse's uniforms was paying off.

'Come on Dave! I won't let you die!' I told him while glancing over to Michaela to make sure she was getting it all.

'It's not working Johnny! You'll have to give him the kiss of life!' Screamed Michaela.

I looked her dead in the eye and tried to tell whether she was taking the fucking piss or not. Unfortunately she seemed genuine enough. Bollocks. All eyes were on me again and the place went deadly quiet. I had nowhere to run now and there was no going back. I was fucked. The loss of my virginity hung on the next decision I made. The way I saw it I could either shoot my way out, making sure, accidentally on purpose, I hit Nicky and those two school girls, and never see Michaela again or put my lips on that mutt and pretend to blow into his little lungs and do my best to fake giving the little shit the kiss of life.

I looked around the room at all the concerned faces. I guess they weren't a bad bunch really. They were clearly very fond of Michaela that was for sure. And they all seemed to care about Dave too. The fucking sentimental idiots. It wasn't their fault that they were all horrible bigots and mental cases. They were just as much a product of their upbringings as me. Apart from the mentals obviously... although saying that look at our Wayne... He went mental because of his upbringing. Maybe I should introduce old Dorothy to the old bag lady and they can lezz off until she's not mental any more?

Up until recently I'd been as bad as them and in many ways I was still a right horrible cunt but at least I was beginning to see the light. It was too late for this lot now anyway and besides by the looks of them ninety percent wouldn't last another winter. Nobody lived to a ripe old age around here.

'Right then, pucker up David I'm coming in! I hope you've brushed your teeth!' I quipped, trying to lighten the mood, but once again not one person even smirked. Those fucking ungrateful cunts. I bet this was the most entertainment they'd had in years.

I then took a paper towel from the little rack, gave Dave's furry little gob a wipe, closed my eyes, slowly put my mouth onto his and pretended to blow. I puffed out my cheeks and then sucked them back in and then did the same routine three times.

Then I got up and said, 'Nope the poor little chap is dead as a fucking Dodo... Right then Michaela let's go babe. Fair well everyone. It was lovely to meet you all and we must do this again sometime. Actually Nicky I think these days you can get your pets cremated and then made into rings and that. Maybe that will bring you some kind of solace. Dave would look nice on you. Anyone know any numbers for cabs around here then?'

'Oh Johnny please give it one more go! For me! I know you can do it! I believe in you! We all believe in you don't we guys?' Michaela pleaded with me again. Her lovely and inspiring words were of of course met with fucking silence and I wasn't even surprised. The wankers.

'Okay for you I will give it one more go. But only because I love animals and I love you.' I replied.

Michaela blushed which made my cock twitch and I felt euphoric again until someone muttered the word nonce under their breath and I didn't catch who it was so I couldn't put a bullet in them. I then took a deep breath and did the same thing. I was just about to get back up when the cafe door opened and I heard a voice shout, 'Oh he's fucking turned up has he!? Del, get the baseball bat out of the boot!'

It was June.

Oh yeah I'd forgotten all about June and Del. Maybe they'd been away for the day. I hoped they'd had a good time. She didn't sound too happy with me though so I thought that the best thing I could do was carry on pretending to give Dave mouth to mouth until she's seen what was going on and then realise that I was actually a hero and then hopefully Del wouldn't come at me with that bat and I wouldn't have to shoot him in the bollocks.

I stayed with my lips on Dave's until I was sure that she'd seen me but just as I was going to take a step back and lament poor Dave's sad demise for the last time someone shouted, 'Oi! What's that in his pocket!? Is that a hard-on? The dirty rotter has got a hard-on from kissing Dave!'

On hearing these ridiculous words; it was obviously Michaela who had given me an erection not Dave, I couldn't help but let out a large gasp of incredulity and horror at the mere suggestion of this accusation and in doing so I blew all the air I'd had safely stored in my mouth into Dave's and then deep into his little lungs which resulted in Dave suddenly and inexplicably opening his fucking eyes.

On sensing this I instinctively opened my own eyes and we stared at each other in mutual shock and disbelieve with our mouths locked in unison until Dave suddenly, without any kind of prior warning, vomited into my mouth. This act caused me to vomit all over Dave and the next thing I knew Dave was bouncing about on what not two seconds ago was his death bed despite being covered in sick and wearing on his head what looked for all the world to be a very large red, nylon thong. I calmed Dave down and then gently picked them carefully off Dave's head and held them up to Nicky.

'I believe these our yours.' I told her.

For a brief moment the room was silent again. Then someone started clapping. Then someone else joined in and before long the whole place was in uproar with people shouting and cheering.

'He's saved Dave!' Somebody shouted.

' The lad has only gone and saved Dave!'

Then everyone started to sing, "for he's a jolly good fellow," which until then I thought only happened in black and white films but rather than being cringy as fuck for some reason I felt overwhelmed with pride and joy.

The next thing I knew Nicky ran over to me and kissed me full on the mouth and told me I was her hero. I had to admire her commitment for that. I gave her back her underwear and told her that it was my pleasure and no big deal.

Then everyone started coming up to me and patting me on the back and ruffling my hair and fucking up my perfect quiff but I didn't mind because due to more luck than judgment I'd somehow saved the day and now I'd been accepted by this mob and it felt great.

Even the two school girls came up to me and though it pained me to do so, as I didn't want to risk being called a fucking nonce cunt again, I made sure to keep my cock well out of their way while they hugged me.

Then Michaela came up to me with a can of coke and after I'd gargled with it and spat it back out into the pint glass she'd had the foresight to provide, she also kissed me and her tongue went right into my mouth and then she pressed her pubic bone hard up against my cock and whispered in my ear, 'You belong to me now Johnny Capone. You're my hero and tonight you're in for a night you're never going to forget.' and I felt happier than I'd ever felt in my entire life. Then I saw June approaching. Michaela slid off me and said, 'I'm just gonna leave you two to chat for a bit. Clear the air like. Be careful she doesn't try and stick a finger in your arse.'

Fuck me you really could not keep a secret around here. June came up to me and kissed me on the cheek.

'Well I hear it was all just a bit of a misunderstanding Johnny so we're friends again and you're welcome here any time you like... but it obviously goes without saying that if you ever harm her that girl in any way shape or form, you're going to have to deal with me.' She told me. Then she squeezed my balls.

My mind went back to our last liaison and it took all my will power not to burst out laughing. June was the first person not related to me that I'd seen naked though and she'd also shown me some kindness at a time when I had sorely needed it so I vowed there and then to be respectful to her.

'Listen June, I replied,' I adore Michaela, surely you must know that. I would never harm here or take the piss. She's the most awesome person I've ever met and I'm privileged just to know her let alone be her boyfriend... Yes, it's no secret that I am clearly a psychopath but I'd have to be a totally different kind of mental to fuck this up.'

Just as I said those words the lady in the dirty rain coat threw a glass at my head and called me a fucking nonce cunt.

'Abby no! He's not a nonce! It's a very nice young man! Now say sorry!' June told her.

'Sorry about that son. She's off her pills again you see? I keep telling her. I say "Abby, you must take your pills or you'll hear all those voices again and we can't have that it in here" I tell her. She's usually good as gold apart from the smell of piss and the random violence.'

   I walked over to her and I took a pill out of my bag and I gave it to her. 'Take that Abby and tell me how you get on' I told her, 'If you like them I've got loads. You can have them on the house.'

Then I said to June, 'Do you and Del want a couple? They make you feel all loved up.'

'Oh do they? Yeah go on then. How much are they?' June replied.

'I'm going to sell them for twenty quid each but you can have these two for free,' I told her as I put two pills into her hand. 'If it wasn't for you then I'd probably never had met Michaela so I owe you one.'

'Well that's very kind of you Johnny. I'll slip one in his whiskey tonight and shave my cunt.' June replied.

'Yeah you do that June and let me know how you get on. And if any of your customers want any drugs just let me know. Pills, coke, weed, hash, speed ... Sanatogen.' I replied.

'You're a cheeky bugger Johnny McQueen. But yes I'm sure I can shift some for you. This lot love to party when they're in the right mood.' June laughed.

'Nice one June. Right then we're off. See you later.' I replied as I watched Michaela putting on her coat. Then I kissed her on the cheek. 'Oh yeah and sorry about the mess! I think it was Hitler over there that did most of the throwing!'

'Don't you worry about any of that, you just concentrate on showing that girl a good time.' June replied. 'Now you take good care of yourself and our Michaela son. Have a lovely evening and don't do anything I wouldn't do!'

'Well that doesn't leave me with many options!' I laughed, although we both knew that June was an absolute cock hound and would literally do anything sexual to anyone.

Michaela ran up to me, jumped into my arms and then smothered me with kisses and then whispered into my ear, 'Take me away from all this and treat me like the princess I was fucking well born to be.'

'That would be my absolute pleasure you fucking goddess.' I replied and then we fucked off.

Chapter Sixteen

As soon as we left June's cafe Michaela put her arm around me and squeezed me and kissed my neck and then she let go and immediately held my hand and then she let go of my hand and put her arm back around me again and squeezed me and kissed my neck. It was awesome and as we walked down the street I felt I was walking on the moon.

'Have you ever been in love Johnny Capone?' Michaela asked me with a twinkle in her eye.

'Well there was this one girl.' I replied, 'She was the most beautiful girl I'd ever seen and she was funny and intelligent and she loved animals, especially scruffy old dogs and her arse was so tiny and pert and her bum hole tasted like sweets...'

'No Johnny! Stop! Oh you were doing so well up until the bum hole bit!' Michaela protested.

'I'm sorry Michaela that was inappropriate but it tasted so amazing I just wanted you to know! I was trying to pay you a compliment !' I replied.

'Yes well thank you and I appreciate the thought but from now on please try and be a bit more discrete!' Michaela replied, 'Especially when we're out... Although when you're cock is inside me you can be as fucking indiscrete as you like! In fact I insist on it! ...Okay now tell me how good my little cunt tastes so you've got it out of your system and then we can go get something to eat because I'm fucking starving and you'll need a full belly because you're going to be fucking me all me all night.'

   I stopped her in her tracks and span here around until she faced me. Then, under the yellow glow of the street lamps, I looked into her beautiful green eyes and said, 'Michaela, your cunt tastes delicious.'

   Then we snogged. It was my first proper snog. At first I think we clashed teeth because of my inexperience and eagerness but after a while we found our rhythm and I was in paradise. I could have stayed like that all evening but after a few delirious minutes Michaela pushed me away and said, 'Well that's my briefs soaked and they were brand new on and we've only gone a few hundred yards. Fuck me you've got the gift.' And then she bit my lip so hard she drew blood.

'Oops, sorry. Hope I didn't hurt you.' She said with a smirk.

'No. It was nice. I liked it. You can do whatever you like to me. And for your information I know that the correct terminology is not in fact, briefs, but dung hampers.' I replied with a grin.

Michaela looked at me and sighed. 'Oh my oh my mister Johnny Capone, you might just be the one. You could be the one I've been waiting for.'

Then she looked left and right in a conspiratorial manner, and seeing that the coast was clear she squeezed my bollocks and said,' I'm assuming that you kept your promise?'

I replied,'If you continue to do that for much longer then you're going to find out young lady and it won't just be your "briefs" that are ruined. I'm fit to bursting.'

'I thought as much when I saw that giving Dave mouth to mouth was giving you a hard-on.' Michaela giggled.'

'Yeah there was just something about that little furry little mother fucker that just got me at it and if it hadn't been for the promise I'd made to you I'd have surely flipped the little cunt over and given him a right good seeing to, right there and then, in front of everyone.' I replied trying not to laugh.

'Oh I don't doubt that for one minute you dirty little boy. You do look like the kind of boy who'd lose his virginity in side an old dog while it was choking to death.' Michaela giggled and then she started barking.

'Woof! Woof! Do you like that Johnny? Hmm? Is that turning you on? Woof! Woof! Or are you more of a yappy kind of boy? Yap! Yap yap! Yap! Is that more your style you absolute rotter?' Michaela asked playfully.

'You're my style.' I laughed.

'Good. I'm glad tot hear it. And you're my style. Now feed me. I haven't eaten a thing all day just so that I'd look good in this dress.' Michaela replied.

As I gazed in awe at this absolute deity of a girl I wouldn't have cared less if she was wearing an old sack to our date. Actually that would have been rather sexy. Everything she said and everything she did was sexy though. I didn't know if it was the drugs wearing off or just the momentous occasion that I now found myself in but I was suddenly close to tears.

'I'm in love with you Michaela.' I told her.

'Good.' And I'm in love with you Johnny.' She replied.

'Well that's settled then.' I said.

'Yes. That's settled then.' She replied.

Then she lifted up my chin into the light and said, 'Hang on. Are you crying?'

'No!' I replied indignantly while pulling my face away.

'Yes you are! She said lovingly. ' You're crying! Oh my God you sweet boy! That's the most adorable thing I've ever seen!'

'I'm not even crying! You're crying! I'm not sweet! I'm a ruthless psychopath! And even If I was crying, which I'm not, it's only because you look so fat in that dress and not at all sexy as hell! So if anyone should be crying it's you! You fat bitch!' I replied furiously wiping away my tears.

Michaela then kissed my face and said, 'It's okay for boys to cry Johnny! ...Hang on a minute! You really do love me! I can tell! Oh my God Johnny! You really do love me! I can actually tell! I can feel it! In my belly! This is really it! You love me and I love you! Fuck it now I'm crying! All my makeup! It'll be ruined!'

'Are you even wearing makeup?' I asked her.

'Well no, but that's not the point. I'm naturally beautiful and I don't need it.' She giggled as she wiped away her own tears.

'That's a fact.' I told her. 'Well what is the point then?' I asked.

'The point is that you love me and I love you and that's the fucking point Johnny Capone!' She replied delightedly.

'You're not really fat.' I told her. 'And even if you were fat and you were standing there wearing an old sack all fat and stupid looking I'd still love you. I want you to know that.'

'You'd probably like that though wouldn't you?' Michaela replied, 'You bloody pervert! I bet if I turned up to this date wearing an old sack and no "dung hampers" you'd probably just get your cock out and start wanking it off until you shot your filthy load all over me! You ruddy little rascal! Ruining my lovely sack on our first date! What a disrespectful little shit cunt! What do I see in you Johnny Capone? What do I ever see in you?'

'Fuck knows but whatever it is please don't ever stop loving me.' I replied solemnly.

Michaela then took my head in both her hands and said, 'Okay then. Now shut up and put your tongue in my mouth my darling baby boy.'

Then we snogged again and I could taste her salty tears and I was sure that she could taste mine. I'd never been happier in my entire life but as we kissed all I kept thinking about was trying not to cream my jeans. After about five minutes I reluctantly pulled away and said. 'You need to keep your tongue out of my mouth until we are somewhere more private because it's taking all my will-power not to cum in my pants.'

Michaela giggled and said,'Okay baby let's go. We need to fix this right away before our little problem starts getting in the way of our date.'

Then she took my hand and started to run down the street. Suddenly she stopped and said, 'This one will do. Right then get down there.' and pointed to a basement flat.

I did as I was told and the next thing I knew we were down the steps. It was dark and secluded and perfect for what she had in mind.

'Take off your jacket and give it to me. I'm not getting dirty knees and who knows what the fuck is on this floor.' She whispered. '...And don't make a noise, we don't want to be disturbed.'

I gave her my jacket and she laid it on the ground and then knelt on it. Then she looked up at me and said, 'I'm going to suck you off. If that's okay obviously.'

'Yes. That's absolutely fine by me.' I replied in a low voice. 'That will be not be a problem at all.'

Then the next thing I knew she'd pulled down my trousers and pants and put my cock in her mouth. Then she immediately took it out again and in a harsh whisper, said, 'Do not push my head up and down! You are not in some ridiculous porno! If you push my head up and down I'm going to stop and you'll have to just have a wank Johnny! If I choke I'm going to puke right into your fucking "bloomers" so put your hands behind your head and let me do what I do best! I've sucked off thousands of lads so I know what I'm doing!'

'Thousands? Really?' I asked her. I tried to be cool but I couldn't help but think that was quite a large figure for one so young.

Michaela took my cock out of her mouth again, looked back up at me and replied, 'I'm seventeen Johnny! What can I say! I was a late starter! I come from a deeply religious family! Well excuse me! I'm sorry that I'm not more experienced like your previous girls! I'll do the best I can with my limited experience, okay! Jesus! Can we just get on with this please?' Then she put my cock back in her mouth.

Eh? Late starter? Deeply religious? What the fuck? Did she think that wasn't even a large number? Oh well I didn't want her to think that I was being judgmental and at least she must have a good idea what she was doing I guess.

   Thousands? Fucking hell I didn't even think that there was even a thousand guys in this town! I had to be cool though or I could blow the whole thing. I loved her and if she'd sucked all that cock before mine then I'd just have to wear it.

'No! I wasn't being judgmental! No that's loads! Thousands is a big number in my opinion! That's a huge number! So well done for managing to suck that amount of cock while coming from such a religious family!' I told her and then inexplicably, I patted her head.

   Michaela took my cock back out of her mouth and whispered angrily and rather loudly, 'Did you just pat my head?'

'Yes but I didn't mean to! I was just trying to be encouraging! Seriously though? Thousands?' Really? You've sucked off thousands of lads?' I replied, but even though I was trying to be laid back about it I couldn't help but picture thousands of other guy's dicks going in and out of my girlfriend's mouth like a conveyor belt and then cumming all over her face. No wonder her skin looked so good.

'Of course not you soppy cunt!'Fuck me Johnny really? Did you really think that I'd sucked off thousands of lads? Do I look like a fucking slag to you Johnny? Do I have stretch marks around my fucking gob?' Michaela replied angrily.

'No!' I replied. 'Oh my God no! You look nothing like a slag!Oh fuck me that's a relief I ain't gonna lie! No! No way! I just thought that you might be one of those 'empowered' geezer type birds like you see on channel four and that! ...You know drinking pints and fighting and fucking loads of men the same way as some men behave just to prove you're as cool as us or whatever! ...I just wanted you to think I was cool about you sucking off thousands of cocks! I'm not really though. I know I should be cool about it but the thought of it makes me want to vomit actually.'

'Johnny you need to stop talking right now.' Michaela replied.' You're digging yourself into a very deep pit babe. Of course I haven't sucked off thousands of lads you cheeky cunt! Are there even that amount of men in this town? So you were quite happy for me to have sucked off the whole town plus a few more is that it? And as for the drinking and fighting and fucking to prove we were as cool as men well...'

   I loved her but I just wanted her to suck me off so I could think straight again. It was torture being this close.

'Oh my God I'm so sorry Michaela!' I replied,'I'm just a fifteen year old boy and I'm ignorant as fuck! I don't know what to say! Tell me what to say and how to behave and I'll do it!'

   Michaela then looked up at me and giggled. 'I'm just fucking with you Johnny. I don't care about the politics of blow jobs I just want your bollocks empty so we can go and eat. I was just having a bit of fun at your expense. Now then, lean up again that front door and keep your hands behind your head and let me do my work. Oh and for your information I've only had one serious boyfriend before you came along. So chill.' Then she put my cock back in her mouth.

   Fuck me what a mind fuck. Was it double standards and sexist not to want your bird to have sucked off loads of men before she got to yours? I mean up until I'd met Michaela I wanted to shag pretty much anyone and everyone with a vagina and a pair of tits. Even Nicky back there and she was definitely no oil painting. Now was not the time for these thoughts though and plus I didn't know and neither did I care to be honest. I was just happy that my own cock was getting sucked at that very moment and as much as I was enjoying it I just wanted to cum so that I could indeed 'chill.'

  I did as I was told and leaned back on the door, closed my eyes and revelled in the sensation of my dick being inside Michaela's beautiful soft, warm mouth. It wouldn't be long now, I thought to myself. I did wonder what she meant by only having one 'serious' boyfriend though. Did she mean that all the others were not serious and just kept pissing about making jokes or did she mean that she had one serious boyfriend before she met me and the rest were just one night stands that had shagged her and then left the next morning?

  Or maybe they just bent her over a skip down some ally and after they'd chucked their muck up her and wiped their filthy cocks on her dress had then gone back inside the boozer to laugh about it with their mates?

Those fucking cunts I'll kill them all! How fucking dare they disrespect Michaela like that?! I was livid.

 Michaela took my cock out of her mouth and asked me if I was okay.

'Yes I'm fine,' I lied. Why do you asked?'

'Well only because your willy has gone all small. Have you got something on your mind?' She replied.

I decided to just tell her the truth.

'When you said you only had one serious boyfriend before me did you mean that all the others were comedians or where the rest all one night stands?' I asked her.

'Jesus Johnny. You're a little bit insecure aren't you? Why does it really matter? I'm here with you now. Isn't that enough? It's not like you didn't come in June's wig while her finger was rammed up your arse hole now was it? Or your auntie didn't sit on your face and whatever else the fuck you got up to now is it?' Michaela replied.

'I wanked off a transvestite.' I replied.

'Well good for you Johnny. Oh look at that! Your cock is starting to get hard again! Would you prefer it if I had a big cock too Baby!' Michaela teased and then she started to wank me off. 'You like that my darling little baby boy?' Then she spat on the end and sucked and licked my helmet. Then she stopped and said,

'It's actually none of your fucking business but I've had one serious boyfriend, which lasted about six months and before that I'd only been finger banged and licked out, and that was at school. Happy now?'

'Yep.' I moaned.

'Right then, let's finish this.' She replied and then she stuck a finger up my arse and sucked hard on my bell-end. 'That's it baby! Good boy. Cum for me Johnny... Cum for me my darling baby boy... My little gangster mother fucker...'

As she was getting more and more into it her voice was getting louder and louder.

'Would you like to watch me finger fuck myself Baby? Would that make you cum? You want me to spread my legs and frig the fuck out of my tiny, wet little cunt? Is that what you want? Let me get that fucking devil juice out of you and down my throat baby! ...Would you like that Johnny? Would you like to give me both barrels down my throat right this instant?'

'Yes.' I moaned.

'Yes what?' Cried Michaela as she furiously wanked me off.

'Yes please baby.' I replied.

By this stage even if she's asked me to call her daddy I would have because there was no turning back now and I was ready to explode.

'GIVE IT TO ME BABY! GIVE ME THAT FUCKING LOAD RIGHT NOW! FUCK MY FACE! FUCK MY FACE JOHNNY! I WANT IT! GIVE ME YOUR FUCKNG SPUNK! NOW! ' She screamed.

And then she started to suck on my balls and wank my cock and run her tongue up and down my shaft and her finger was still embedded in my arse. Maybe June had taught her that move? Finally, after all this time, I'd reached the point of no return. Here we go. Lift off!

Just then the front door opened and a voice shouted. 'Who is it! What's all this racket? What's going on out there!'

As the door opened I went flying backwards and Michaela, still being on her knees, with one hand inside her knickers fell backwards in the opposite direction and onto the concrete floor. This mother fucker's timing could not have been any worse because as they came outside to see what the fuck was actually happening I couldn't help but shoot my considerable load all over them. Three full days worth and some change cascaded all over the poor cunt. Wave after wave of hot salty man fat covered the poor bastard and there was nothing that I could do to stem the tide.

  I'd had my eyes screwed up tight just as I'd always done a million times before as I shot my load so I couldn't really gage the situation until I'd finished but when I saw what had actually occurred I prayed to all the saints that I would be able to go back in time and for none of this to have ever happened.

  As I lay there in the doorway with my jeans and pants around my ankles and my rapidly shrinking cock in one hand, instinctively squeezing out the last remnants of my bollock babies, I looked up and to my horror discovered that I'd just emptied my pods over a child! A really ugly, wrinkled and grotesque looking little boy!

'Oh my God! I'm so sorry son! For fuck's sake please don't don't tell your mum! It was an accident! Oh fuck me I'm so sorry!' I said as quietly as I could. It was now my turn to be doing the loud whispering just in case his fucking parents came to see what all the fuss was about only to find that I'd given their kid a cum bath.

'Listen mate it was all a misunderstanding! Look! That's my girlfriend! Over there! Um Tracy! Yes that's it! Her name is Tracy!' I told him and pointed to Michaela who was still sprawled out on the concrete in front of us.

 'Yeah and my name is ... fucking.... hang on ... what is it again? I know! It's David! Yes we're Tracy and David! And we're not from around here either! We are out of towners! We came here for a dirty weekend you see and we'd had a couple of drinks and then we came down here, as in your parent's gaff, for a quiet little nosh because my bollocks ... I mean my balls were so full it was driving me mental, you must know what that's like mate! What are you, about twelve? Thirteen maybe? You're probably wanking half a dozen times a day minimum right?' I babbled, and was about to give him a high five until I remembered he was now covered in my spunk.

'Yeah, but I haven't had a wank in three days! I continued. 'Four really! So you must know how fucking insane I was feeling right? So anyway I started to get all insecure and lost my erection right so then Mich... Tracey, started giving it the old sex talk which, give her her due, immediately got me right back on track but it seems like Tracy here is a bit loud, anyway I had every intention of cumming in her mouth and not over you but then you opened the door and I stumbled and fell behind it and just at the exact moment I was about to cum so when you popped your head round there was fuck all I could do to stop myself from giving you a right royal pearl necklace by the looks of it!' It then fumbled for my wallet and said, 'Here you go son look! How about I give you one hundred pounds and you don't tell your mum and dad anything about what just happened here? Tracy, do you have a tissue in your purse for this young man's boat please?'

'I don't own a purse Dave. Maybe you've got one in YOUR purse? ...David.' Replied Michaela.

'Twelve or thirteen? Twelve or fucking thirteen? You cheeky little cunt! I'm fifty four I'll have you know!' Replied the recipient of my 'devil juice.'

'Fuck me' I replied, 'you've had a hard paper round ain't you mate?!' I thought that this little joke my lighten the mood but if anything it just made matters worse.

'I'm not a boy I'm a dwarf! He replied.

'Oh thank fuck for that!' I replied,'What a relief!'

'What a relief? What a fucking relief?'' replied the dwarf. 'So it's okay to cum all over a dwarf is it?'

'Well if I had the choice between cumming over a child and cumming over a dwarf then yes I'd say it was mate! People don't take kindly to covering there kids in dirty concrete around here you know! In fact they veritably frown upon it! Don't they Tracy?'

'Och I the noo!' Replied Michaela, 'now then bonny lad don't you be tryin' tae drag me into your wee mess Davy boy! Twas your idea to come to this town for a wee dirty weekend so it was and nooo mistake, gawd blimey love a duck, so it was, and no the mine! And it wasne me who shot their load over this fine gentleman either so it wasn't … the noo … so I'd thank you to keep me out of this please and let's get back to bonny Scotland!'

Oh it was a Scottish accent she was trying to do! Fuck me that was awful, but still a good idea disguising her voice. What a gal.

'You an Indian lady?' Replied the dwarf. 'I've been to India. I was in the merchant navy. Been all over the world I have. I've seen a lot of things I have. Things that would make your hair curl some of them. Cor blimey, love a duck and no mistake? What's that mean then? Never mind. This isn't even the first time someone has emptied his bollocks over me either. Or the second.'

'Really?' I asked him.

'Well of course it is you dumb arse! Fuck me, how unlucky would that be?' The dwarf replied. 'And I'm sorry 'son' but would you mind pulling up your trousers and pants and putting your penis away please. It's really quite distracting... Which is surprising what with it being so small and all.'

'Yeah well it's only small now but it wasn't a minute ago before I came all over you. Accidentally came all over you.' I replied grumpily, while quickly doing as he'd asked.

Then the dwarf peered through the darkness at Michaela and said, 'Hang on, is that you Michaela? From June's cafe?'

'Steve? Oh God Steve! Hello! Oh God this is embarrassing! Yes it's me! I didn't know you'd moved back here! How long have you lived down here then?'Michalea replied.

'Michaela! I should have guessed! I thought that sex talk rang a bell but I couldn't place it!' Replied Steve.

Then he looked back at me and said, 'Did she suck your balls mate? Finger up the arse? Was that the bit that made you shoot your load son? She's very good isn't she?'

Fuck me gently. Trust me to come all over Michaela's fifty four year old, dwarf, ex boyfriend. Unless this fucker was one of the jammy bastards who fingered her or licked her out when she was a school girl? He's old as fuck though so unless he used to dress up like a school boy in order to get his tiny little mitts on school girls, which by looking at him, even I doubt, he must have been one of her teachers.

Teachers were always trying to shag the fit birds at my school. And even some of the more ropey ones too. Especially the PE teachers and the drama teachers. The dirty bastards. It was no wonder that half the girls in my year were already mums with that lot preying on them from all sides. And if they did manage to fend off the teachers, sooner or later there would be a good chance that at least one of the hotter ones would be kidnapped and murdered by the care taker.

Caretakers were always child killers or potential child killers. It was part of their job description. If a kid went missing the caretaker would always put his hand up first to join the hunt and you would actually see the cunt on the six o'clock news being interviewed and he'd be saying, "yeah it's a dreadful shame that Sandra has gone missing, she was a cracking young girl and an absolute delight to be around, she always used to pop into my shed and we'd smoke fags and I'd buy her little gifts …" and then he'd lick his lips and say … "Yeah so if anyone has any information please come forward" etc. etc. while he's probably wearing her skin under his overalls. If I was a detective and I had to investigate the disappearance of a school girl the first thing I'd do would be to kick down the front door of the school's caretaker and arrest the cunt and even if he wasn't guilty I'd lock him up just out of principle to be on the safe side. Come to think about it, this little prick looked a bit like a caretaker actually.

'You two know each other then?' I asked him.

'Yes. I know Michaela very well.' Steve smirked and then they both laughed.

   After hearing this I instinctively put my hand on my gun and thought very hard about shooting the cunt in the throat but I didn't want to risk spoiling our date.

'Cool! Glad to hear it.' I lied.

'Oh yes Johnny me and Steve go way back!' Michaela laughed.

   Maybe I should shoot them both? I decided to give them one more chance to explain what the fuck was happening here before I abruptly ended our date due to one of the participants being recently deceased.

'Wow guys this is great! You know what, I would really love to know how you two met and your relationship!' I asked them trying to sound light hearted and fucking jovial as a mother fucker.

   I didn't care if they'd constantly fucked the shit out of each other and carried vials of each other's blood around their fucking necks at this point, it was the smirking and these little in- jokes that was winding me up now.

'Me and Steve used to fuck Johnny!' Michaela replied matter of factly.

'Oh yes Johnny me and Michaela fucked for a good six months in all sorts of ways!' Said Steve.

'Oh wow that's so great!' I replied. 'Well done you two!'

I was trying to be cool because even though that news made me feel physically sick I did understand that people fucked and then broke up and not everyone was a virgin like me, even dwarves. I would just have to suck it up and be mature about it. It was another learning curve and a life lesson and I decided to do my best not to sulk about it.

'Yes it was great! Sometimes we would fuck twice a day! Three times on the weekends!' Continued Michaela full of fucking merriment.

'Sometimes we'd get a round of applause and even a standing ovation!' Steve laughed and then they both doubled up.

So they were exhibitionists! Erotic entertainers in a circus! Clown fuckers! I bet they fucked on elephants and

Steve here stuck his little dwarf cock into the mouths of lions while Michaela sucked his balls and put her fingers up his arse! It all started to make sense.

'Well good for you two!' I told them still not sure whether to murder them both and then go back to see if Sally still wanted me to shag her. Or her mum. Or the pair of them.

'We're just teasing you Johnny!' Michaela suddenly shouted and came over and hugged me.

'I'm sorry for being cruel but it was just too good an opportunity to miss! I'm sure you would have done the same under the circumstances! Oh my God and you were so sweet about it!'

'Hang on so you're not a clown fucker?' I replied, dazed and confused.

'Clown fucker? So you think I'm a clown? Is that it? Because I'm a dwarf? I'm an actor you horrible little prick!' Said Steve all disgruntled and upset.

'No! Of course not! Don't be ridiculous Steve! I told him while doing my best to frantically think on my feet.'That would be a dreadful thing to suggest! No, I naturally thought that you and Michaela fucked on an elephant and then you jumped down and put your knob inside a lion's mouth ... and then... well... and then Michaela sucked your balls and stuck her fingers up your arse ... while getting scuttled BY clowns! So I didn't think you were a clown at all! You were just you! A dwarf! Not a clown! See? Actually it was a little bit rude of you to think that of me but no harm done. I accept your apology.'

'Apology? Fuck off! I'm not apologising!' Replied Steve indignantly. 'You should be the one apologising for assuming that just because I'm a dwarf I was some kind of fucking circus act! And a very dark, odd circus act as well by the sounds of it!'

Michaela then stopped hugging and kissing me and said, 'Scuttled by clowns? Let me get this straight. You thought that me and Steve were some kind of circus act in which we fucked on an elephant and then Steve jumped down and put his knob inside the mouth of a lion while I licked his balls and stuck my fingers in his arse, while getting scuttled by clowns?'

'Sucked.' I replied.

'Sucked?' asked Michaela.

'Yes.' I told her.

'Sucked?' She asked again.

'Well you said 'licked' by what I said was 'sucked.' I replied. 'But it's okay I understood what you meant.'

Then I looked at my watch and said, 'Shouldn't we be going babe? Please to meet you Steve. We really must do this again soon!'

And then I tried to kiss her but for some reason she seemed upset, and then she headbutted me. She was probably hungry and this was making her a bit moody. Steve was probably a bit peckish too because then he came over and kicked me in the nuts, and surprisingly hard too for someone taking such a small swing.

'Right then, if we're all done her I think we should eat!' I said to Michaela.

'Well I think you need to apologise to Steve first.' Michaela replied.

Even though I wasn't really sure why I should be the one to apologise seeing as though it was Steve that had kicked me in the nuts I decided to be the bigger man and do as I was asked.

'Sorry Steve.' I told the cunt.

'And what are you sorry for exactly?' Asked Steve.

Sorry that I didn't put a fucking bullet in your massive fucking head about ten minutes ago. That was what I wanted to say anyway but instead I said, 'I'm sorry I got all jealous thinking about you and my girlfriend shagging twice a day and three times on weekends while everyone around you was clapping and cheering. My imagination ran away with me because I'm so insecure and also so in love with Michaela, and the thought of anyone, especially a handsome man such as yourself, even looking at her with even the slightest hint of sexual intent, let alone putting their fingers inside her vagina or licking her vagina or god forbid, actually fucking her vagina feels me with such anguish and sadness right deep down in the pit of my soul that it made me react in a vulgar and disrespectful way towards you.'

There was a moment's silence as I waited for another kicking but mercifully that didn't happen. Instead Michaela said, 'So I'm officially your girlfriend then? Okay I accept!' And then she kissed me on the mouth. And then Steve said,' So you think I'm handsome then eh? Okay I accept your apology son. And I apologise for winding you up.' Then he shook my hand.

Well fuck knows how I got away with that but I did.

'Come on baby let's go.' Michaela said and put her arm around me.

'See you soon Steve! Pop into the cafe and we can have a proper catch-up without Johnny and his fucked up imagination getting in the way!' She told him,

'Yes see you soon Michaela! By Johnny! See you soon too I hope son!' Shouted Steve as we made our way up the steps and back out onto the street.

'Sorry for spunking all over your face and neck Steve!' I shouted back just as an old lady was walking past. Without even looking up the old lady just shrugged and said, 'Don't tell me son, it's a long story and not what I'm thinking! Don't worry I've heard it all before!'

'Nope, It's pretty much exactly what you're thinking! My girlfriend was noshing me off down there when a dwarf came out to see what all the noise was, which was mostly me moaning in ecstasy due to getting wanked and sucked off while having a finger rammed up my arse, and when he shoved the door open and popped his head out, my girlfriend, who was fingering herself at the same time, fell backwards and I somehow ended up coming all over him! He's an actor by all accounts.'

'Oh that's nice son.' The old lady replied.' Well as long as no one got hurt. That's all that matters love. It's very good for the skin, Harry Monk is. Good for the complexion. If you're girlfriend is too prudish to swallow it you should bottle it. I'd buy a jar of teenage spunk and so would my friend Gladys! And Mavis...' She didn't break her stride.

'I fell backwards and it came out of my mouth just as he was cumming!' Michaela shouted after her. 'I would have swallowed it! I was looking forward to it all day!Even though he smokes and his diet is dreadful! I wanted three days of his nut custard down me as an aperitif! I'm starving! I haven't eaten all day so that I'd look good in this dress!'

'Let it go babe. Let it go. She's gone now.' I told her.

'Yeah but I don't want her to think that I'm the kind of girlfriend who doesn't swallow Johnny!' She replied.

'It's okay baby. It's okay. Anyone only has to look at you to know that you're a swallower.' I reassured her.

'Do they Johnny? Really?'

'Yes baby.' I replied.

'Thank you baby. That means a lot. I love you baby.' Michaela replied.

'And I love you too baby.' I told her.

'Did you really think that I was a clown fucker baby? Michaela asked.

'No baby.' I replied, but we both knew that I did.

Chapter Seventeen

It had been a full day to say the least and hopefully the evening would also be as eventful. I took my girl's hand and we strolled along the street just being happy to be in each other's company.

'I like it when I hear you tell people I'm your girlfriend.' Michaela told me.

'Good because I love telling people.' I replied.

'What do you think people think when they see us together? Do you think that we look good together?' Michaela asked.

'They probably look at you, then they look at me and think that I'm either hung or rich!' I laughed.

'No way! I bet they don't think you're hung Johnny!' Michaela replied.

'Why the fuck not?' I asked her. The cheeky bint.

'Well a girl can tell if a man is hung by the way they walk.' She replied.

'And how do these hung mother fuckers walk then?' I asked her.

'Well like they've got a big dick!' She said.

Then she ran in front of me and started strutting about, presumably pretending like she was a man with a big cock.

'No you look like a man who has just shit their pants.' I told her.

'Well you'd know all about that wouldn't you baby!' She laughed.

'Well how do I walk then? Can you tell how big my cock is by the way I walk?' I asked her studiously ignoring her last remark.

'Yes.' She replied.

'Well? Go on then?' I demanded.

'Well I've seen it haven't I? It's been in my mouth! So you could accuse me of cheating.' She replied.

'Okay then let's imagine that you hadn't seen it or had it in your mouth and you see me walking towards you, how big would you think my dick is?' I asked.

'Well I'd know that it was exactly the size it is!' Michaela replied. 'Why are men obsessed with the size of their dicks? Girls don't care about that! They'd rather a boy was nice and kind and considerate and thoughtful than a boy who was hung but an absolute cunt bubble! In the long term anyway!'

'Fuck off! I replied. 'That's what girls say to guys with tiny cocks! Oh fuck me do I have a tiny cock Michaela? How do I compare to all your other boyfriends? The serious one and all the others who just fingered you and licked you out? Hang on, what do you mean by, in the long term anyway?'

'I was joking Johnny!' Michaela replied. 'You have a lovely penis babe! And it's a very respectable size! Yours is pretty which I'd take all day long over a big, fat, ugly one! If they're too big it hurts anyway! So relax. You should have seen the size of that one of the clowns who was fucking me! Those big shoes he wore were taking the fucking piss! Little titchy thing it was! I'll tell you that! What a swizz! It did honk when pressed though!'

'Would you not rather have bigger tits then?' I asked her.

'What the fuck Johnny! Well not until right this very minute you massive dickhead!' She replied and then slapped me around the head.

'I was just making a point!' I protested. 'I love your tits! They are perfect! You are perfect! I wouldn't care if your tits were huge or non-existent! I'd still love you even if you had a row of teats running down your belly! The thing about your tits are that they're pretty! I'd rather have a girlfriend with small, pretty tits than some bird with huge big veiny ones, all covered in stretch marks and hairs all over her nipples! Big tits hurt!'

'Touché' needle dick. Touché!' Michaela replied.

'Touché yourself tiny tits!' I replied.

Then we both swaggered down the road like we both had big dicks and huge tits.

'What do you want to eat then baby? I would have booked us somewhere but because you're so skinny I didn't know if you had some kind of eating disorder and would rather sit in the park and eat some bog roll or munch on a bit of grass or whatever you lot do for sustenance. Plus I don't know how to make a reservation for a restaurant but I'll ask the cunts so I know for next time.

'I'm not skinny you cheeky cunt. I'm slim.' Michaela replied. 'And I'll have you know I have a perfectly healthy appetite. I eat like a fucking horse actually and you're just about to find that out. And you'll need to eat too because I'm not going to put up with you just climbing on me and immediately cumming as soon as you enter my sacred treasure like a two pump Charlie mother fucker and expecting that to be it. You won't be running off to tell your mates you've finally lost your virginity until you've sexually satisfied me and that may take all night. Or even days due to your tiny little clown cock. So you'd better eat up bitch.'

That sounded absolutely fine by me. I was happy to spend the rest of my life trying to sexually satisfy her or die trying.

'Well that sounds like a plan baby.' I told her. ' We both know it's my first time so neither of us is going to be surprised if I'm initially shit at it. Especially me. This takes the pressure off me as both our expectations are going to be low.'

'Well I'm not exactly experienced either!' Michaela replied.

'Well Steve seems to think you know your way around a cock.' I told her.

'Fuck me Johnny that was a joke! We were in this play and we had to be lovers! It was hilarious! I was dressed like a sheep and Steve was dressed up like a lion! It was avant guard! It was supposed to be a serious play but everyone just laughed there heads off!'

'So you didn't suck his balls and put your finger up his arse?' I asked her.

'Well yes of course I did because it was in the script!' Michaela replied.

'Was it?' I asked.

'No! Of course fucking not you absolute bell-end!' She laughed.

'Yeah well I knew that I was just playing along.' I lied.

   then took my head in both of her hands and said, 'Listen Johnny. This is everything. I got licked out twice by the same boy. Both times we were drunk on cider and both times it was shit. Then I got fingered one time by another boy for about ten seconds when I was in Geography. And then I had a relationship with another boy and it was shit most of the time and we argued more than we fucked. Okay?'

'Well what about the clown?' I asked her.

'Yeah well the clown fucked me loads of times! Right in my arse too Johnny! And guess what? While he was busy rupturing my colon, Steve, for some reason, known only to you, kept sticking his knob in a lion's mouth while I sucked and licked his fucking ball bag you soppy cunt! I've already done more with you than I've ever done with anybody so chill the fuck out! The past is the past and if you're going to get all sticky about it then maybe we should finish this before it gets too deep. Jealousy will kill even the best relationship so bear that in mind.' Michaela replied.

'I'm sorry Michaela. I'm sorry I'm so insecure.' I told her. ' I can't help it. Nobody has ever given a shit about me before. Especially someone as hot as you! You're not even niche hot! You're what everyone would describe as being hot, hot! I love you that's all and it's bringing out parts of me that I don't like but I'm dealing with it. I've dealt with it. It's done. I've got my head around it now. I just have to deal with dating a really hot girl and I need to come to terms with all that means and I hope you can still find it in your heart to piss on my face while you use me as some kind of living, breathing dildo.'

'You are forgiven but if you still keep fucking moaning about the past I reserve the right to headbutt you because I won't be having it ruining what we've got.' Michaela replied.'Do we have a deal?'

'Yes, we have a deal.' I told her.

'Now feed me bitch.' Michaela replied, so we headed into town.

'I've never been to a restaurant before Michaela so you're going to have to forgive my ignorance in these matters.' I told her. 'I've been to loads of pubs though and recently I've been frequenting a rather lovely little cafe but that's only because I wanted to shag one of the waitresses.'

'I'm not just a waitress you rude little prick I'm the assistant manager!' Michaela replied indignantly.

'How do you know I was talking about you? That place is full of hot chicks! Fuck me there's nothing wrong with your ego is there?!' I replied.

'It's funny that all the staff who work at June's cafe had put a finger up your arse hole isn't it Johnny?' Michaela replied with a smirk.

  That was quite cool actually and even though she'd only said it to make me squirm I was still quite pleased with the progress I was making in my quest to be a super stud swordsmith. It was a shame that my plan to shag all the beautiful women in the world had come to an abrupt end even before it had started due to falling in love with Michaela but she was definitely worth it. I really couldn't believe my luck and I was going to do everything in my power to keep her.

'Oh and just so we're on the same page Johnny I must let you know that I've never been to a restaurant either. I think my dad took me and my sister to Wimpy once when we were little but I don't remember it. And soon after that we never saw him again. So we're both just going to have to wing it babe.' Michaela told me.

'Who cares!' I told her. ' We'll just have to make the best of it. I'm just happy to be in your company. I'm more than happy to get fish and chips and take them back to mine and eat it off your naked body but I forgot to turn on the heating so you'll freeze by the time its warmed up...Oh and sorry about your dad leaving. Although if he was anything like mine it was probably for the best. I wished my dad had fucked off years ago. And my mum too.'

'If you're going to eat yours off me then when am I going to eat? Before? Yours will be cold! And I'm certainly not waiting until you've finished or mine will be cold! No fuck that we are going to a restaurant and eat off plates. You can stick a mars bar up my pussy later if you must but I insist that our main shall be eaten at a table like classy folks!' Michaela replied.'And fuck my dad, he's a cunt.'

'I think they're all cunts actually. Parents I mean.' I replied.

'I love my mum.' Michaela said.

'Lucky you. You're lucky. My mum is a bit shit.' I told her.

'Well I'm sure that you wouldn't have kicked the shit out of her if she wasn't babe.' Michaela replied.

   Whether it was right or whether it was wrong it was done and now wasn't the time to dwell.

'The way I see it is that we have a number options. French, Italian or Indian... Or Wimpy for the flashbacks. What do you fancy out of those four?' I asked.

'So basically it's either, snails, pizza or curry... or Burger and chips.' Michaela replied.

'Well I can't help thinking that you've over simplified it but basically you're right.' I replied.

'It's a difficult one baby. What do you think?' Michaela replied.

'It's the lady's choice! You're my princess so you get to decide. I'll tell you what, I'll shout out the choices and you shout out the first thing that comes into your head? How does that sound?' I asked.

'Okay! Good idea. Go!' Michaela agreed.

'French!' I yelled at the top of my voice.

'Snobby Wankers!'

Italian!'

'Greasy mummy's boys! ...And thieves!'

'Indian!'

'Perfect!'

'Wimpy!'

'Childhood trauma! Flashbacks! Daddy! Why did you leave us!!!?'

'Wimpy it is then!' I laughed.

Our local curry house was called the Taj and even though I'd never been in it from the outside it looked exotic as fuck. I'd past it many times and always peered in hoping to see fit Indian birds like Pali who would see me and invite me in to give them one. I was very glad that that had never happened now because that would have been a bit awkward. "Hey Johnny where have you been baby? Me and my three sisters have missed you giving us all one as we lezzed off!" Yeah that was a lucky escape.

We got to the door, looked at each other and took a double deep breath.

'After you babe. Ladies first.' I told her while giving her a slight nudge.

'Fuck off! Fuck that shit! After you mate! I'm not going in first!' She replied harshly and pushed me through the door.

'Welcome my friends!' Said a beaming waiter.

'Two?' He asked.

'Two what?' I replied.

'Table for two sir?' The waiter asked.

'Oh yeah. That makes sense. Yes please. Table for two!' I replied enthusiastically.

'Come this way sir and lady please.' The waiter beamed and took us to a table in the middle of the crowded room. And what a room it was. It looked to me like a palace. It was regal as a mother fucker and the atmosphere was amazing but for some reason I didn't feel intimidated at all. Maybe it was all the red flock wallpaper that was giving off a womb like feel. Not my mum's womb though obviously. Or maybe it was the Bollywood sound track which made me think of beautiful Indian girls with pierced belly buttons dancing and smiling behind trees as they hid from their prospective lovers like I'd seen in those late night channel four films and wanked off to while thinking about Pali. Or maybe it was the waiters were so un- cunt like and nice. Fuck knows what it was but I immediately felt right at home. Actually it was a million times better than my home.

Before the waiter had chance to do it, I helped Michaela off with her coat and then pulled out her chair in order for her to sit down.

'Michaela giggled and said, 'This charming man.'

Just when I thought that she couldn't get any sexier, my girlfriend was quoting Morrissey.

'You are my princess.' I told her.'Are you okay? Is this better than the Wimpy?'

'I feel fantastic! What a place! It's so opulent! Michaela replied while looking around open mouthed. 'We must eat her every night until the day we die baby!'

'We can do that baby! Your wish is my command.' I replied with a solemn bow of my head.

Michaela then leaned in towards me and whispered, 'you are going to fucking get it later Johnny Capone.'

'Yeah and so are you my darling queen.' You'll be walking like John Wayne tomorrow.' I replied.

'That's big talk for such a little virgin.' Michaela laughed.

The waiter came back with two menus and asked us if we would like any drinks.

'Baby?' I asked. What drink would you like?'

Michaela quickly scanned the drinks menu and said, 'please can I have a beer please? Cobra. A pint. And my boyfriend will have a lemonade top!' And then she let out a big dirty laugh and then I laughed too but the waiter just looked confused.

'She thinks she's funny mate. I'll have a pint too! Of Cobra.' I told the waiter even though I didn't know what the fuck Cobra beer tasted like I just didn't want to look like a cunt.

'Two cobras. Very good sir. I'll give you a few minutes and then come back for your order.' Said the waiter and then he fucked off.

Thanks to Pali's mum and the meals she used to give me and our Wayne I had quite a good knowledge of what to order which was good because Michaela admitted to being out of her depth.

'Baby you're in safe hands' I'll order for both of us if you like?' I offered.

'Oh god yes please Johnny. It all looks so good but I wouldn't know where to begin.' Michaela replied, and I loved her for her honesty. If it hadn't been for Pali's mum I wouldn't have known what the fuck any of the things on the menu were either.

'Do you like spicy food? Is there anything you don't like? Are you allergic to nuts?' I asked her trying to keep a straight face.

'Only when they're not resting on my chin!' She replied and let out another big dirty laugh.

'Jesus you're so childish Michaela! I was only saying how childish you were to my dollies whilst we were having a pretend tea party in my bedroom the other day!' I replied gleefully and then it was my turn to laugh out loud. Michaela, on the other hand, just surreptitiously threw me the internationally recognised sign of me being a wanker before changing it to the internationally recognised sign of someone holding an ice cream cone and then licking the tip which made my cock hard. Then the waiter came over with a plate of poppadoms and three little jars of pickles and asked if we were ready to order.

'Baby. Please order for me.' Michaela said shyly.

I picked up a menu and quickly perused it before saying, 'Okay, to start could we get some lamb samosas, some crab and prawn cakes, Amla and beetroot tikka, Aloo Pakora, Aloo Tikka, Kakori Kebabs, Hariyali Chicken, Aloo Gobi and two plates of Asparagus and Pea soup with parsnip Crisps please... And for her main, my beautiful girlfriend would like Butter chicken tandoori and I'll have a chicken Tikka masala also with rice and can we get some Roti and Chapati too please? Both with Jasmine rice.' Then I gave him the menu back.

'Very good sir.' Replied the smiling waiter.

'Fuck me Johnny. Just as my panties were beginning to dry out too.' Michaela giggled.

Little did she know that I was just reading things out randomly from the menu and didn't really have much of a clue what most of it was. Chicken was chicken though so I thought that whatever the rest of it was like we could always eat that and if not there was always the Wimpy.

The two beers came and we clinked our glasses and toasted each other. I hadn't eaten anything but drugs for days and that pint went straight to my head and I think Michaela felt it too because before long we were getting quite boisterous.

I was having the best day of my life and as I looked over at Michaela laughing and joking and giving off this infectious and glorious energy that seemed to permeate the entire place, I tried to picture what the future would look like for us. I wanted her to have the best of everything; a big posh house with a pool and a big posh car and nice holidays and all the money and things she's ever dreamed of. She could be a lady of leisure while I went out to work as a criminal overlord. All she needed to do was to be herself. She was my muse and my inspiration.

We would have kids and we would love them and cherish them and they would never know what it was like to be hungry or beaten or neglected and then and one day they would have kids and my empire would grow and grow and then I'd pass down my empire and abdicate and then me and Michaela would retire in the sun and spend the rest of our days wrapped up in each other's arms.

We were having the time of our lives when suddenly this red faced fat cunt of an old man on the next table tapped me on the shoulder and told me to keep the noise down.

'Sorry sir. It's very noisy in here. What did you say?' I asked him. Even though I knew exactly what he'd said.

'I said keep the fucking noise down you little cunt. If you can't behave like civilised people why don't you fuck off down the Chinky!' He replied with a snarl.

'Oh yeah! A Chinese!' Me and Michaela shouted in unison.

'Listen sir, I replied, trying to remain calm. 'I'm on a first date with my girlfriend and I'm in a very good mood because of many things but one of them is that hopefully I'm going to lose my virginity tonight so I'm going to overlook the fact that you just called me a cunt and not shoot you. Now if you'd like to go back to eating your meal then all you need to do is apologise.'

'Apologise? Are you taking the fucking piss son? He snarled. ' What are you twelve? Thirteen? Shouldn't you be in bed by now?'

Then he turned to, who I assumed was his wife; although it could just has easily been his sister they were so alike, and said, 'Get a load of this little cunt! Who does he think he is? Al Capone?'

And then she laughed too. Then I laughed, but it was a different kind of laugh.

'I'll give you one more chance to apologise before my food gets here.' I told him.

His wife then chimed in.

'And what the fuck is a little drop- balled' shit cunt like you or your slag of a girlfriend going to do about it if he doesn't then?' She asked, starting to get herself at it.

On hearing this Michaela turned to the woman and said, 'what did you call me you fat fucking cunt?'

'How dare you speak to me like that!' The fat cunt replied.

'Well to be fair to my girlfriend' I replied, 'you are actually rather fat and it does also seem that you're also a cunt. ....And your fella looks like a fat fucking nonce while we're throwing insults about. Although that's more of a fact than an insult. I bet you like to watch the kiddies down at the pool and fiddle with yourself don't you sir! I bet you've fucked your own kids too sir haven't you! It's actually a well known fact that if a kid is going to get fiddled it's usually by a member of its own family and looking at you I'd agree with that fact because you look like the fucking definition of one. You fat... fucking... nonce... cunt.'

Well neither of them took too kindly to that and the man got up to give me a dig but I got up first and pulled out my gun and then I put my my gun to his head. It was cheating really but I'd only had a few poppadoms up to that point and I was hungry as fuck and that was making me a little bit fractious.

'I gave you a chance sir. You can't say that I didn't give you a chance.' I told him. 'Now I'm going to shoot you in the head.'

On hearing this the fat cunt let out a loud fart. I couldn't blame him. Having a gun put up against your head can be quite a life changing moment and people react in different ways.

Then Michaela suddenly stood up and threw her hands up into the air and screamed, 'No Johnny! Please don't!'

On hearing this the fat cunt let out an audible sigh and his body visibly relaxed.

Then Michaela shouted, 'Shoot his fat cunt of a wife first so he sees her die! Then shoot him!'

On hearing this the fat cunt's wife farted.

'Oh God! Please no! Please son! Don't shoot me!' Pleaded the man. 'I'm sorry! I'm sorry! We are both sorry! Aren't we love? Tell him we're sorry love!'

'Love? I'm not your love! Don't you dare call me love! Don't shoot you? Don't shoot you? What about me you soppy fat cunt?' Shouted the fat cunt's wife at the fat cunt.

'Come on now lady don't be like that he probably meant to include you but can't you see he's upset?' I told her trying to calm her fat arse down.'Hey! Wait up! Hang on a minute!' I continued, 'I hope this isn't some big scam where you trick me into shooting your wife! ...Are you trying to get me to shoot your wife sir?'

Then I addressed the fat cunt lady and said, 'Has he taken out life insurance on you lately babe? Does he have any reason to want you dead?'

'I want her dead Johnny.' Michaela said coldly.

'Apologise to my girlfriend for calling her a slag or I'm going to shoot your husband.' I told her.

'You can shoot the cunt for all I care.' She replied flatly. 'He probably has been fiddling the kids because he hasn't come near me in years so he's getting it from somewhere! ... My sister is convinced he's a nonce! Look at him with his bald head and those little glasses. Proper noncey they are!'

'Oi! Don't you go calling me a nonce! I've never touched those kids!' Replied the fat cunt husband. ' Especially the ginger one! The ugly little bastard! He stays in his room all day and all night! Never comes out he don't! What's he do in there? Eh? It's not right I tell you!'

At that point I think if I'd handed him the gun he would have gladly shot his wife himself. I was getting bored and hungry by this point and it was all making the waiters nervous; although to give them their due, they never stopped smiling throughout this whole unfortunate farce.

'Come on now why don't you do us all a favour and go and have this argument somewhere else because you're spoiling everyone's evening.' I told them.

'Don't you speak to us like that! We were here first!' Screamed the guy's wife.'Stanley! Are you going to let him talk to us like that? You're nothing but a cowered Stanley! ...My mother warned me all those years ago not to marry you and now I can see that she was right!'

'Well to be fair to Stanley, he does have a gun pointed at his head.' I told her.

Well he did. It was okay for her to expect poor old Stanley to do something heroic when she was not the one having to keep it together while death could be seconds away. And little did they both know that he was closing in on death, and so was she because I was just about done with their shit by this point. Right then all I could think about was our fucking starters. In my mind's eye I could see the waiters, patiently waiting behind the kitchen doors with them in their hands and they were all getting cold and congealed. I'd had enough of their bickering so decided that enough was enough but just as I was seriously thinking about putting a bullet in the pair of them fate intervened. Well when I say fate I really meant Michaela.

'Oh for fuck's sake leave poor Stan alone! No wonder he's so angry!' She shouted at Stan's wife. 'I would be too if I had to put up with your rabbit morning, noon and night! Fucking give it a rest Fatty Arbuckle!'

'Don't you speak to me like ...' Stan's wife began but before she could finish her sentence Michaela headbutted her and she hit the floor with a dull thud and silence prevailed once more. Everyone in the restaurant then clapped, including Stan, and within a couple of minutes she was back on her feet, dazed and confused but, thanks to my girlfriend, still alive and after a couple more minutes, with the help of the still smiling waiters, Stan got her outside and we reassumed our meal.

When the starters came I thought that we'd never get through them as there was so many but Michaela was like a furnace and just kept shovelling food into her beautiful mouth until it was all gone. Then she did the same to her main course and even finished mine. She also drank four pints of Cobra lager and both of the little shots they brought out along with the bill.

'That was lovely Johnny. Thank you baby.' Michaela told me and then she theatrically yawned and stretched and said, 'Oh my oh my I'm really tired now! Will you walk me home please my darling man?'

There was a moment of silence before she burst out laughing. 'Oh baby you should have seen your face!' She laughed.

'Yeah. Good joke. You should seriously think about doing a bit of stand-up.' I told her. Then I said, ' yeah well I'll have you know that if you really were tired I would have happily walked you home because you are much more to me than a living, breathing, receptacle for my spunk.'

'Well that's the most romantic thing I've ever heard Johnny Capone.' She replied.

She was trying to sound sarcastic but I knew that she was pleased that what I felt for her was more than lust. Much much more.

Then she said, 'Oh yes I nearly forgot! I've got a present for you!'

'Oh yeah? 'I replied.'Let's see it then.'

Then she giggled and said, 'It's under the table.'

'Under the table?' I asked.

'Yes! Go and have a look!' She replied with a glint in her eye.

'Okay. I'll play along. Oh fuck you're not going to run out on me are you? Please don't run off.' I laughed.

'Of course not baby! You and me forever. Always and forever my darling! Always and forever. Until death do us part.' Michaela replied and then she winked and pointed to the floor.

'I love you baby.' I replied. 'I'll be right back.'

I then took a deep breath and held my nose like I was just about to jump into the sea and then pulled back my chair and scrambled under the table. There was nothing obvious on the floor but when I looked up I saw Michaela furtively wriggling out of her knickers and the next thing I knew they were provocatively dangling off one of her stilettos. I slipped them off and instinctively inhaled them before stuffing them into my jean's pocket.

All I needed to do now was get off the floor, pay the bill, help Michaela on with her coat, leave the restaurant, go back to mine, slowly undress her, kiss her all over and loads of other stuff, and then, finally, after all those near misses, we'd make love, and then during that love making I'd penetrate her vagina with my penis and hopefully after an embarrassingly amount of time, I'd ejaculate and then that would be that. Goodbye virginity. Simple. Even with my luck surely nothing could go wrong from here on in. I did need a shit though.

As I knelt on that restaurant floor I could help but grin. Not only was I about to lose my virginity I was about to lose it to the most amazing girl in the world. Michaela was perfection. She was beautiful and sexy and funny and intelligent and rude as fuck and she knew how to headbutt a motherfucker. I'd hit the jackpot and I was looking forward to spending the rest of my life showing her how grateful I was that out of all the boys in this world she could have picked to spend her life with, she'd chosen me.

Everything I did from this point on would be for her. I worshipped her and I didn't care who knew it. For all I cared, rather than being known as the entertainer, everyone could call me that sad, cunt-struck mother fucker who is totally under the thumb of his missus. I did not care about anything but making Michaela happy and I would do anything to keep her by my side.

'Baby, I need a shit.' I told her as I got back off the floor.

'I'm going to nip to the bogs and then we can get the fuck out of here because I cannot wait any longer to penetrate your vagina with my penis...'

As I got back in my chair and sat down I saw that Michaela had her head bowed. Maybe she was religious and was now deep in silent prayer, giving thanks to a higher power for the amazing meal we'd just had or for the pounding she was just about to receive from me? Fuck me I loved her so much I didn't even care if she was a Protestant. We'd only really just met and there was so much more for us to get to know about each other and I couldn't wait.

I waited for a couple of minutes out of respect and then I coughed. Then I coughed again. And then I said her name. And then I shouted her name. Then I noticed that something was dripping from her head. Maybe she had a nose bleed?

'Baby... Baby... Michaela... Michaela... MICHAELA! You okay? Baby are you okay?' I asked her, my voice becoming more and more urgent.

Still nothing. I then ran around the table and lifted up her head. I held her head in my hands and looked down at her face. Her eyes were open but she looked like she was dead. How could she be dead? I'd literally seen her less than a minute ago and she was alive.

How could she now be dead? How could Michaela be dead? I brushed her hair away from her forehead and that's when I saw it. Michaela had a small hole in the middle of her forehead. She'd been shot. Someone had shot Michaela in the forehead and now she was dead. My darling Michaela was dead.

I looked around the restaurant. Everything seemed normal enough. People were sat down eating and chatting like everything was fucking normal. But everything was not normal. Nothing would ever be normal again. Who would shoot my girlfriend? Why was I alive and Michaela was dead? I should be dead too. What was the point of me being alive now? Why were all these people just eating and chatting away like nothing is wrong? Why are these fuckers alive and my Michaela is dead? What the fuck is happening? Maybe I'm dreaming?

Yes! That's it! This is a dream and I'm going to wake up and Michaela will still be alive and I'll go to the cafe and tell her that I had a dream about her and she'll ask me what the dream was and I'll make something up in case my real dream upset her and I wouldn't like her to be upset. I never want her to be upset.

Everything looked real though. Those two over there look real and the smiling waiters look real and the bullet wound in Michaela's forehead looked real and all that blood looked real. I decided to ask one of the smiling waiters if everything was real and called one over.

'Hello. Excuse me!' I said to one of the smiling waiters. 'I don't mean to bother you, and I can see that you're extremely busy, but would you do me a favour and check whether my girlfriend has been shot in the head please?'

The smiling waiter just looked at me and smiled. 'I'm sorry sir? I don't understand.' He replied.

'Well you see that just a moment ago my girlfriend was alive and she asked me to go under the table as she had a surprise for me so I went under the table and then she took off her knickers... they were the surprise you see? It was like a sort of sexy joke between two people in love. We are in love you see? So anyway Michaela, that's her name, or that was her name, anyway you see she has a really good sense of humour and she took down her knickers and put them on her shoe and then I took them off her shoe and then I inhaled them and put them in my pocket.'

As I said that bit I took Michaela's knickers out of my pocket and showed them to him and then I mimed inhaling them.

'Anyway, when I came back up from being under the table I told her that I needed a shit but she didn't respond, she was all silent and still and her head was bowed and at first I thought that she was praying and then I noticed that there was something dripping from her head so I went over to her to see if she was okay and then I lifted her head and that's when I saw that someone had put a fucking bullet in it. Her beautiful head has a bullet in it now.'

At this point I could feel tears rolling down my face and I noticed that my hands and legs were shaking uncontrollably and I also felt very cold.

'As I said, I can see that you're busy but I really must insist that you look at my girlfriend's fucking head and tell me if there's a bullet hole in it. Please.' I asked the smiling waiter again.

The smiling waiter just stood looking at me and kept smiling. Maybe it was actually all just a dream and this smiling waiter cunt has some kind of unconscious meaning? Just as I was trying to figure out what a smiling waiter might represent somebody screamed.

'Blood! I'm covered in blood!'

'Excuse me a moment sir.' I said to the smiling waiter and I went over to the screaming woman who was sat directly behind Michaela and she was indeed covered in blood. Michaela's blood.

'See!' I shouted over to the smiling waiter. 'I was right! That's my girlfriend's blood! This lady is covered in my girlfriend's blood because she's been shot in the head! This isn't a dream! It's not a dream! It's real! Somebody has shot Michaela in the head and she's dead! Michaela is dead!'

The waiter then stopped smiling and that's when everything went dark.